Activating Human Rights

Elisabeth Porter & Baden Offord (eds)

Activating Human Rights

PETER LANG
Oxford · Bern · Berlin · Bruxelles · Frankfurt am Main · New York · Wien

Bibliographic information published by Die Deutsche Bibliothek
Die Deutsche Bibliothek lists this publication in the Deutsche Nationalbibliografie; detailed bibliographic data is available on the Internet at ‹http://dnb.ddb.de›.

British Library and Library of Congress Cataloguing-in-Publication Data:
A catalogue record for this book is available from The British Library, Great Britain, and from The Library of Congress, USA

INCORE international conflict research

The United Nations University

Southern Cross UNIVERSITY

Cover design: Thomas Jaberg, Peter Lang AG

ISBN 3-03910-509-4
US-ISBN 0-8204-7515-7

Hochfeldstrasse 32, Postfach 746, CH-3000 Bern 9, Switzerland
info@peterlang.com, www.peterlang.com, www.peterlang.net

Printed in Germany

Contents

Part III Human Rights in International Contexts

Part IV Activating Particular Rights

Preface

The Centre for Law, Politics and Culture at Southern Cross University, Australia, hosted an international conference, *Activating Human Rights and Diversity: Local and Global Voices*, in Byron Bay, July 2003. We would like to acknowledge here the team behind this conference, which brought together scholars, activists, students and community workers: Judy Atkinson, Greta Bird, Vivien Clear, Janie Conway-Herron, Kierrynn Davis, Sam Garkawe, Karen Hanna, Christopher Macfarlane, Mark McDonell, Ros Mills, Baden Offord, Elisabeth Porter and Michael Reid.

This book represents a select sample of the themes addressed during the event. Each chapter has been especially written for this collection (bar Stychin). The publication of this book has been made possible by funding from the Graduate Research College, Southern Cross University, Australia in support of the Centre for Law, Politics and Culture (www.scu.edu.au/research/clpc/index.html) and from INCORE, an International Centre of Excellence for Conflict and Peace Studies at the University of Ulster, Northern Ireland associated to the United Nations University (www.incore.ulster.ac.uk). The editors would like to thank Annie Abegg at Southern Cross University for her desktop work and Andrew Ivett and Graham Speake at Peter Lang for their editorial assistance and support in bringing this book to publication.

Elisabeth Porter and Baden Offord

ELISABETH PORTER AND BADEN OFFORD

Introduction: Activating Human Rights

The leader of Burma's National League for Democracy and Nobel Prize winner, Aung San Suu Kyi, has made the important point in relation to human rights that

> Actions without ideational content lose their potency as soon as the situation which called for them ceases to be valid. A series of pragmatic moves unconnected by a continuity of vision cannot be expected to sustain a long-term movement. (Suu Kyi, 1991: 128)

In light of this, what kind of vision for humanity and the world is necessary for the harsh realities of the twenty-first century? What connects and sustains action with vision? How is the vision of human rights activated in the individual and in society? The purpose of this book is to probe these questions, and in doing so, to offer contemporary perspectives on what inspires human rights thinking as well as providing examples of how human rights are practically activated in specific contexts.

The vision, language and culture of human rights have become integral to the survival of the individual, community and society in the twenty-first century. Human rights are the international benchmark of normative frameworks of governance and morality as well as the primary language of amelioration shared by networks of transformative political, social, economic and cultural activism. A fundamental feature of human rights institutionalisation through international law has been, in fact, the widespread acknowledgment that law is only one field of its realisation, that there is indeed a kaleidoscope of contexts in which human rights as principle, value and moral framework are realised. The literature in this field is extensive (see Meckled-Garcia and Cali, 2005; Gready, 2004; Cowan, Dembour and Wilson, 2001; Ignatieff, 2001; Falk, 2000; Offord, 2003; Turner, 1993). The vision and activation of human rights points to the importance of what moves us to think, reflect and act on human rights law, culture, education, principles and values.

The twenty-first century challenges the vision of human rights. The war in Iraq, terrorist bombings in Washington, Bali, the Middle East, Madrid, London and elsewhere, the continuing rise of poverty and destruction of the environment, the inequalities of globalisation, the advent of greater surveillance by governments, the devastating consequences of the tsunami, and more – all contribute to uncertain times. Certainly, in the wake of the twentieth century, which itself was characterised by genocide and violent conflict, the twenty-first century faces these and new challenges that require clear, thoughtful, intell-igent responses to a range of human rights issues and problems.

This book is a conceptual and practical toolkit for facing these challenges. There are three themes that run through the book. First, there is a reflection on what inspires and activates human rights thinking. Second, there is a focus on practical considerations of how that vision can be translated into a range of contexts. Third, there is a concern for what is being done about human rights by individuals, organisations, countries and cultures. Our purpose in this book is to invoke and explore the lived connections between our humanity and inhumanity, between action and thought, and between the universal and particular. We propose that it is through understanding diverse perspectives on human rights that we are able to get beyond narrow and restrictive interpretations of human rights discourse to acknow-ledge lively connections between theory and activism, and between ideal and reality.

Many scholars, philosophers, activists, lawyers, community and NGO workers, students and politicians, now regard the language of human rights as an indispensable tool in protecting, explaining, ex-ploring and nourishing the rich diversity of our humanity. In current times, this moral language has become even more fundamental to survival and the transformation of humanity. As we face the ominous bio-technological revolution, which Australian High Court Justice, Michael Kirby calls the greatest challenge of this century, as well as all the other challenges of how human beings conduct themselves together, and with their environment, we cannot fail to notice the importance of seeing the connections between the vision and the activation of rights. Human rights language thus can be considered a map about the nature of human well-being, of being well on this planet earth (Birch and Paul, 2003). How well that map works for us depends on the connection between vision and action, and the commitment to ensure a sustainable, dignified life for all people.

This book is divided into four parts: first, human rights, theory and action; second, organisational defences of human rights; third, international contexts of human rights in practice; and fourth, specific examples of activating rights. Part One addresses the relationship between human rights theory and specific action taken by activists, legal practitioners and human rights advocates. Many human rights activists are motivated into action as a direct response to injustice, oppression, repression and intimidation. Most frequently, the relationship between human rights theory and action is vibrant, where ideas inform responses and both are transformed in the process. Such a dynamic relationship changes with culture, time, place and individuals, affirming the richness of diversity as a way of understanding human rights.

Baden Offord begins Part One by situating human rights within the landscape of ongoing human suffering. The authors in this book accept the importance of understanding cosmopolitan interconnections, including the relationship between human rights abuse and suffering. We share the vision of human rights, as Upendra Baxi has put it, to give expression to human suffering (Baxi, 1999). The suffering of humanity is not something to be pushed aside; of concern only when parochial or national interest comes to the fore. Rather, as Offord maintains, as humans we are implicated in a community of suffering which prompts a desire to alleviate suffering. Accordingly, Offord explores the role, validity and strength of human rights values in contemporary times. Offord's argument is that to activate human rights, due consideration must be given to the relationships between individual activists, human rights sufferers and responsible social activism.

The question of what human rights we possess vexes human rights theorists. Yet, the question is not merely academic. The answer provides parameters of what it is reasonable to expect in law, policy and practice. Additionally, in transitional democracies, in post-conflict situations of institutional and governmental reconstruction, and in communities that have been ignorant of the scope of human rights, it is important to clarify the nature of human rights. Further, rights emerge in specific community contexts. Jim Ife criticises Western constructions of rights that privilege civil and political rights. Instead, he defends the need for human rights to be sufficiently broad as to be applicable across cultural and ideological divides. To this end, he proposes seven categories of rights: basic survival rights; social rights; economic rights; civil/political rights; cultural rights; environmental rights; and spiritual rights. He argues that collective rights should not be a distinct category, as all seven categories operate in both individual and collective domains.

Diverse viewpoints throughout the subsequent chapters offer different ways to activate human rights. Carl Stychin's chapter on communities of difference may seem to contradict Ife's argument that collective rights should not be a distinct category. However, Stychin argues both that rights transcend the particular and that the language of rights can appeal to difference, specificity, history and community. He draws on examples of same-sex activism in an array of cultural contexts, particularly in Tasmania, Australia and in Romania in order to demonstrate how gay activists operate from local, communitarian strategies through to cosmopolitan, global claims. He returns to the tension between the universalising nature of human rights discourse and the validity of claims to cultural difference within specific communities. Such tensions are of course conspicuous for all oppressed minority groups and have quite different political demands. Stychin comfortably defends the need for gay activists to engage in both the cosmopolitanism of rights and the communitarian engagement with political institutions through which rights can become meaningful. The struggle to realise political identity is a struggle for citizenship and belonging in the communities in which we participate. These struggles and the intense need to belong are common themes shared by the contributors in all parts of the book.

While the realisation of human rights is difficult in all countries, divided societies, conflict zones and societies undergoing radical political transition face additional burdens. Monica McWilliams explains the perceived difficulties in reconciling an emphasis on justice and human rights in peace agreements with the strategic concerns of conflict resolution. She argues strongly for the complementarity between human rights enforcement and conflict resolution and explores alternatives to antagonistic, adversarial approaches to law and community relations. McWilliams explains the benefits of the restorative justice model to transformative relationships between individuals, communities and the state, using Northern Ireland as an example. Along with Garkawe, she meshes human rights issues with processes of reconciliation.

Part of the rich diversity of being human is the range of ways in which activists, academics and advocates work to realise human rights. There are multiple ways to defend human rights and Part Two provides some different institutional and organisational examples drawn from South Africa, East Timor and a well-known international NGO. The defence of human rights is rarely easy.

An example frequently explored by the international community is South Africa's Truth and Reconciliation Commission. Sam Garkawe presents a tight argument based on his visits to South Africa. In particular, he scrutinises the criticism made of the idea of an amnesty for truth, that amnesty breaches international legal obligations; it contributes to impunity; and amnesty violates the rights of the victims of apartheid. Garkawe also highlights the importance of diversity. He stresses that any accountability mechanism for perpetrators can only be assessed in light of the social, political and cultural context of the state at the time of the mechanism's establishment. Thus, he argues that the Truth and Reconciliation Commission was the culturally appropriate model of accountability.

Michael Morison offers an example of democratic inclusion. Morison's example is East Timor, where he coordinated the 2001 United Nations Civic Education program, which trained young, university-educated Timorese women and men to teach 50,000 local villagers about constitutional and political transition. Morison maintains that at a village level, this project succeeded in emphasising the important role all Timorese people play in the democratisation process. Yet, at a national level, many decisions made by the broader UN administration undermined the work done at village level. He argues that the democratisation processes that are integral to national self-determination must aim toward a 'ground up' approach. He suggests that this occurs with genuine capacity-building that supports civil society groups in local communities.

The international community increasingly is becoming aware of the widespread human rights abuses against women. Lara Fergus analyses Amnesty International's appeal cases for representation of human rights abuse against women. She outlines some troubling findings and suggests that Amnesty International has failed to include women's experiences of human rights abuse in some appeal cases. However, she notes the welcome changes in the organisation that have caused it to respond more sensitively to gender issues and to extend its mandate to include abuses by non-state actors. Fergus proposes some changes to Amnesty International's practices so that it might more fully include women's experience of human rights abuses. Inclusion as full citizens with the full range of human rights is a central concern for the book's contributors.

Whatever the theoretical framework for understanding rights or the organisational means to defend rights, the real test comes in everyday practical lives. In Part Three, global examples of human rights in practice focus on the suppression of human rights in Singapore, on the crisis of property for refugees and displaced persons from Bosnia and Herzegovina and Kashmir and on the environmental degradation in Nigeria. While very different international examples, the themes of political immorality, globalisation, refugees and ecology cut to the core of contemporary international politics. Each example highlights a human rights abuse, namely, the suppression of freedom of expression, the displacement of refugees and the threatened livelihoods for indigenous people. The need for, and the actualisation of human rights, emerges through diverse practices.

One author who has endured enormous personal hardships because of his active defence of human rights is Chee Soon Juan. He offers an acutely disturbing account of the degree of repression, control and intimidation that the ruling party in Singapore employs. This subjugation includes access to free and open media, curtailing freedoms of public speech and preventing the watching of any visual media that has political content. Even Internet users are intimidated into exercising self-censorship. Chee's chapter on the human rights violations in Singapore is an important reminder that the defence of human rights is never easy, but indeed often has deeply personal costs.

Kulwant Singh writes of the need to gain the property rights of refugees. Singh compares the effects of international intervention in Bosnia and Herzegovina to secure property rights for refugees and displaced persons with the situation in Kashmir where no similar steps have been taken. Singh maintains that there are lessons to be learnt from Bosnia and Herzegovina in formulating policy guidelines that may assist the stalemate in Kashmir for those displaced following the partition of India in 1947. Unresolved tensions compound the likelihood of terrorism, hence Singh's suggestions are of paramount importance. An early return of refugees and displaced persons to their homes and a careful management of pending ethnic crises may hasten peace and progress. Peace with justice is integral to obtaining human rights in practice.

The issue of oil exploitation by transnationals is explored by Kiikpoye Aaron who writes of the violation of the rights to health, a healthy environment and natural resources for people in Nigeria. Aaron shows how the livelihoods of fisher folks and farmers have been threatened by the ecological devastation in the area. Deprivation and poverty often spark desperate measures, including sabotage-induced oil spills in order to benefit from compensation for oil pollution. Aaron demonstrates the curious irony that oil exploitation in the Niger Delta leads to human rights abuse, and yet the attempt by the region's inhabitants to reassert their lost human rights leads sadly to environmental degradation.

While Part Three examines international examples of human rights in practice, Part Four provides specific examples of ways to activate human rights. The chapters examine disability rights, same-sex domestic rights and rights for Indigenous peoples.

Christopher Newell and Gerard Goggin reaffirm the importance of diversity within a vision of an all-encompassing civil society. Such a vision presupposes the ethical inclusion of all citizens, yet people with disability are not represented in leadership or conspicuous positions in Australia. These authors show how we need to see disability not as uncivil or distressing, but as a normal, positive part of the diversity of Australian society. This ethical vision of inclusion extends of course, to all societies.

An affirmation of diversity strengthens inclusive citizenship. Chantal Nadeau reinforces these ideas through exploring the implications of gay and lesbian claims for equality in terms of the representation of citizenship. She uses contemporary debates around same-sex marital and domestic institutions in North America and Europe and argues that the growing extension of rights to same-sex families cannot be separated from the ways that nations reinforce political platforms around pro-family and assimilationist discourses. The nature of equality needs to be questioned in the light of what nations constitute as desirable citizens. Such questions are linked additionally with integration, ethnicity, immigration and the inclusion or exclusion of citizens and asylum-seekers.

Those with disabilities, same-sex families and Indigenous Australians feel the pain of exclusion from full citizenship. The realisation of pain often is a trigger to begin to activate human rights. Irene Watson writes of this pain from an Indigenous Australian perspective, explaining the foundational nature of the basic human right to survival as a commitment to care for nature and the sustainability of ongoing generations. She argues that human rights and human obligations are tied intimately to a respect for the land and first peoples. Yet, as Watson argues, the language of human rights has failed to incorporate the concerns of Aboriginal peoples. Watson calls for a future that embraces the diversity of humanity and addresses the need of Aboriginal peoples. Listening is a precondition of a non-patronising activation of rights. In sharing the stories of pain, there is some release in acknowledging common ground. The journey of healing should be shared. Healing is integral to truth-telling expounded also by Garkawe and to reconciliation explored by McWilliams.

The goal of activating human rights in a post-9/11 global context is both urgent and daunting. We live in a world in need of a careful balance between international, national and human security. Activating human rights is a crucial challenge we face in the twenty-first century. We need to understand what inspires and moves us to activate human rights sensibilities and what sustains the vision. We must examine and see how human rights are enacted in a range of highly diverse contexts and to understand what institutions, individuals and cultures are doing. We ought to move human rights thinking beyond simply the law section of libraries, to embrace a moral vision of humanity that is inclusive of cultural, social and political concerns and that meets people's basic universal needs. Through an abundance of perspectives, this book provides an important axiological toolkit on human rights for the twenty-first century. The eminent scholar Edward Said once noted, 'Survival is about the connection between things' (1993: 408). We believe the survival of humanity depends on our ability to connect a vision – of caring about human rights – with the reality of activating human rights.

References

Baxi, U., 1999, 'Voices of Suffering, Fragmented Universality, and the Future of Human Rights', in Burns H. Weston and Stephen P. Marks (Eds.), *The Future of International Human Rights,* (New York: Transnational), pp. 101–157.

Birch, C. and Paul, D., 2003, *Life and Work. Challenging Economic Man,* (Kensington, Sydney: University of NSW Press).

Cowan, J. K., Dembour, M. and Wilson, R. A. (Eds.), 2001, *Culture and Rights: Anthropological Perspectives* (London: Cambridge University Press).

Falk, R., 2000, *Human Rights Horizons* (New York: Routledge).

Gready, P. (Ed.), 2004, *Fighting for Human Rights* (London and New York: Routledge).

Ignatieff, M., 2001, *Human Rights as Politics and Idolatry* (Princeton: Princeton University Press).

Meckled-Garcia, S. and Cali, B. (Eds.), 2005, *The Legalisation of Human Rights: Multidisciplinary Approaches*, (London and New York: Routledge).

Offord, B., 2003, *Homosexual Rights as Human Rights* (Berne: Peter Lang).
Said, E., 1993, *Culture and Imperialism* (London: Vintage).
Suu Kyi, A., 1991, *Freedom from Fear* (London: Penguin).
Turner, B., 1993, 'Outline of a Theory of Human Rights', *Sociology*, 27(3): 489–512.

Part I
Human Rights
Theory and Action

BADEN OFFORD

Activating Human Rights through Questions of Value and Activism

Introduction

The principles of human rights have become ubiquitous to any consideration of national and international governance, and they now underpin all serious contemporary challenges to pathologies of power that affect human dignity (Farmer, 2005). As rhetoric human rights are frequently invoked as a means of ameliorating a specific situation of the human condition. There is even a sense that the idea of human rights has triumphed as a universally accepted moral imperative and language (Robinson, 1998: 59), despite significant critiques of its depth and coherence (Sen, 2000: 227). It is also clear that there are various realities to the idea of human rights. The legal and political structures of governance that bind human rights into instruments, treaties and law, are not the same as the cultural, social, economic and spiritual realities of everyday life. This is where human rights translate into individual and community survival communicated through specific moral and ethical worlds, power relations and identities.

Human rights we can acknowledge is an idea that has become embedded in both institutional and subjective positions. As A. Belden Fields has remarked

> Human rights rank along with democracy and free markets in the normative language of our age. Human rights are often used as the ultimate normative reference point. (2003: 1)

Institutionally, this is evident in the recognised work done to bring about an acceptable, humane and responsible society – embedded within a human rights framework – through the expression of law, treaties and covenants. Human rights have become subjective in the sense that they help construct interiority, which is simultaneously both feeling and 'the most acute political event' (Mansfield, 2000: 179). Thus, human rights are a subjective, local, national and global language.

It is noteworthy, however, that any search in a library for books on human rights will lead almost immediately to the law section. This is despite the fact that the idea of human rights is essentially derived from literature, poetry, philosophy, art, as well as through (and not limited to) studies on health, culture, society, politics, animals, ethics, ecology, and the media. The presence or absence of human rights, is experienced in the everyday human condition, not in the abstract.

Following these considerations, the purpose of this chapter is to investigate the value of human rights theory and practice in the context of its paradoxical characteristics. My aim is to look at how the human rights activist is formed through the praxis of suffering, through an enquiry based on the axiological nature of human rights. First, I question the values behind the idea of human rights and link it to the imperative of survival through an ethics of engagement. Second, I invoke several moments that provide contexts through which the activation of human rights might be viewed. Third, I propose an argument that activating human rights is driven by both the need to *contextually think* human rights as well as the *responsibility to speak* to human rights.

An ethics of engagement

I would like to propose in this chapter that if human rights are fundamental to our understanding of the human condition, then there needs to be a human rights framework that operates beyond its institutional station, in fact at the level of homeomorphic (cultural) realities (Pannikar, 1982: 202), where human beings are activated, in their understanding and interpretation of the human condition, by a shared concern for justice, freedom, responsibility and compassion. In this sense, I am following the suggestion of Zillah Eisenstein that the universality at the heart of the modern human rights movement is fraught with the dangerous legacies of a 'colonial', 'Western' gaze and a project of empire built on the United States' liberal, democratic, capitalist ideology. Eisenstein's critique against this empire is based on her argument for a radical notion of polyversality, and an approach to human rights that is aware of its colonial roots (2004: 38).

The field of human rights is a difficult and complex one, therefore, and to understand what underpins this 'modern phenomenon' (Farmer, 2005: 220), to ask what activates its theory and practice, is to confront questions about being and acting human. Certainly, it is about going beyond the 'lawlike character' of human rights, beyond their ensemble of governance, to the reality of the human condition in all its fullness and nuance.

What is needed in the attempt to translate human rights across cultures, across societies and communities in which difference is celebrated and not reduced to a universalist ideology – countenanced by whatever 'ism' is the dominant paradigm of the day – is an ethics of engagement that is robust enough to fashion a meaningful exchange about the relevance of questions such as justice, peace, respect and dignity in human life and relationships. In this consideration, there is nothing self-evident about human rights (Fields, 2003: 1), as they issue out of real everyday concerns and contexts that are frequently unregarded and unquestioned.

Presently, around the globe, human rights might be invoked like a cynical mantra without substance, but their significance issues from face to face encounters with human suffering. As Bryan Turner has eloquently stated as a key sociological argument underpinning human rights, 'Human beings [...] are ontologically members of a community of suffering from which they cannot escape' (1993: 503). This has resonance with Buddhist ideas, which are taken up later in the chapter. Human rights as concept and practice, therefore, are complex and rooted in survival, relationship and co-existence, the exploration of interconnectedness (between *self* and *other*) and its realisation. Ultimately, it is about linking the idea of human rights to the question of what it means to be human.

In this perspective, human rights is an implicative theory and practice, one that demands responsibility for being human as well as for others. This definition is thus predicated on a profound axiology of being human, which extends to a rich diversity of enquiry and principled exposure of how human beings interact with each other as well as with the non-human world. Although not central to the discussion here, such a definition signals that there is an ecology at work in the field of human rights, which resists the tendency towards the anthropocentric. Central to this present discussion, however, is that such a definition reflects principled exposures, for example, of sexuality (Beger, 2004; Offord, 2003; Stychin, 1999), of health (Farmer, 2005), of refugees and asylum seekers (Dechian, 2004), of trauma (Atkinson, 2002; Tutu, 1999), and of poverty (Sen, 1999). A core feature of the praxis of principled exposure is the relationship with the *other*.

Consequently, this approach to human rights thinking also requires a non-colonising ethics of engagement. In the spirit of the late Palestinian activist and scholar Edward Said, an ethics of engagement requires an approach where we learn

> to live in a certain sense *with* the land, not *on* it, not like Robinson Crusoe whose goal is to colonise his little island, but more like Marco Polo, whose sense of the marvellous never fails him, and who is always a traveller, a provisional guest, not a freeloader, conqueror, or raider. (1994: 44)

The critical link that exists between human rights, colonialism and culture is crucial to any discussion of the ethics of engagement. Colonialism remains at the heart of contemporary definitions and debates of what it means to be human.

In Australia, for example, Indigenous activist/thinkers such as Aileen Moreton-Robinson argue that Indigenous Australians have an incommensurable ontological belonging with the land called Australia (2003). Human rights language has become a possible means by which respect for this ontological belonging can co-exist with the non-Indigenous presence in Australia. Moreover, respect for Indigenous Australian ontological belonging can potentially assist in ameliorating the colonial aftermath in Australia, where de-colonisation remains stymied by a 'collective amnesia' (Gandhi, 1998), 'legacies of whiteness' (Jayasuriya, Walker and Gothard, 2003) and therefore a continuing colonialist dominant culture (Hage, 2003). The challenge in Australia is that the very framework of human rights and democracy, embedded in the core (dominant) institutions of that society, and which articulate those values as normative references, do not deliver these values in practice (D'Cruz and Steele, 2003).

An ethics of engagement – necessarily an engagement with difference – has demanded a continual re-assessment of definitions of being human over the last century and more. As the international community has attempted to organise itself according to the principles of the Universal Declaration of Human Rights (UDHR), conceptions of what being fully human implies have led to pressures for a sustained and principled exposure of the *other*. The momentum of this exposure has produced extensive and rigorous scholarly and activist enquiry into markers of difference such as (but not limited to) slavery, gender, sexuality, indigeneity, age, disability, genetics, and the refugee. Incorporating a forensic enquiry into these markers has brought us face to face with the polyversal nature of being human. The paradox of human rights language lies in its ability to provide both a means of ethical intervention as well as the normative reference.

Boutros Boutros-Ghali has captured this paradox and the challenge of the ethics of engagement thus,

> Indeed, human rights, viewed at the universal level, bring us face-to-face with the most challenging dialectical conflict ever: between 'identity' and 'otherness', between the 'myself' and 'others.' They teach us in a direct, straightforward manner that we are at the same time identical and different. (1994: 7)

Nothing could be more important, nor relevant to humanity's survival, it seems to me, than this dialectic. The field of its concern lies in the interconnectedness between ethics and culture. It is my contention that activating human rights is much more than legal or legislative reform (although these are crucial features of survival), and must include a practice of human rights that is nourished and guided by universal concerns for the specifics of humanity. In other words, human rights need to be considered as ethical interventions on behalf of humanity and practiced in their social, ecological and cultural contexts.

The contemporary human rights framework or ethical map is the result of many hundreds, perhaps thousands, of years of deliberation on how human beings can live together and co-exist peacefully.

The relatively recent development of the UDHR in 1948 is one moment in the continuous attempt to marry ethics with industriousness, and represents one of the primary stories of the twentieth century (Farmer, 2005: 220). Together with the consolidation of globalisation (through late Capitalism) and the entrenchment of the international networked society (Castells, 1997), human rights sit paradoxically at the helm of 'progress'. And this most powerful story now confronts us in the twenty-first century. It is a challenging story that has all the hallmarks of realisation, rhetoric, hypocrisy and pathos, a story that can both deepen humanity's intelligence or its self-deception. For Arundhati Roy that story is presently held hostage by the economic imperative that relegates the ethics of engagement to a largely tokenistic and minor role (2004). It is difficult to assess therefore the implicit and explicit value of human rights and how their activation can deeply ameliorate the human condition. The next part of this chapter, however, seeks to draw our attention to the praxis of human rights as an imperative at the heart of human well-being.

What activates Human Rights?

The need for human rights is learned. Human rights are learned through the absence of dignity and freedom or through the governmentality of discrimination.[1] It has arisen as a crucial element of survival through the effects of war, abuse, dislocation, poverty or deprivation. Or, its request is a response to the denial of community and identity, where survival has become imminent due to perceived or actual processes of exclusion.

The language of survival is a complex and immediate one with lasting effects. When, through the social and historical forces of a time and place, a person or community becomes aware of the need to survive; the attachment to life, expressed through the need for recognition, respect, justice, integrity and dignity, is invoked against the lie that there is no immediate (or continuing) danger. In this manner, human rights are clearly about the face-to-face encounter underpinned by an ethics of engagement across culture(s).

The insights of Edward Said reverberate in this language of survival. In his classic text, *Culture and Imperialism* (1993: 408), he concludes

> Survival in fact is about the connections between things; in Eliot's phrase, reality cannot be deprived of the 'other echoes [that] inhabit the garden'.

This statement is worth considering carefully in relation to the idea of human rights. Human rights do not exist within a vacuum but are historically and contextually dependent. They offer a means of connecting human beings together through a universal matrix of shared (moral and ethical) concerns. But, importantly, as human rights have become cogent, contested, convergent and critical features of twenty-first century sensibilities, their central paradox, that is, their *modus operandi* – the crucial connection between vision and practice, between ideal and action – has been threatened by the irony of legitimacy. In other words, as human rights have become part and parcel of contemporary legal, cultural and political landscapes, and thereby legitimised, their value has been compromised. The very fact that human rights literature is mainly found in the field of law attests to the removal of human rights praxis from everyday reality.

The language of human rights that have their lineage drawn from the twentieth century, developed in response to horrendous crimes by humanity against itself, not to sideline the impact humanity also had upon the planet. With well over 203 million people killed in that century by genocide, wars and other forms of 'cleansing' and 'clearing', collective humanity's response was to institutionally inscribe an international standard of principles by which protection and affirmation could be declared (Rummel, 1994: 5). The UDHR became a moral map of survival, a means of legitimising core human rights concerns across the spectrum of humanity's activities.

A key argument in this chapter is that the UDHR is an attempt at stabilising humanity's most important connections, bringing into focus that crucial dialectic between the *self* and *other*. In relating this universal map to the concept of survival, the UDHR's value takes place in specific social, cultural and political contexts. This implies that whenever we consider the meaning of human rights language and instruments in our lives, we must explore the axiological nature of those human rights. To understand the fact that 'survival is about the connections between things', is to see what value human rights language, practice and knowledge has in our everyday lives.

Another key argument is that Said's ultimate analysis of survival expresses a claim of and for humanity in the face of de-humanisation. The ethics of engagement spoken of earlier is contingent on a forensic analysis of how de-humanisation occurs. Recent work by Australian scholars who examine the de-humanisation of Arab-Australians in the wake of September 11, terrorism and refugees, demonstrate the power of de-humanising ideologies that conflate the 'other' with the 'barbarian'. Their analysis of the production of the 'evil incarnate' 'Arab other' in Australian society, shows a 'systematic dehumanising of those involved, whether they be criminals, terrorists or refugees' (Poynting et al., 2004: 38). A society interpreting itself through ideologies of de-humanisation sits in clear contradistinction to the language of human rights. The activation of human rights against de-humanisation arises immediately as a language and ethical engagement that, in the poignant words of Upendra Baxi, 'give voice to human suffering' (1999: 103).

Principled exposures of the human condition

An effective way to examine the axiological nature of human rights is through reflecting on the role of the human rights activist. Eleanor Roosevelt perhaps states this best in an address she gave in 1958

> Where, after all, do human rights begin? In small places, close to home – so close and so small that they cannot be seen on any map of the world. Yet they are the world of the individual person: the neighbourhood [s]he lives in; the school or college [s]he attends; the factory, farm or office where [s]he works. Such are the places where every man, woman and childe seeks equal justice, equal opportunity, equal dignity, without discrimination. Unless these rights have meaning there, they have little meaning anywhere. Without concerted citizen action to uphold them close to home, we shall look in vain for progress in the larger world. Thus we believe that the destiny of human rights is in the hands of all our citizens in all our communities.

In this rendition of an activist, the underpinning value and usefulness of human rights is in their contextualisation; in their application, connection to, and realisation in, everyday life. In recent work done in the field of disability and human rights, Gerard Goggin and Christopher Newell have contextualised the position of people with disability in everyday Australia. Following Roosevelt, they examine and, importantly, expose, the social, cultural, economic and political apartheids that exist for people with disability. By looking at the intersection between human rights, disability and refugees, for example – a severely under-researched area – they expose 'the creation of disability through the brutal penal and exclusionary mechanisms of Australian detention policy' (Goggin and Newell, 2005: 169).

In my view, human rights are activated by insights into normative references that are unquestioned and systemically legitimated through governmentality. Once human rights thinking is activated in a given context, however, the dialectic of *self* and *other* becomes alive. It is in this sense that John Berger writes about the work that Indian writer/activist Arundhati Roy does in the face of human rights violations in India and across the world. Berger argues that Roy is an embodiment of what we need to do in awakening the 'voice of human suffering'. What does he mean by embodiment?

> Of being fully alive in our world, such as it is, and of getting close to and listening to those for whom this world has become intolerable. (Berger in Roy, 2001: xxiii)

Interestingly, Roy, at a lecture given in 2004 as a recipient of the Sydney Peace Prize, opened her thoughts by denying that she was an activist; rather, she was a literary figure. Her conception of an activist, it became evident, was someone who carried placards and participated in explicit and visible protests. I would argue with Roy, however, that her literary works are in fact profound ethical engagements. Her critical essays on the devastating effects of the Narmada Dam project in India upon millions of people, together with her recent incisive investigations into the industrial/militarist imperial United States, demonstrate powerful principled exposures of the dominant forces at work in the world today. In my view, then, Roy is clearly an activist. What I would like to emphasise here is that I think there is a fundamental need for activism to be understood more comprehensively, to recast our material view of an activist into a nuanced appreciation of its range and possibilities.

There are, therefore, many forms of human rights activism; they all have in common the basic drive towards the amelioration of the human condition. In the final section of this chapter I would like to extend these thoughts by drawing on an example of how human rights are activated through the interdependence of self and world transformation. My interest here is in the spiritual dimension of being an unruly human rights activist.

Achyut Patwardhan (1905–1992) was one of India's famous freedom fighters. I was fortunate enough to have him as a mentor for several years through the 1980s until he died. In Patwardhan's early years following his education, he became a Professor of Economics at the Central Hindu College in Varanasi. But, in 1932 his serious interest in politics saw him enter into the Independence Movement and he became a close associate of Mahatma Gandhi as well as a leading Congress Party member. Infused with socialist ideology, Patwardhan eventually quit Congress to form the Socialist Party of India. Until 1950 he was involved in many sustained underground activities against colonial rule and for a decade he was in and out of prison. The esteem in which he was held was apparent when he was asked to consider taking up the position of President in post-colonial India. However, an event happened towards the end of the Second World War that changed his regard for politics fundamentally. The bombing of Hiroshima led Patwardhan to consider the futility of politics and of any ideology.

Following the thoughts of his friend, the Indian philosopher J. Krishnamurti, his conception of revolution as an outward, political event changed entirely towards a position that the only worthwhile revolution was psychological, ecological and spiritual. From 1950 until his death Patwardhan worked to bring change through education. His principled exposure consisted of enquiring into the source of human suffering, which for him lay in the 'brain of man' (1982: 31). Patwardhan's strong commitment to equality and freedom, which had been central to his quest for an independent India, remained unchanged throughout his later life, but his regard for the value of political and legal architecture in bringing about realistic and actual amelioration of the human condition waned. His activism radically transformed from an outward focused to a holistic approach to peace and conflict resolution based on awareness, dialogue, and loving kindness. Patwardhan would say that this is where human rights begin, where they are activated, in the convergence of *self* and *other*.

In a similar vein, the Tibetologist Robert Thurman has written about this in his work on the Buddhist philosopher Nagarjuna. Thurman writes that

> The primary Buddhist position on social action is one of total activism, an unswerving commitment to complete self-transformation and complete world-transformation. (1983: 19)

Nagarjuna and Patwardhan shared a passion for such an ethical engagement with the world based on principles that went further than the Universal Declaration of Human Rights. Commenting on Nagarjuna's approach to ethics, equally applicable to Patwardhan's, Thurman states

> It was revolutionary in its transcendentalistic critique of ideology, in its stress on individualism, in its pacifism, in its universalistic missionary zeal to spread enlightenment. (1983: 30)

The individualism spoken of here sits in contradistinction to the individualism as expressed through ideologies such as capitalism. Nagarjuna's view is that true individuality is based on recognition of indivisibility, that the *self* and *other* are interdependent. The response to the dialectic between *self* and *other* is thus explicated in principles that clearly focus on 'giving voice to human suffering' through a spiritual engagement. This is one response to that 'ontological community of suffering' to which humanity belongs. Becoming aware of the need for a comprehensive understanding of human rights activism is something that requires a great deal of energy and consideration. Vaclav Havel has commented

> Becoming a dissident is not something that happens overnight. You do not simply decide to become one. It is a long chain of steps and acts. And very often during this process, you do not really reflect upon what is happening. You know that you want to avoid any debt that would put a stain on your life. You don't want to become involved with the dirt that is around you and one day, all of a sudden you wake up and realise that you are a dissident, that you are a human rights activist. With me the story was rather similar. It was only much later, while I was in prison, that I started reflecting on the process of why I had done what I had done. There must be some, call it 'transcendental,' source of energy that helps you overcome all these sacrifices. Now some people may disagree with this idea of a transcendental source, but I feel it. While I was in prison, I often thought about why a man decides to remain decent, a man of integrity, even in situations when he or she is on his own, and nobody knows your actions or thoughts – except you yourself. Even in these situations a man can feel bad, can have a bad conscience, can feel remorse. Why is this? How is it possible? And my answer to this is that there must be another eye looking on – that it's not just the people surrounding you that make the difference. I have

> no evidence of the existence of such an eye, but I'm drawing on the archetypal certainty of such existence. (cited in Cuomo, 2000: 134)

Through this chapter the point has been made that human rights are translated through the lens of being human and in everyday life more than we think. They do not simply lie in the legal or political theatres of our lives. Indeed, as has been argued throughout, human rights are absolutely about the human condition. They are about survival, connection as well as transformation.

What remains central to this discussion is that activating human rights demands a concerted effort to 'give voice to human suffering.' I have outlined how human rights are contextually driven through ethical interventions. The importance of human rights, it seems to me, does lie in the dialectic between *self* and *other* that Boutros Boutros-Ghali speaks about. And perhaps that is the point of human rights – they bring us face to face with the everyday moral and ethical questions of co-existence and relationship. In the praxis of human rights we are most of all tested for our humanity. As Paul Gilroy so poignantly states

> The […] challenge defined here is that histories of suffering should not be allocated exclusively to their victims. If they were, the memory of the trauma would disappear as the living memory of it died away. […] This difficult stance challenges that unnamed group to witness sufferings that pass beyond the reach of words and, in so doing, to see how an understanding of one's own particularity or identity might be transformed as a result of a principled exposure to the claims of otherness. (Gilroy, 2000: 114–115)

The value of human rights, therefore, lies in their activation. Only through our ability to translate the human condition in a contextual and responsible manner will it be possible to transform the self and the world.

Endnotes

1 Following Michel Foucault, I am suggesting that the language of human rights is caught within a matrix of governance, which is both objectively constructed through an ensemble of sites, mechanisms and instrumentalities, as well as subjectively, through the interiorisation of self-governance.

References

Atkinson, J., 2002, *Trauma Trails: Recreating Song Lines*, (Melbourne: Spinifex).

Baxi, U., 1999, 'Voices of Suffering, Fragmented Universality, and the Future of Human Rights', in H. W. Burns and S. Marks (Eds.), *The Future of International Human Rights*, (New York: Transnational), pp. 101–157.

Beger, N., 2004, *Tensions in the Struggle for Sexual Minority Rights in Europe*, (Manchester: Manchester University Press).

Boutros-Ghali, B., 1994, 'Human rights: the common language of humanity. Opening statement of the United Nations Secretary-General,' *World Conference on Human Rights*, (New York: United Nations Department of Public Information), pp. 5–21.

Castells, M., 1997, *The Power of Identity*, (London: Blackwell).

Cuomo, K., 2000, 'Speak Truth to Power', in N. Richardson (Ed.), *Human Rights Defenders Who Are Changing the World*, (New York: Crown Publishers), p. 134.

Dechian, S. et al. (Eds.), 2004, *Dark Dreams: Australian Refugee Stories*, (Adelaide, Wakefield Press).

D'Cruz, J. V. and Steele, W., 2003, *Australia's Ambivalence Towards Asia*, (Monash: Monash University Press).

Eisenstein, Z., 2004, *Against Empire*, (Melbourne: Spinifex Press).

Farmer, P., 2005, *Pathologies of Power: Health, Human Rights and the New War on the Poor*, (Berkeley: University of California Press).

Fields, A. B., 2003, *Rethinking Human Rights for the New Millennium*, (New York: Palgrave Macmillan).

Foucault, M., 1979, 'Governmentality', in B. Turner and P. Hamilton (Eds.), *Citizenship: Critical Concepts*, (London: Routledge), pp. 437–451.

Gandhi, L., 1998, *Postcolonial Theory*, (St Leonards: Allen and Unwin).

Gilroy, P., 2000, *Between Camps: Race, Identity and Nationalism at the End of the Colour Line*, (London: Allen Lane).

Goggin, G. and Newell, C., 2005, *Disability in Australia: Exposing a Social Apartheid*, (Kensington: University of New South Wales Press).

Hage, G., 2003, *Against paranoid nationalism: searching for hope in a shrinking Society,* (Annandale, N.S.W.: Pluto Press).

Jayasuriya, L., Walker, D. and Gothard, J. (Eds.), (2003) *Legacies of white Australia: race, culture and nation*, (Crawley, W.A.: University of Western Australia Press).

Jayakar, P. and Patwardhan, S. (Eds.), 1982, *Within the Mind: On J. Krishnamurti*, (Madras: Krishnamurti Foundation India).

Mansfield, N., 2000, *Subjectivity: Theories of the Self from Freud to Haraway*, (St Leonards Allen: and Unwin).

Moreton-Robinson, A., 2003, 'Introduction: resistance, recovery and revitalisation', in M. Grossman (Ed.), *Blacklines*, (Melbourne: Melbourne University Press), pp. 127–131.

Nguyen, H., (2004) 'Journey to Freedom', in S. Dechian et al. (Eds.), *Dark Dreams*, (Adelaide: Wakefield Press), pp. 198–204.

Offord, B., 2003, *Homosexual Rights as Human Rights*, (Berne: Peter Lang).

Poynting, S., Noble, G., Tabar, P., and Collins, J., 2004, *Bin Laden in the Suburbs*, (Sydney: Sydney Institute of Criminology).

Robinson, F., 1998, 'The Limits of a rights-based approach to international ethics,' in T. Evans (Ed.), *Human Rights Fifty Years On*, (Manchester: Manchester University Press), pp. 58–76.

Roosevelt, E., 1958, *The Great Question,* (New York: United Nations).

Roy, A., 2001, *The algebra of infinite justice*, (London: Penguin).

Roy, A., 2004, *The Ordinary Person's Guide to Empire*, (London: Flamingo).
Rummel, R., 1994, 'Power, Genocide and Mass Murder,' *Journal of Peace Research*, 31(1): 1–10.
Said, E., 1993, *Culture and Imperialism*, (London: Vintage).
——, 1994, *Representations of the Intellectual*, (London: Vintage).
Sen, A., 2000, *Development as Freedom*, (New York: Anchor Books).
Thurman, R., 1983, 'Guidelines for Buddhist social activism based on Nagarjuna's "Jewel garland of royal counsels"', *Eastern Buddhist*, 16, Spring: 19–51.
Turner, B., 1993, 'An Outline of a Theory of Human Rights,' *Sociology*, 27(3): 489–512.
Tutu, D., 1999, *No Future Without Forgiveness*, (London: Rider).

JIM IFE

Human Rights beyond the 'Three Generations'

It has become common to refer to three categories of human rights, sometimes also referred to as the three 'generations' of human rights, namely *civil and political rights* (first generation), *economic, social and cultural rights* (second generation) and *collective rights* (third generation) (Ife, 2001). The distinction between the first two categories reflects UN usage, and also more or less coincides with the distinction between 'positive' and 'negative' rights (Gewirth, 1996). Civil and political rights (negative rights) are seen as generally requiring protection against abuse, whereas economic, social and cultural rights (positive rights) require more positive action on behalf of the state or civil society in order for those rights to be attained and realised, for example through the provision of health, education, housing and social security. The addition of the third 'generation' of collective rights is an acknowledgement of the essential individualism in the way first and second generation rights have been constructed, and the need also to incorporate more collective understandings of rights, especially in light of the so-called 'Asian critique' of rights as a western preoccupation (Bell, Nathan and Peleg, 2001; Meijer, 2001; Bauer and Bell, 1999; Van Ness, 1999). This has represented an important attempt to broaden the discourse to include non-western understandings and has facilitated cross-cultural dialogue about human rights, though it should be noted that the three generations also reflect the trinity of 'Liberty, Equality, Fraternity' of the French Revolution and thus remain squarely within the western tradition.

While the three generations have proved to be a useful typology for conceptualising rights, and have helped to extend the idea of human rights beyond a narrow western liberal construction, it is the contention of this chapter that this does not stand up to close scrutiny, and is a limited and inconsistent framework. A broader perspective on human rights can be achieved from a critique of the traditional three generations, and the development of a more conceptually consistent alternative.

Before attempting this task, however, it is important to acknowledge the problematic nature of any such categorisation. Allocating rights to particular categories can create artificial distinctions, and is in line with the modernist, rationalist (and some would add patriarchal) urge to classify, which can discourage holistic and ecological thinking. It erodes the notion of the indivisibility of human rights. On the other hand, classifications of rights (or of anything else, for that matter) can be a useful analytical tool, can encourage people to think about the breadth and complexity of the field encompassed by the idea of human rights, and can lead to further questioning and understanding. Indeed, debating and arguing about classification can be an important form of intellectual inquiry, and can encourage critical analysis of what we really mean when we define or describe a certain right. The three generations classification, though it has significant weaknesses which will be explored below, has itself been useful in helping people to see beyond traditional 'civil and political' framings of human rights, and also to think about collective understandings. The position of this paper, therefore, is that such classifications can be useful, and indeed important, while at the same time acknowledging their potential limitations, especially if they are understood as static, rigid definitions, rather than as categories which can themselves be contested, with permeable conceptual boundaries between them. Categories of human rights might thus be seen as representing different aspects of the totality of rights, consistent with the idea of indivisibility, rather than as distinct definitions of different types of rights. From a human rights education perspective, opening up such classifications to scrutiny and debate is itself a fruitful basis for education and conceptual development.

The first and most obvious problem with the three generations is their labels of 'first', 'second' and 'third'. The three are named in that way simply because that is the order in which they emerged in western thought since the Enlightenment, and by assuming and privileging this context, the 'three generations' typology still locates the human rights discourse firmly within the modern western intellectual tradition. It thus does little to address the critiques that human rights need to be understood from other cultural traditions than the western. There is a further problem with the numbering of the 'generations', in that denoting them as first, second and third can be seen to imply a priority for civil and political rights, as if they somehow 'come first' in any consideration of human rights. A hierarchy of rights is therefore assumed, and this reinforces the tendency, supported by media usage, by dominant legal discourses of human rights, and by western liberalism, to give priority to civil and political rights, and thereby to marginalise other categories of rights.

Johan Galtung (1994) has suggested that the three generations be labelled blue, red and green, rather than first, second and third. This of course overcomes the above objection, removing any necessary primacy for civil and political rights, but it causes additional problems by associating the three categories of human rights with particular ideologies. While indeed there is some association of 'first generation' rights with liberalism, 'second generation' rights with socialism, and 'third generation' rights with green ideology and communitarianism, the association is not necessarily as strong as such labels would imply. Galtung's view also accepts the legitimacy of the three categories, but a further examination suggests that, quite apart from the problematic numbering, the categories themselves are conceptually inconsistent, and thus an inadequate analytical tool.

The next section of this paper explores in more detail some of the problems inherent in the three generations (even without numbers), and proposes a reformulated typology. There are five arguments that underlie this approach.

Individual and collective rights

In the traditional 'three generations' typology, the creation of a separate category for collective rights represents a different basis of classification from the creation of categories for civil and political, and economic, social and cultural rights. The first two generations are based on a classification of *rights to* certain things, whereas the third generation is based on *rights of*; the emphasis here is on a characteristic of those claiming the right (in this case collectivities), rather than, as with the first and second generations, a characteristic of the claimed rights themselves. This creates considerable difficulties. The most obvious, and significant, is the implication that if third generation rights are different from the other two because they are collective, then the first and second generations must, by definition, consist of individual rights. This forces an individualistic construction on all rights belonging in the first two generations, ignoring the fact that many of these can also be understood as applying collectively. To take a classic first generation right as an example, the right of freedom of expression can apply to collectivities as well as to individuals, as in claims for the rights of Indigenous groups, or the rights of people with disabilities *as a group,* to be heard. Similarly, classic second generation rights, such as the rights to education and to health, can be seen as applying to communities and societies (e.g. the right of a community to the benefits of education, the right of Indigenous People *as a group* to adequate health care), as well as to individuals. In addition, some rights understood as typically third generation can also be appropriately categorised as 'civil and political' or as 'economic, social and cultural'. For example, a typical third generation right – the right to benefit from economic development – also belongs in the second generation, as it is properly an economic right.

The standard 'three generation' classification can thus be seen as effectively marginalising collective rights, by placing them in a separate category, and thereby allowing civil and political rights, and economic, social and cultural rights, to be understood as essentially individual rights. It thus reinforces the very problem it aimed to solve, and far from incorporating collective understandings of rights, it marginalises them by removing them from the whole range of civil, political, economic, social and cultural rights.

A more consistent and useful classification of rights would accept that most if not all human rights can have both individual and collective dimensions, and that therefore collective rights should not constitute a separate category of classification. Rather, all categories of rights can be understood as applying both individually and collectively: it is effectively a different dimension of analysis. Further, we can understand that both individual and collective constructions apply to the duties implied by rights, as well as to the rights themselves. Just as rights can be individual or collective, so can duties (see figure 1). Classic liberalism tends to emphasise individual rights and individual duties, and because of the dominance of liberalism in western political discourse, this has been the dominant western framing of human rights. But other ideological traditions of human rights take a different view: socialism tends to emphasise individual rights but collective duties, especially the duties of the state to provide for the individual. Confucianism, on the other hand, emphasises collective rights and individual duties, with the onus on the individual to contribute to the society and to preserve the rights of the collective. And communitarianism tends to emphasise both collective rights and collective duties, as it is in the collective experience that both rights and duties are seen to be enacted. Of course such statements represent over-simplification, and there are variations within each ideological tradition, but this perspective draws attention to the way in which liberal individualist understandings of human rights have pervaded the discourse, and have resulted in the inconsistencies of the 'three generations' framework, and also suggests that other positions will privilege collective understandings of rights, or duties, or both.

Figure 1: Rights and responsibilities: individual and collective

		Rights	
		Individual	Collective
Responsibilities/ Duties	Individual	LIBERAL	CONFUCIAN
	Collective	SOCIALIST	COMMUNITARIAN

Disaggregating economic, social and cultural rights

The inclusion of economic rights, social rights and cultural rights in a single category seems to have little conceptual justification. Originally this category seems to have been created by the UN as a grab-bag for all the other rights that could not be readily included under the heading 'civil and political'. However economic rights, social rights and cultural rights are clearly distinct. Economic rights are of a fundamentally different nature, given their essentially material base, when contrasted with social and cultural rights. Indeed it could be argued by advocates of the market that economic rights should have primacy over some aspects of social rights; if our economic rights are met, it might be suggested, we will be able to purchase education, health care, housing, and so on. Economic rights – rights to employment, to earn an adequate wage, to social security, to freedom to spend one's money as one wishes – hardly fit in the same category as social or cultural rights. Indeed, in a world dominated by market theory and neo-liberalism, to include the three together is likely to marginalise social and cultural rights, as economic rights will inevitably assume a greater importance.

Indigenous writers, and writers from non-western traditions, have emphasised the importance of cultural rights, and rights to freedom of cultural expression (Garkawe, Kelly and Fisher, 2001). These have little in common with economic rights, and insofar as they are conceptually distinct they deserve a category of their own. Indeed, not to validate cultural rights with their own distinct category might be seen as devaluing different cultural traditions, including Indigenous wisdom. Culture, indeed, is central to human rights (Bell, Nathan and Peleg, 2001; Schmale, 1993). Our rights are constructed, protected, realised and respected in different cultural contexts, which are themselves dynamic and pluralist. It is often through different forms of cultural expression, and through debates about cultural practices, that our assertion and attainment of human rights are realised. The right to belong to a culture, to participate in a culture, and to a range of forms of cultural expression is therefore necessary for the achievement of human rights. From this perspective, to include cultural rights in a single category with economic and social rights is not only inappropriate and inconsistent, but it devalues cultural diversity and the significance of culture as the context for human interaction.

Social rights are appropriately linked neither with economic nor cultural rights. They include rights to education, to raise a family, to freedom from discrimination, to adequate social services, to adequate leisure, to choice of lifestyle, and so on. They are distinct from cultural rights, in that social rights themselves can be seen as transcending cultural boundaries, though the way they are realised and protected will, of course, vary significantly according to cultural context.

In summary, an argument can be made that economic rights, social rights and cultural rights should be disaggregated, and become three separate categories in any revised typology of rights. Linking them within a single category is more a function of the historical politics of the UN than a considered analysis, and indeed serves to marginalise the importance of each.

Survival rights

The traditional category of 'social rights' contains a number of rights that do not naturally carry a label of 'social'. Included here, probably because they did not really fit anywhere else in the UN framework, is the set of rights that might more properly be labelled 'survival rights' – rights to food, water, clothing, shelter and basic health care. Some writers do not categorise these as 'rights', but rather as basic human needs (Doyal and Gough, 1991), from which one might develop a theory of rights. However, to do so confuses the categories of rights and needs, which I have explored elsewhere (Ife, 1997, 2001). While there is not space in this chapter to develop the argument fully, the position I have taken suggests that all 'needs' that are asserted normatively (that is, there is an expectation that the defined 'need' should be met) imply an assumption – usually implicit – of rights. Hence rights are implied by statements of needs, and represent the normative aspect of any need statement. Needs then become the local contextualisation of universal rights (for example, the right to education can be translated into very different educational needs, depending on context). In this light, to talk about basic human needs masks the reality that one is really talking about basic human rights, and so in the case of survival rights the language of rights, rather than needs, is still appropriate. Survival rights are actually derived from the basic 'right to live', and are the rights to those things without which life would be impossible.

Survival rights are not really 'social', as they do not necessarily imply social interaction with others, but rather are the rights that we claim as basic human rights in order that a person may actually survive to enjoy and exercise her/his other rights. While such rights may (like others) be understood individually or collectively, 'social' is not really an appropriate label. Indeed, to include such rights in a 'social rights' category can serve to devalue the other social rights – education, choice of lifestyle, family rights and so forth – as there is an inevitable imperative to meet survival rights before bothering about others. Some rights traditionally regarded as 'civil and political' might also be included here as survival rights, for example the right not to be killed or severely tortured, which is of a rather different order from other civil and political rights such as the right to vote and the right to free speech.

Human rights are commonly claimed to be indivisible, and claims that one set of rights is more important than another are usually based on some contestable ideological principle. However, a strong case can be made for this limited group of rights – survival rights – to have primacy over all others, simply because their attainment is a necessary precondition for any other right to be realised. Therefore it seems appropriate to place them in a separate category, in acknowledgement of their unique status, and also allowing those rights that might more properly be labelled 'social rights' to be considered on their own merits.

Environmental rights

If the traditional 'third generation' of collective rights is to be dispensed with, it is important to ask what might happen in any new typology to the rights commonly understood within this category. Some of these rights can be easily accommodated elsewhere, for example the right to benefit from economic development is an economic right, and the right to enjoy a cohesive, harmonious social order is a social right. One category of rights, however, which have been seen as belonging to the third generation, and which do not readily fit elsewhere, is environmental rights. No categorisation of human rights can afford to ignore environmental rights, given the central place that they now occupy in human rights discourse. The recognition of intergenerational rights – our responsibilities to address human rights violations in the past and to protect the human rights of future generations (Falk, 2000) – gives environmental rights a particular importance, and the scale of current environmental degradation gives them particular urgency.

It can be argued, therefore, that environmental rights warrant a category of their own. This has the added advantage of removing environmental rights from the 'collective' category, as clearly environmental rights can also be claimed, enjoyed and violated at an individual level, as well as collectively. Environmental rights relate to our interaction with the physical world, and in that sense they are distinct from other commonly claimed human rights.

Spiritual rights

A further group of rights which can be proposed as warranting a separate category is spiritual rights. This is contestable, as it might be argued either that spiritual rights can be subsumed as part of cultural rights, or that the right to practise one's religion of choice belongs in civil and political rights, hence there is no need for a separate category. Both these, however, represent a limited view of human spirituality. While there are clearly cultural aspects to the experience and expression of spirituality, for many people spirituality is more than culture, and extends beyond the bounds of any cultural context. For some, spirituality is a deeply personal and individual experience, while for others, spirituality is part of the experience of the natural world, and hence spiritual rights might be closer to environmental rights than to any other category. For some, spirituality is experienced primarily through organised religion. For others, cultural practices, such as music, poetry and art, can be a profound expression of spirituality. And for some, the simple experience of human community and connectedness with others is essentially spiritual. Spirituality, therefore, can cover more than the cultural. And the right to freedom of religious expression covers a wider field than we would normally associate with civil and political rights.

But there is a further argument for the inclusion of spiritual rights as a separate category of human rights. The secular rationalist assumptions inherent in the western world view have devalued spirituality as an important aspect of the human condition, and this is reflected in human rights discourse. If human rights are to move beyond their characteristic western framing, to include other traditions and world views, the marginalisation of spirituality cannot be justified. For Indigenous People, spiritual rights represent one of the most important aspects of human rights, and their claims for land rights, for rights to sacred sites, for rights to sacred artefacts, and rights to repatriation of artefacts and human remains stored in museums, can only be understood properly within some conception of spiritual rights (Garkawe, Kelly and Fisher, 2001). If one regards spiritual rights as human rights, that is, the rights of all people to their own forms of spirituality, then claims by Indigenous People to land, artefacts, sites and so on cease to be 'special pleading' on the part of a particular group, and instead become a claim to the realisation of fundamental human rights. If human rights are an expression of what makes us human, spiritual rights have a clear place alongside the other rights discussed above.

A seven-fold typology

The arguments above lead to a typology of human rights containing seven categories, rather than the traditional three:

- Survival rights
- Social rights
- Economic rights
- Cultural rights
- Civil and political rights
- Environmental rights
- Spiritual rights

It should be noted that no attempt has been made to disaggregate or redefine civil and political rights, the traditional 'first generation'. This is because, unlike the other traditional categories, this seems to be a clearly understood category, which lends itself to analysis. Seeking to divide it into separate categories of civil and political rights, however, presents further difficulties. The boundary between civil rights and political rights is unclear, and it might well be argued that it is an artificial distinction. Certainly the rights commonly claimed within the category of 'civil and political rights' – the traditional 'first generation' of human rights – belong readily together, and any attempt to separate them seems pointless.

Human Rights and community development

There is a natural connection between human rights and community development. This argument has been developed in more detail elsewhere (Ife, 2001), but in brief, the connection develops out of the link between rights and duties or obligations. Rights cannot 'exist' in isolation, associated with a single individual; rather the link between rights and obligations suggests that rights can only exist within a community of interlocking responsibilities (Gewirth, 1996). The obligation associated with a right may be seen as held by another individual, by a community, by civil society or by the state, but in whatever form, it implies people, either individually or collectively, interacting with each other, and constructing their rights and responsibilities in their daily human interactions. From this perspective, a strong human rights regime requires a strong community. Further, there is, arguably, an obligation to exercise one's rights; there is not much point in having rights if they are not exercised, and so a society that values human rights is an active participatory society where those rights are not only protected, but are realised.

While the argument is more complex than has been presented here, the point for present purposes is to emphasise the link between human rights and community development. Indeed, to the extent that human rights are about articulating our *common humanity*, and that community development is about achieving *human community*, the two might be regarded as closely related, given that the terms are effectively synonymous. Community development requires a human rights framework, and human rights require strong communities. This close link suggests that community development theory may have something to contribute to human rights, and it is notable that, working from a different set of assumptions, at a different time, and from a different disciplinary perspective, I derived a list of 'dimensions' of community development (Ife, 2002) that is remarkably similar to the above list of human rights categories; the six dimensions are: social, economic, political, cultural, environmental and personal/spiritual (only the 'survival' category is missing), and this has proved to be a quite robust and useful categorisation of community development. Yet this similarity is really not so surprising, given the commonalities between human rights and community, and given that each is an attempt to understand the different ways in which human beings relate to each other and develop interlocking connections of mutual rights and responsibilities.

Using the typology: a matrix for human rights education

Developing such a typology of human rights may have academic interest, but it can only really be justified if it proves to be useful in practice. As was indicated at the beginning of the chapter, a typology of human rights can be justified only if it can create a space for dialogue, and enable people to think about human rights in new ways. For the concluding section of this chapter I will briefly describe how this typology can be used as a basis for human rights education and awareness-raising.

A simple matrix can be drawn, with the seven categories of human rights listed horizontally, while vertically a number of sets of analytical questions about human rights are listed to be applied to each category (see figure 2). Such sets of questions might be:

- What might count as human rights in each category.
- Questions about the religious, philosophical and ideological traditions of rights and obligations.
- Questions about individual and collective understandings of rights.
- Questions about how rights are understood in both public and private domains.
- Questions about the justiciability of human rights, and the role of legislation, courts and legal processes.
- Questions about how structures and discourses of oppression affect rights and their violation: class, gender, race, age, disability, sexuality and so on.
- Questions about responsibilities/obligations associated with rights, including obligations of the individual, the family, the community, civil society, the state, the private sector, and the global community.
- Questions about inter-generational rights; obligations to redress past human rights violations and the responsibility to respect the rights of future generations.
- Questions about the way dialogue about rights can be facilitated, encouraging the rising of community awareness.

Figure 2: The Human Rights Matrix

	Survival Rights	Social Rights	Economic Rights	Civil/ Political Rights	Cultural Rights	Environ-mental Rights	Spiritual Rights
List rights in each category, for example: (not exhaustive lists)	life, food, water, shelter, clothing, health, safety	family life, privacy, recrea-tion/ leisure, educa-tion, choice of: partner, lifestyle, sexu-ality, housing	basic living standard, earn a living, work, social security, savings, choice of spending	free speech, free assembly, vote, fair trial, stand for office, join organis-ations, join union, strike	cultural expres-sion, cultural practices, clothing, religious ex-pression, intel-lectual property, land rights	pollution free, poison free, wilder-ness, beauty, sustain-ability, access to land	choice, religious expres-sion, rituals, experience nature, personal fulfilment, sacred land/ objects
Cultural, religious, philoso-phical and ideological traditions and under-standings							
Individual and collective under-standings of rights							
Rights in the private/ domestic and in the public/ civil domains							
Rights and protection through courts & legislation, justici-ability, etc							

Rights and oppres-sion: class, gender, race, age, disability, sexuality							
Responsi-bilities: individual, family, com-munity, civil society, state, world							
Intergene-rational responsi-bilities to past & future genera-tions							
Education, facilitating dialogue, conscious-ness raising, awareness							

Such a matrix can be used as a basis for human rights education, whether with a school group, university students, community groups or any group interested in exploring the meaning of human rights. Small groups can work on completing all the cells of the matrix, sharing ideas with each other, and debating how the various analytical questions apply to each category of rights. Such a process, of course, will take different forms, depending on the group and the time available. One can use the traditional 'small-groups-with-butchers-paper' approach, or (for a smaller group) simple brainstorming, or a modified Delphi approach by email, or email discussion groups, and so on. To complete the task thoroughly, including informing the group about the analytical questions, can occupy a workshop of several days duration, though more abbreviated or simplified forms could be used where necessary. Initial trials of such a matrix have shown that it can be highly successful in three ways:

- Encouraging people to think about and understand conceptual issues relating to human rights.
- Encouraging people to understand the diversity of human rights.
- Encouraging people to have a sense of ownership of human rights, and to appreciate that rights do not merely 'exist' in treaties, conventions and legislation, but are constructed in our day-to-day lives and interactions with others.

This last point is critically important. Using this approach to human rights education enables people effectively to construct their own declaration of human rights, which may differ in significant respects from the Universal Declaration, but which is grounded in the reality of their own experience, and which derives from their own debates and struggles about what might be involved in sharing a common humanity.

Such a matrix is a tool, not a final word on the definition and categorisation of human rights. Indeed a human rights educator – certainly at university or adult education level – would want to problematise the matrix itself, and allow the participants in a workshop to debate the matrix and, if appropriate, develop an alternative. It thus becomes a tool for creating the space for a dialogue about human rights, in all their complexity. If we reject the positivist account of human rights, and accept an argument that rights are constantly constructed and reconstructed through discursive and reflexive processes, then using the matrix to create a space for dialogue becomes part of the on-going human rights agenda, and reinforces the view that human rights are not located in conventions, treaties and legislation, but in how people live together, work together, play together, respect each other, and both build and experience human community.

References

Bauer, J. and Bell, D. (Eds.), 1999, *The East Asian Challenge for Human Rights*, (Cambridge: Cambridge University Press).

Bell, L., Nathan, A. and Peleg, I. (Eds.), 2001, *Negotiating Culture and Human Rights*, (New York: Columbia University Press).

Doyal, L. and Gough, I., 1991, *A Theory of Human Need*, (London: Macmillan).

Falk, R., 2000, *Human Rights Horizons: The Pursuit of Justice in a Globalizing World*, (London: Routledge).

Galtung, J., 1994, *Human Rights in Another Key*, (Cambridge: Polity Press).

Garkawe, S., Kelly, L. and Fisher, M. (Eds.), 2000, *Indigenous Human Rights*, (Sydney: Sydney Institute of Criminology).

Gewirth, A., 1996, *The Community of Rights*, (Chicago: Chicago University Press).

Ife, J., 1997, *Rethinking Social Work: Towards Critical Practice*, (Melbourne: Longman).

——, 2001, *Human Rights and Social Work: Towards Rights-Based Practice*, (Cambridge: Cambridge University Press).

——, 2002, *Community Development: Community-based Alternatives in an Age of Globalisation*, (Melbourne: Longman).

Meijer, M. (Ed.), 2001, *Dealing With Human Rights: Asian and Western Views on the Value of Human Rights*, (Oxford: World View).

Schmale, W. (Ed.), 1993, *Human Rights and Cultural Diversity*, (Goldbach: Keip).

Van Ness, P. (Ed.), 1999, *Debating Human Rights: Critical Essays from the United States and Asia*, (London: Routledge).

CARL F. STYCHIN

Same-sex Sexualities and the Globalisation of Human Rights[1]

Introduction

Only a few years ago, it was sometimes queried whether 'sexual orientation' raised any human rights issues.[2] Today, those questions have largely ceased to be asked, as sexuality has permeated human rights consciousness. For that, an enormous collective debt is owed to those many courageous activists around the world who have struggled in difficult and dangerous circumstances to articulate their claims openly in a discourse of human rights in order to better people's lives. That is, they have used 'human rights' as a way to connect with others in and out of struggle, and to make a collective difference.

These human rights claims have also connected to the academic and judicial interpretations of human rights. In the past decade, we have witnessed a far more receptive attitude from courts and legislatures in a range of different ways. Same-sex sexuality cases have come to receive a more positive response from many national courts through the interpretation of domestic constitutional rights documents; through the development of the common law; through transnational legal regimes, such as the European Union (EU); and through the discourse of international law and international human rights. Moreover, these different levels and frames through which the language of rights can be mobilised often intersect and interact. As a consequence, rights proponents can claim that the strategy of deploying human rights in the sexuality arena has met with considerable success (but setbacks as well), and believers in liberal legal progress will argue that there is nowhere to go but forward in the making of human rights arguments.

A double movement of globalisation

This story of success and progress can be explained, I argue, through a double movement of globalisation. First, we have witnessed a globalisation of human rights, whereby human rights become, as Peter Fitzpatrick (2001: 120) has argued, the 'pervasive criteria' by which nations approach a universal standard of civilisation, progress and modernity. Rights transcend the particular (despite the fact that human rights discourse presumably must come from a particular place), and become the marker and measure of a global civil society embracing all 'humans' (itself a historically contested concept).

But there is another globalisation move that has occurred: the universalising of same-sex sexualities as identities (Altman, 2002; Manalansan IV, 1993). There are many examples that demonstrate the export of an Anglo-American, 'Stonewall' model of sexuality, identity and liberation.[3] In the Stonewall model, same-sex sexuality marks an identity category that comes to be labelled as gay, lesbian or both (and the two are often problematically conflated). Put crudely, who (in terms of gender) one has sexual relations with is the key to who you are, and the 'coming out' is the central moment of identity formation. The sexual relations model has increasingly transcended its own cultural and historical roots to become universalised as *the* paradigm of sexual identity. This paradigm, however, is a dramatic oversimplification of the dynamics of sexual identity outside of a western (or, more specifically, Anglo-American) frame.

Despite this globalisation movement, activists in many non-Western countries travel between the universalising and essentialising discourse of sexual identity ('we are everywhere'), to a local, historically- and culturally-specific reading of sexuality that resists the bluntness of the Stonewall model (see Cruz-Malavé and Manalansan IV, 2002). Nevertheless, as gays come to appropriate that sexual identity, the universalising language of human rights neatly fits the globalising movement of sexual identity that seems to be occurring (most obviously in urban spaces around the globe). Furthermore, this fusion of the two movements of globalisation has been advanced by human rights law and international human rights experts, who have assisted activists in many parts of the world, and have brought to the attention of the world the abuses to human dignity that have been experienced (see eg Human Rights Watch, 1998; Offord, 2003). Claims to privacy, equality and dignity for those who have been constructed as less than human because of their same-sex sexual practices and desires, clearly lend themselves to these universalising and globalising currents. In this way, they become cosmopolitan claims to justice, which transcend the particularities of time and place through the powerful argument that flows from the desire to be 'who we are'.

Although the ways in which these human rights claims are made is important, what is no less interesting are the ways in which they have been *resisted* in a number of different cultural locations (see Stychin, 1998): we consistently find opposition to *cosmopolitan* claims to human justice firmly grounded in a *communitarian* language that speaks to the preservation of a particular community's 'way of life', tradition, and often, national or local culture. Of course, 'nation' (like sexuality and human rights) is a socially constructed, historically specific identity, which has come to be universalised. To use Benedict Anderson's (1991) famous phrase, nations are 'imagined communities', and it is this imagining that provocatively has been deployed to resist claims for universal human rights through a reverse discourse that employs the language of difference, specificity, history, community, and ultimately, the language of rights itself.

None of this should be surprising. It is well documented how the construction of the imagined community of 'nation' has frequently been realised through the deployment of gender, race, and sexuality. Women have been constructed as 'mothers to the nation', a discursive device by which procreation becomes central to national survival (Yuval-Davies, 1997). Race has also been part of the constitutive formation of the nation, summed up memorably by Paul Gilroy's (1992) phrase 'there ain't no black in the Union Jack'. Less widely known are cases that demonstrate how, when the nation state perceives a threat to its existence, that danger is frequently translated into homosexualised terms. Male same-sex sexuality, for example, has been deployed as the alien 'other', linked to conspiracy, recruitment, the 'third column', and ultimately, constructed as a threat to Western civilisation itself (Moran, 1991; Edelman, 1994).

Interesting inversions of this discourse of civilisation can be documented within a post-colonial context. The southern African region provides perhaps the best known example, particularly as demonstrated by the discourses employed by Robert Mugabe in Zimbabwe, most famously around the Zimbabwean International Book Fair in 1995 – for which the theme was 'human rights', and which was to feature a presence by the organisation Gays and Lesbians of Zimbabwe ('GALZ') (see Engelke, 1999; Stychin, 1998: 89–114; Phillips, 1997). On the eve of the opening, a letter from the state director of information advised the book fair trustees that the government strongly objected to the presence of GALZ. The trustees, claiming that they had been placed in an impossible position, cancelled GALZ's registration. A storm of protest ensured, much of it emanating from South Africa. In this example, Mugabe used a discourse of colonial contamination to shore up the post-colonial state, wherein homosexuality is attributed to the white coloniser, and homosexual relations were the means he used to exploit and contaminate the colonised sexually. Homosexuality becomes an abhorrent Western import.

This discourse is also an important means to strengthen the identity of the beleaguered nation state and the masculine subject, under threat in the current conditions of post-colonial globalisation. The expulsion of homosexuals from the imagery of the nation state becomes metaphorically equated with the erasure of the white coloniser and, with him, his degenerate influence on a mythologised, pre-colonial, 'pure' African (hetero) sexuality. Condemnations of sexual perversion thus are made in the name of an Afrocentric and specifically Zimbabwean national tradition. In this trope, the defence of heterosexuality becomes essential to securing the group right of self-determination of a people protecting its cultural heritage, pre-colonial way of life, and very survival. This is a communitarian claim in defence of community against threats from globalisation and (neo) colonial powers, and it also lends itself to the language of international human rights (ie, the right of a community to preserve its way of life).

One can find parallel movements in the West, for example, in the campaign in the mid-1990s over the decriminalisation of same-sex sexual acts in the state of Tasmania, Australia (see eg Stychin, 1998: 145–193; Morgan, 1994; Morris, 1995). The goal of this struggle was explicitly achieved through the deployment of a discourse of international human rights (cosmopolitan claim) which, it was successfully argued, had been incorporated into a set of Australian cultural values (a communitarian argument) that trumped the particular claim to a uniquely Tasmanian, heterosexual way of life. Australia has long entered into a range of treaty obligations and has sought to abide by their terms domestically, such as the *International Covenant of Civil and Political Rights*, which proved relevant in the case of same-sex sexuality in Tasmania through its protection of the right to privacy. The explanation for the Tasmanian laws – an anomalous legal situation in Australia – was, as Australians will readily explain, the cultural 'peculiarity' of Tasmania, an island state removed from an island continent. Gays, like other 'outsiders' such as environmentalists, have been consistently constructed as those who had arrived in Tasmania to undermine the traditional values of 'the people'.

The implicit, and sometimes explicit, argument of opponents of decriminalisation was that to be an authentic Tasmanian was to be heterosexual. This was a somewhat more complex and nuanced battle over communitarian and cosmopolitan claims, but the language of rights – states' rights – was often deployed in defence of the anti-gay laws (Tenbensel, 1996). In this resistance to gay rights claims, the community itself is constructed as under siege from powerful, metropolitan interests seeking to undermine the rights of a disadvantaged and disenfranchised, 'politically incorrect' community. Moreover, it was argued that the federal system of Australia was intended to protect states from these majoritarian impulses.

Thus, theoretically, we can often find ourselves in a cul-de-sac of rights claims spawned by the globalisation of human rights and sexual identities. Resistance to gay rights is grounded in communitarian claims to difference, specificity, cultural authenticity, and history, which are also, in turn, grounded in the language of rights of self-determination of a people. The question is then about which self, which group, and which right to protect. What 'trumps' what?

Although this may seem to be a theoretical dead end, a closer examination of social movement struggles reveals that activists have had relatively little difficulty rhetorically manoeuvering through the cul-de-sac. Gay rights activists, in quite an array of cultural contexts, have become highly skilled in answering claims to cultural difference and cultural authenticity. Specifically, I refer here to local activists engaged in social struggle resisting nationalist, heterosexist discourses, rather than international lobby groups, which may themselves fall into the trap of a highly cosmopolitan discourse that gives away too much of the communitarian ground to their opponents. Moreover, international gay rights activism, particularly in some forms that emanate from the United States, is sometimes itself in danger of forms of neo-colonialism in relation to local contexts through its adoption of a discourse 'in which a premodern, pre-political non-Euro-American queerness must consciously assume the burdens of representing itself to itself and others as "gay" in order to attain political consciousness, subjectivity, and global modernity' (Cruz-Malavé and Manalansan IV, 2002: 5–6).

By contrast, local activists have adopted a number of effective strategies in making claims to human rights, chief among which is a redeployment of the very communitarian arguments that have been used against them (see generally Stychin, 1998, 2003; LaViolette and Whitworth, 1994). Rather than speaking solely in cosmopolitan terms, we find gay activists first turning to local history and the cultural past to question the idea of an authentic, opposite-sex sexuality and tradition. In other words, they retell the story of nation, but with some new characters introduced (or they redefine well-known characters in terms of sexual desire). It is a reclaiming of a same-sex sexual history that challenges the idea that homosexuality has polluted a sexually pure culture (see Murray and Roscoe, 1998). This, of course, is closely tied to discourses of colonialism. Activists sometimes claim to have discovered an authentic gay past, prior to its condemnation by the coloniser and the missionary in the name of civilisation and Christianity. It may, for instance, involve reclaiming words within indigenous languages to describe same-sex desire. This strategy has proven to be extremely rhetorically powerful, albeit anthropologically problematic. It often falls into the trap of reading Western, twentieth-century identity categories, such as the 'homosexual', back into history and across cultures, which renders the analysis dubious. In response, it can be argued that historical accuracy is not particularly the point, and that the argument is not aimed at anthropologists. Rather, the rhetoric is politically salient and powerful. It rewrites the history of community, allowing for its re-imagination in more inclusive terms.

A second strategy that again tackles communitarian claims on their own terrain has also proven powerful. Gay activists have devised a rhetoric that adopts the theoretical idea of multiple and intersecting identities, which often provides an effective response to the idea of a homogeneous, one-dimensional identity. For example, placards at demonstrations in Tasmania that read 'GAY and TASMANIAN' provide an important counter to claims that these identities are mutually exclusive (Morris, 1995). This is often an important dimension of strategy. It forces opponents to concede that, in their construction of the imagined community, indigenous gays *do* exist, and that they have been expelled from the bounds of community, rather than having never existed within it. In this way, gays are constituted as the disenfranchised, and turned into non-citizen 'others'. They have been forced to migrate to more hospitable surroundings and denied their right to participate as full political citizens of the broader community, unless their sexuality is closeted within the private sphere. To strip your own people of citizenship – and this, I suggest, is crucial to gay rights arguments – is a move which is difficult to justify except in the defence of the survival of a people (although anti-gay discourse often in the past has merged quite seamlessly with an anti-communist discourse, which was described in precisely those terms). That argument itself begins to unravel when gay rights arguments are framed in the language of privacy and equality. These are liberal values that most communities are loathe to dissociate from rhetorically (although part of the difficulty with cosmopolitan rights claims is the assumption of a liberal, universalist consensus, which does not necessarily exist within communitarian discourse).

This leads to the third activist strategy. Activists construct the language of human rights as an essential feature of the community in which the claim is being advanced. In this moment, the cosmopolitanism of rights becomes part of the self-constitution of a people and a community. It makes us who 'we' are. This again proved very effective in the Tasmanian context, in which international human rights discourse was deployed as characteristic of the national law and of the Australian people (Stychin, 1998: 171–193). More dramatically, it has been used very effectively by gay activists in the Republic of South Africa, in which respect for human rights is a leitmotif of the Constitution of the Rainbow Nation, with its extensive constitutional guarantees of equality and rights (de Vos, 2000). International legal standards thereby become part of the essence of a people. This can sometimes also provide a means to conveniently erase egregious abuses of rights that have occurred in the very self-constitution and imagining of the nation. For example, aboriginal peoples might have something to say about the rights-respecting *essence* of white settler societies.

The strategy also may involve the attempt to universalise and essentialise the concept of human rights, as activists claim a history of human rights in a non-Western context. In other words, human rights, like homosexuals, existed prior to the imperialist mission that devastated both – as part of a history of a community – and, therefore, are culturally *authentic* today. Once again, this is undoubtedly anthropologically problematic, for both 'human rights' and 'homosexuality' are historically and culturally contingent (Dembour, 1996; LaViolette and Whitworth, 1994). They are a product of a time and place. Nevertheless, it may be a rhetorically and politically useful strategy.

In sum, we find activists operate at different registers simultaneously: from local, communitarian discourses through to cosmopolitan global claims. They argue from the local level on behalf of grassroots social movements to the transnational level, through organisations such as the International Lesbian and Gay Association ('ILGA'). It is this seamless movement between the local and the global which best describes human rights activism around same-sex sexualities today.

From national communities to supranational standards

A somewhat different activist strategy unfolded recently in Romania, a country that has a shocking history of human rights violations, including against lesbians and gay men, extending from the Ceausescu era (and before) through the post-Communist period. The abuse of human rights was demonstrated by draconian laws against same-sex sexual acts and, moreover, against same-sex sexual expression (Stychin, 2003: 117–118). Most infamously, the 1968 Penal Code saw the enactment of articles 200–202. Under article 200, sexual relations between persons of the same sex were punishable by imprisonment of one to five years. Article 201 declared that acts of sexual perversion were illegal and subject to the same penalty as prescribed by article 200. Article 202 dealt with the sexual corruption of a minor. Human rights organisations have produced extensive and appalling documentation on the ways these laws were enforced during and after the Communist era (Human Rights Watch, 1998). Although the post-Ceausescu government repealed the laws prohibiting abortion, it showed no similar desire to repeal anti-gay criminal laws.

With time, this intransigence dissipated as it became increasingly clear that Romania's future lay westward. It also became apparent that any invitations to join the institutions of the West would come with both political and economic conditions attached. With respect to homosexuality, this was true as early as 1993, when *rapporteurs* from the Council of Europe, visiting Romania following its application for admission, began raising the issue of the treatment of homosexuals. Shrewd political activists in Romania, who formed an NGO called ACCEPT, managed after many years of social struggle to take advantage of a European Union accession agenda in which respect for human rights has become one of the criteria for entry into the EU. In this regard, ACCEPT had the active support of Dutch gay groups, and funding from the Dutch state (Stychin, 2003: 120–122). Originally, funding was obtained from the Embassy of the Netherlands, and subsequently from the Dutch Ministry of Foreign Affairs, as part of a program designed to strengthen institutions in the target countries of

Central and Eastern Europe through their 'twinning' with institutions in the Netherlands. The Romanian activists were twinned with the federation of Dutch associations for the integration of homosexualities ('COC') and this partnership would continue, formally and informally, into the future. The COC-ACCEPT project funding and expertise were crucial in the setting up of an organisational infrastructure, the opening of office space, developing programs and activities.

The arduous character of the Romanian struggle can be explained by the opposition of many nationalist members of parliament, as well as a hostile press, and an Orthodox Church asserting its role in political life. For all of these forces, resistance to change would be characterised consistently in terms of the protection of a religious-cultural way of life, against outside influences and conspiracies seeking to undermine traditional Romanian values (Gallagher, 2001; Roman, 2001). These tropes have a long history in Romania and have been consistently deployed in the name of ethnic nationalism. As well, for the Orthodox Church, the issue of homosexuality provided a means to claim its authority, which enabled it to draw attention away from its own dubious past association with the Ceausescu regime. Within this narrative of nation, many groups – not only homosexuals, but also Jews, Hungarians, and Roma – are constructed as 'other' to the essence of a Romanian identity. They become undeserving of human rights because they have been constructed as *less than human*. The eventual repeal of the anti-gay laws and the enactment of anti-discrimination law (which includes 'sexual orientation' as an enumerated ground of non-discrimination) occurred in January 2002. ACCEPT executive members will readily admit that it was pressure from the institutions of the EU, which they fostered and encouraged, that ultimately led to legal change (Coman, 2001).

The turn to the institutions of the European Union, which have also placed pressure on the Romanian state regarding the human rights of the Roma, institutionalised children, and other minorities, becomes part of a reimagining of identity focused on a highly constructed notion of 'Europeanness', in which respect for human rights becomes a condition of, and an inherent aspect of, what it means to be European (van Bogdandy, 2000). Quite obviously, the boundaries of Europe are currently up for grabs in the circumstances of EU expansion. In this reading, 'Europe' is emblematic of civilization itself because of its respect for human rights. Outside of the fortress of Europe, by contrast, one enters the non-rights respecting, uncivilised 'other'. That other desires entry into civilisation, which, of course, is currently subject to EU immigration control that seeks to protect European civilisation from the barbarians at the gates.

The acceptance of 'European values' has been explicitly described by EU politicians as a precondition for entry into the Union, and this was strategically highly useful for gay activists in Romania, as anti-gay laws become perceived as incompatible with those values. For example, in a letter from eight members of the European Parliament, Prime Minister Nastase was told that '[w]e look forward to welcoming Romania into the European Union, but an essential prerequisite is that we must share the same values. Discrimination on whatever ground may never be permitted' (van der Laan et al., 2001). In this way, European institutions have a civilising and disciplinary function, but human rights are only a small part of that role. The imposition of neo-liberal economic policies as a condition for EU accession is of far more interest and importance to the EU, and to the West more generally. This is apparent also in the relationship between Romania and the International Monetary Fund and the World Bank, throughout the post-Communist period. Conditions for financial support have included privatisation and industrial restructuring; the creation of a climate conducive to foreign investment; the elimination of government price controls and industrial subsidies; and the liberalisation of the foreign exchange market (Jones, 1997: 41).

While the Romanian state agreed to repeal its anti-gay laws – as with the neo-liberal agenda, what choice did it really have? – this was only after some years of resistance on the basis that this was an internal, domestic matter. The irony was not lost on many observers of this struggle that the civilising club of Europe itself has a far from illustrious history of human rights protection on this, or many other grounds. After all, the idea of 'European values' has a chilling historical pedigree. That is, the imagining of Europe is often on the basis of a highly selective memory. In this way, human rights can become a marker of the civilised European and globalised order and, as Peter Fitzpatrick (2001: 200) has compellingly argued, as human rights become 'the self-constituting mark of the global', this is simultaneously 'a mark of differentiation, a mark of exclusion and marginalisation'. The 'other' to European civilisation continues to be produced, as it has been throughout the history of 'European civilisation' (which could then justify the imperialist mission). Within the Romanian, and more widely, the Eastern European context, this is all too apparent. The EU and its human rights law are 'exalted as epitomes of the universal and progressive in opposition to the particular and reactionary realms of the nation' (Fitzpatrick, 2001: 136–137). The post-Communist nation states of the region become, from the perspective of the EU, undisciplined, reactionary, non-rights respecting, particularistic, uncivilised nations that require the discipline of the EU to transcend their particularity and approach the universal, rights respecting dimension of nationhood. In this way, the EU becomes the civilised version of nationhood, while simultaneously transcending the idea of nationhood. Human rights discourse, as Fitzpatrick (2001: 122) has shown, is deeply implicated in these discourses of nationhood, civilisation, and savagery, and there is some considerable evidence for Fitzpatrick's thesis in the context of EU accession in Eastern Europe.

Human Rights or special rights?

The EU's self-image as civilising non-rights respecting 'others' brings me back to the central problem of human rights as political claims: the tension between the constitutively universalising character of human rights discourse (despite its inevitably socially constructed and historically specific reality), and the validity of claims to the cultural difference and specificity of communities. Moreover, these claims to difference can also be framed in the language of rights, which underscores the political indeterminacy of the discourse of rights more generally. Within the context of the EU, this is apparent in terms of the 'rights of member states' in the face of EU law, and language such as the 'margin of appreciation' and 'subsidiarity' underscores the concern for a right of *national* communities to be different. Within federal systems, the language of 'states' rights' has a long history, and certainly was invoked in Australia during the Tasmanian human rights dispute. Similarly, for the post-colonial state resisting gay rights claims, one can find resort to a right of the self-determination of a historically colonised people (group) to resist a westernised and oppressive language of individual, bourgeois rights.

The particularised right of the nation often proves a remarkably inventive use of the language of rights in a range of different cultural contexts. In these narratives, we find the homophobic state fuelling an anti-gay rights discourse by constructing its 'self' and its (homogenised and essentialised) people as oppressed by the claims of a privileged elite undeserving of 'special rights' (see Goldberg-Hiller, 2002; Herman, 1997: 111–136). Rights are grounded in the particular and unique contribution of heterosexuals (and their reproduction) to the common good. In this way, rights and duties connect, and the promotion of the common good is located in the heteronormative private sphere of the nuclear family. These narratives rely upon the defence of a right to a traditional way of life for a people (composed of heterosexual families) under threat from a variety of privileged sources, which are selectively invoked depending upon the political context: urban elites; liberal, white political correctness; individualism; the West; neo-colonial powers; wealthy gay men and so forth. Anti-gay discourse here relies upon the right to defend an oppressed, geographically based community from powerful interests seeking to sweep away ways of life and belief systems shared by a people that simply want to be left alone, with their lives uncomplicated by gay rights (and, for that matter, modernity).

What these rights-grounded discourses underscore is not only the centrality of rights discourse, but the political manipulability of human rights talk. As Costas Douzinas (2000: 375) has incisively concluded

> human rights as a principle of popular politics express the indeterminacy and openness of society and politics. They undermine the attempt to police some social identities and sanction others and their indeterminacy means that the boundaries of society are always contested and never coincide fully with whatever crystallisations, power and legal entitlement impose.

Struggles around sexuality rights neatly demonstrate this very important point. Human rights claims by gays can trouble the anti-gay communitarian discourse, but simultaneously, claims by communities of difference, grounded in the language of human rights, challenge the logic of cosmopolitan claims made in the name of a universalising discourse of sexuality rights. Rights discourse may have become 'the fate of postmodernity' (Douzinas, 2000: 1) and, for that matter, the product of a global consumerist society, but as a consequence, they are open to *all consumers equally*, and their deployment is limited only by the imaginations of those who wish to make claims.

From rights to politics

It is tempting to end the story there, and to conclude that rights are politically indeterminate, socially constructed (as are sexuality and nationhood), and open to both cosmopolitan and communitarian claims. But if that is the conclusion, then we are left – perhaps particularly *because of* the language of rights – with a tendency toward polarisation and irreconcilable political demands. Ultimately, though, I expect gay rights arguments will win the day because of their easy articulation as part of globalisation discourse. They represent the triumph of the global and of modernity itself. The language of rights cannot, however, apolitically provide resolutions to these moments. Legal claims *have* led to results but a turn to law does not mask the political character of the dispute and its outcome. If anything, it exacerbates both.

In this respect, gay rights disputes demonstrate a wider point made by Richard Bellamy and Dario Castiglione (1996) concerning politics and the state today. They suggest that both cosmopolitan and communitarian pressures are engendered by globalising currents, which push the state in opposite directions. Furthermore, they argue that the cosmopolitanism of rights must be tempered by a communitarian belief in democratic debate and engagement with political institutions leading to a spirit of compromise between previously polarised groups. This must be achieved through a politics of reciprocity, compromise and toleration (see also Bellamy, 1999). The focus thus turns to political practices and institutions through which rights can be given meaning. Bellamy and Castiglione (1996) provide, in this way, a more communitarian account of liberalism as a means through which to embed rights within a network of relationships, and thereby, to provide a bridge through the cosmopolitan-communitarian divide.

In my experience, gay rights activists aspire to engage in precisely this politics of the wider communities of which they are a part, and to do so explicitly from their positions as lesbians and gay men (as well as from other politicised identity positions). Their struggles are for citizenship and belonging to a wider collectivity in which they can have voice and participate. The difficulty is that anti-gay rights campaigners so often seek to exclude them from politics except to the extent that homosexuality is depoliticised and closeted.

This was particularly true in Romania. The struggle over the decriminalisation of same-sex sexual activities clearly was a crucial human rights issue on its own terms. The law was brutally applied to deny fundamental dignity to individuals. However, activists also saw this struggle as a precondition to achieving wider political change towards the creation of something akin to Bellamy's (1999) politics of reciprocity and compromise (Coman, 2001). The term I use to describe this politics is 'civility'. In interviewing lesbian and gay Romanians, I found a deep desire for a politics that was based on reciprocity, compromise and civility. In this regard, many saw the struggle over human rights as a means to achieve a more 'civil' society, rather than only the realisation of cosmopolitan, universal rights. Indeed, ACCEPT explicitly sees its role, now that basic human rights have been achieved, as participation in a dialogue within civil society and with the state as part of a wider participatory politics (Coman, 2001). In this way, the politics of rights activism is grounded in recognition of the wider *potential* of human rights beyond the immediate claim itself.

There is considerable irony in my use of the term civility. Critics of human rights discourse point to the way in which human rights have become the measure of 'civilisation' and that, in turn, is derived only through its opposite: 'It was created in the divide between "the

European family of nations" and "savages or barbarians" who were beyond the pale of nationhood, speech and history' (Fitzpatrick, 2001: 122). Despite the rhetorical power of that critical analysis, what struck me in Romania – a prime example of a nation state constructed in EU discourse today as lawless, chaotic and backward – was the yearning for civil society and the belief that human rights were a necessary step to achieve a politics of civility. The term civility usefully highlights the political indeterminacy of human rights. While we can accept and appreciate Fitzpatrick's (2001) trenchant critique of human rights discourse in the world today, we also need to recognise the powerful popular imaginary of rights and the *desire* to deploy rights for transformative effect.

From the struggles of human rights organisations mobilised on the ground around sexuality, we can find operating within activism a response to the theoretical difficulties in the use of the globalising cosmopolitanism of rights discourse when it meets rights claims made by communities of difference. The key may be to see the deployment of human rights as a 'calling card' to enter into political and civil society; indeed, a calling card to enter what was constructed as a community of difference (or, to put it differently, to heterogenise a community). Activist strategies in practice move between cosmopolitan and communitarian discourses, and this is an important moment in bridging this divide. It allows for claims, not to abstract cosmopolitan rights, but to participation as full members of a wider community, and to have specific grievances emanating from same-sex sexualities recognised and heard as legitimate citizenship claims made by full members of that community.

Concluding thoughts

In conclusion, the implications of this analysis are multi-faceted. While we will, I predict, increasingly see lesbians and gay men achieving human rights victories and successfully making claims to full citizenship, with these rights to participate within wider society come responsibilities to engage in struggles for political transformation. In my view, it is easy for gay politics to become politically conservative in an era of gay marriage and same-sex partnership benefits. These arguably assimilationist political moves also lead to the construction of some 'queers' as the rights undeserving – the dangerous, and the uncivilisable. It becomes far too tempting for 'citizen gay' to consume human rights and then withdraw from any kind of progressive politics, especially when those who have bestowed the rights are also pursuing policies which are eviscerating the human rights of others on issues from migration to counter-terrorism. In this regard, my claim has always been that law (including the law of human rights) can operate in an explicitly juridical way through repression and social control (the enforcement of anti-gay sex laws exemplifies this), but also that legal discourse can operate in a more subtle, disciplinary mode by encouraging individuals, in an infinite variety of ways, to conform to how the law constructs proper – even civilised – behaviour. The way such behaviour is constructed by law is informed, I would also claim, by a wider neo-liberal economic hegemony that emphasises the privatisation of responsibility for others and the withdrawal of the state from many aspects of care. In this way, law acts as a force for the discipline and normalisation of the self. To gain rights in such a political context, and to be satisfied with them as a final result, thus would be a hollow victory indeed, and would undermine the transformative potential (since it is only a potential) of human rights discourse. In other words, to be included and to be brought within a community does not by itself transform that community in terms of its ongoing need to construct boundaries of membership; to construct 'insiders' and 'outsiders'; the rights 'deserving' and the rest. So too, same-sex sexual communities must themselves continue to be interrogated for their own exclusions and marginalisations (such as around race, gender, and social class). For the privileged within communities who are achieving the most from inclusion (that is, those who are not disadvantaged along other vectors of oppression), there are particular responsibilities to fight for those who are constructed as rights undeserving.

In my view, this is the challenge and the potential of human rights discourse. The critique of rights is that lesbian and gay human rights struggles have become disconnected from politics and, moreover, that we have become depoliticised consumers through the fetishisation of rights. But, to the extent that rights may provide a key that opens the political realm on the basis of full citizenship, the language of human rights does remain a valuable discourse in today's political tool box.

Endnotes

1 This chapter originally appeared in the *McGill Law Journal* and can be found at (2004) 49: 951–968. The author gratefully acknowledges the permission of the journal to republish a revised version of the original article in this collection.

2 I was asked this very question by a law professor in 1994 at an academic conference on human rights.

3 In using the term 'Stonewall', I am referring to the birth of contemporary American lesbian and gay identity politics at the Stonewall riots in New York City in 1969.

References

Altman, D., 2002, *Global Sex*, (Chicago: University of Chicago Press).

Anderson, B., 1991, *Imagined Communities*, rev edn (London: Verso).

Bellamy, R., 1999, *Liberalism and Pluralism: Towards a Politics of Compromise*, (London: Routledge).

Bellamy, R. and Castiglione, D., 1996, 'The Communitarian Ghost in the Cosmopolitan Machine: Constitutionalism, Democracy and the Reconfiguration of Politics in the New Europe', in R. Bellamy (Ed.), *Constitutionalism, Democracy and Sovereignty: American and European Perspectives*, (Aldershot: Avebury), pp. 111–129.

Coman, A., 2001, Personal Interview with author (former Executive Director, ACCEPT), Sinaea, Romania, 7 August.

Cruz-Malavé, A. and Manalansan IV, M. F., 2002, 'Introduction: Dissident Sexualities/Alternative Globalisms', in A. Cruz-Malavé and M. F. Manalansan IV (Eds.), *Queer Globalisations*, (New York: New York University Press), pp. 1–10.

Dembour, M. B., 1996, 'Human Rights Talk and Anthropological Ambivalence: The Particular Contexts of Universal Claims', in O. Harris (Ed.), *Inside and Outside the Law: Anthropological Studies of Authority and Ambiguity*, (London: Routledge), pp. 19–40.

de Vos, P., 2000, 'The Constitution Made Us Queer: The Sexual Orientation Clause in the South African Constitution and the Emergence of Gay and Lesbian Identity', in C. Stychin and D. Herman (Eds.), *Sexuality in the Legal Arena*, (London: Athlone Press), pp. 194–207.

Douzinas, C., 2000, *The End of Human Rights*, (Oxford: Hart).

Edelman, L., 1994, *Homographesis*, (New York: Routledge).

Engelke, M., 1999, '"We Wondered what Human Rights he was Talking About": Human Rights, Homosexuality and the Zimbabwean International Book Fair', *Critique of Anthropology*, 19: 289–314.

Fitzpatrick, P., 2001, *Modernism and the Grounds of Law*, (Cambridge: Cambridge University Press).

Gallagher, T., 2001, 'Nationalism and Romanian Political Culture in the 1990s', in D. Light and D. Phinnemore (Eds.), *Post-Communist Romania: Coming to Terms with Transition*, (Basingstoke: Palgrave), pp. 104–126.

Gilroy, P., 1992, *There Ain't No Black in the Union Jack*, (London: Routledge).

Goldberg-Hiller, J., 2002, *The Limits to Union,* (Ann Arbor: University of Michigan Press).

Herman, D., 1997, *The Antigay Agenda,* (Chicago: University of Chicago Press).

Human Rights Watch and the International Gay and Lesbian Human Rights Commission, 1998, *Public Scandals: Sexual Orientation and Criminal Law in Romania*, (New York: Human Rights Watch and the International Gay and Lesbian Human Rights Commission).

Jones, C., 1997, 'Rumbles felt in Romania', *The Banker*, June: 41.

LaViolette, N. and Whitworth, S., 1997, 'No Safe Haven: Sexuality as a Universal Human Right and Gay and Lesbian Activism in International Politics', *Millennium: Journal of International Studies*, 23: 563–588.

Manalansan IV, M., 1993, '(Re) Locating the Gay Filipino: Resistance, Postcolonialism, and Identity', *Journal of Homosexuality*, 26 2/3: 53–72.

Moran, L. J., 1991, 'The Uses of Homosexuality: Homosexuality for National Security', *International Journal of the Sociology of Law*, 19: 149–170.

Morgan, W., 1994, 'Identifying Evil for What it is: Tasmania, Sexual Perversity and the United Nations', *Melbourne University Law Review*, 19: 740–767.

Morris, M., 1995, *Pink Triangle*, (Sydney: University of New South Wales Press).

Murray, S. O. and Roscoe, W., 1998, *Boy-Wives and Female Husbands*, (New York: St. Martin's Press).

Offord, B., 2003, *Homosexual Rights as Human Rights*, (Berne: Peter Lang).

Phillips, O., 1997, 'Zimbabwean Law and the Production of a White Man's Disease', *Social & Legal Studies*, 6: 471–491.

Roman, D., 2001, 'Gendering Eastern Europe: Pre-Feminism, Prejudice and East-West Dialogues in Post-Communist Romania', *Women's Studies International Forum*, 24: 53–66.

Stychin, C. F., 1998, *A Nation by Rights*, (Philadelphia: Temple University Press).

——, 2003, *Governing Sexuality: The Changing Politics of Citizenship and Law Reform*, (Oxford: Hart Publishing).

Tenbensel, T., 1996, 'International Human Rights Conventions and Australian Political Debates: Issues Raised by the "Toonen Case"', *Australian Journal of Political Science*, 31: 7–23.

van der Laan, L. et al., 2001, Unpublished letter by eight Members of the European Parliament to Prime Minister Nastase, 29 May.

von Bogdandy, A., 2000, 'The European Union as a Human Rights Organisation? Human Rights and the Core of the European Union', *Common Market Law Review*, 37: 1307–1338.

Yuval-Davies, N., 1997, *Gender and Nation*, (London: Sage).

Monica McWilliams

Human Rights and Conflict Resolution: Are They Mutually Dependent in a Divided Society?

Peace-making, which culminates in the signing of an agreement, and peace-building, which includes the implementation of an agreement, are well recognised in transitional societies as two very different processes requiring different inputs and different skills. However, what is less acknowledged is that the demands of justice and the enforcement of human rights, at the heart of most peace agreements, are not easily reconciled with the strategic concerns of conflict resolution, at the heart of all peace-building. The pursuit of one is often perceived to be possible only at the expense of the other. But human rights enforcement and conflict resolution need to be complementary rather than contradictory (Jarman, 2003). Unless they become mutually dependent, a peace process will stumble from crisis to crisis. That has been my experience in implementing the peace agreement in Northern Ireland.[1] However, as I show in this chapter, it is also possible to create positive change particularly where communities are prepared to adopt an alternative route to reconciliation.

When a conflict comes to an end, as it has in Northern Ireland, entire communities have to begin to reorient themselves from the antagonistic, adversarial relations of war to the more respect-based relations of cooperation. Similarly, the implementation of the peace agreement means that new relationships have to be built – not simply those between parliamentarians or leaders, but between whole communities. Conflict resolution has to involve a much wider group of people than those who are labelled as victims or perpetrators because they have been directly implicated in the conflict. So in activating human rights, there is also a pressing need to underpin it with working relationships built on a real understanding of each other's needs, fears and aspirations alongside new habits and patterns of cooperation.

Too often we hear people in conflict situations who are frustrated with all the political wrangling, admonishing others simply to forgive and forget (Rigby, 2001). But the resolution of a conflict is a long-term objective that can only be reached after all the important ingredients of justice, truth, healing and so on have been addressed. One of the many lessons of peace-building is that conflict resolution takes time and its pace cannot be dictated. It involves a process of what Lederach calls 'remembering and changing' (1997: 10) and this is a vast and often painful challenge that cannot be rushed or imposed. To give one example, the members of the 'Justice For the Forgotten Group' in Ireland waited over 30 years for the inquests into the deaths of 26 relatives, killed in the Dublin bombings in 1974. One of the victims, who was aged eight at the time her mother was killed by a loyalist paramilitary bomb planted in the city shopping centre, summed up the group's feelings: 'The families have been fighting for this for 29 years – I'm hoping that we will get some closure and I hope that all the families will be able to get on with their lives.'[2] Some of these families have been involved in a dialogue project, called LIVE or 'Let's Involve The Victim's Experience', which helps them to understand the political context in which this violence took place (Bloomfield, Barnes, Huyse, 2003). A number of dialogue sessions between former paramilitary combatants and victims/survivors have now taken place and the first step in conflict resolution has begun.

But conflict resolution has to be a deep process as well as a broad one. It has to apply to everyone. It is not just a process for those who suffered or those who inflicted that suffering. In Northern Ireland, we have had to accept that the attitudes and beliefs that underpinned our violent conflict spread throughout the community and must be addressed at that broad level (McEvoy and Gormally, 1997). We now have to question the attitudes, prejudices and negative stereotypes that we all develop about the 'enemy' during violent conflict – or about the 'other' as we move through a transition. As Porter puts it, without 'strong reconciliation' (2003: 35) then conflict resolution in Northern Ireland as elsewhere will remain 'an elusive quest'. If we are to safeguard against a return to violent division, then human rights, inclusion and reconciliation have to be intertwined.

Although the focus of this chapter is on activating human rights and conflict resolution, there are other important ingredients that make the transition from a segregated to a more integrated society have some meaning for the people involved. Concepts such as equity, diversity and interdependence are at the core of tackling the cauldron of sexism, sectarianism, racism, disability, ageism and homophobia. From the mid 1970s the issue of religious discrimination in employment was being addressed in Northern Ireland, but the other issues such as sexual orientation or disability came much later in the late 1980s and early 1990s. 'The right of women to full and equal political participation' is written into the Good Friday Agreement but it was put there during the final hours of negotiations and at the insistence of the Northern Ireland Women's Coalition (Fearon, 1999: 116). It was an acknowledgement that women in Northern Ireland had to endure years of living in what Harkin calls an 'armed patriarchy' (1985: 40). The Women's Coalition took the view that action would be needed to counteract the predominance of men (in the security forces or paramilitaries) in decision-making roles in the post-conflict politics in Northern Ireland.

Overall, the peace negotiations that led to the Good Friday Agreement should stand as a model of how strong community relations and strong affirmative action duties can be enforced through government policies (Robinson, 2002). The equality legislation which results from the Agreement attempts to untangle all the issues that make up one's identity, such as gender, religion, ethnicity, marital status, sexual orientation, having dependents, age and disability (Harvey, 2001). The enforcement of equality legislation is a difficult but not impossible task and it will be important for others to see how these policies have the potential to activate a truly transformed society.

In Northern Ireland there had to be a deal made. The essential pre-condition for the peace process was that all sides recognised that no further political gains could be made by violence. The state recognised that military victory over its enemies was unlikely and the insurgents recognised that violence had reached the limits of its effectiveness (Morrissey and Smyth, 2000). Since no-one had won the war then all must be involved in winning the peace. Once a process of conflict transformation had begun, then the faults on all sides had to be addressed and things needed to be fixed. In the end, people had to agree, do a deal and make the contract work.

Each package of institutional reforms that go into a peace deal depends on the circumstances of the conflict. The main platform of the deal is usually an agreed form of governance but it may need wheels like human rights, equality, justice, social and economic opportunities to move the wagon forward. Some of these wheels in the Northern Ireland context were the institutional parts of the Good Friday Agreement, for example a new Assembly, a new Human Rights Commission, an Equality Commission and a reformed police system. But an essential piece had to be the 'people' part – the reconciliation piece needed for genuine conflict resolution (HMSO, 1998: 18). It is still too often the case that after a bitter conflict, most victims tend to pursue their rights through the more formal justice system. Although this is necessary it may not be sufficient in reassuring the victims that the conflict will not happen again. So a healing, reconciliatory and restorative system may be the complementary process to the more prescriptive one of formal human rights investigations.

Northern Ireland: a legalistic or restorative approach?

Northern Ireland endured a violent political conflict for over thirty years in which 3,500 people were killed, 30,000 were seriously injured and 300,000 people regard themselves as victims in a population of 1.6 million people (Smyth et al., 2004; Victims Unit, 2001). If the numbers killed and injured proportionate to the population were to be applied to Great Britain (population approximately 54 million), then the figures of 108,000 deaths and 1,188,000 injured give us some idea of the scale of the problem. The conflict inevitably produced wholesale breaches of human rights, not least that of the right to life. Irrespective of whether it was the state or non-state combatants that were mainly responsible for human rights breaches, this fact meant that restoring human rights had to be part of any resolution of the conflict (Mageean, 1997). In Northern Ireland, the restoration of the rule of law and the institution of a state regime and political culture based on human rights and equality became indispensable constituents of the peace process (Harvey, 2001). But some 'just' closure is also necessary before a conflict can be regarded as finally over. In this context, 'justice' also tends to imply 'truth', that is a full disclosure of all the 'crimes' committed by combatants during the conflict. However, there is no consensus, at least in Northern Ireland, on the character of the justice or the truth that may be appropriate to close the conflict.

The natural place to look first is at the body of international human rights law. The main principles of this body of law are: first, violations of human rights or humanitarian law should always be properly pursued. Second, amnesty or impunity should only be granted in the most exceptional circumstances and after full investigation and disclosure. Third, a lack of this formal justice will distort society and prevent genuine reconciliation (UN Reports, 1997, 1999).

What is also fairly clear, however, is that international law is mainly concerned with violations of human rights by states. The principle is that where a state has been engaged in the wholesale oppression of its people, or a section of it, it should be thoroughly reformed, the guilty individuals weeded out and held to account and firm measures put in place to prevent repetition. It is hard to argue against this principle and, indeed, in Northern Ireland a number of enquiries are engaged in investigating certain alleged abuses by the State. The most notable of these is the Enquiry into Bloody Sunday, led by Lord Saville, which is examining the killing of thirteen people by the British army in 1981.

However, we cannot ignore the reality of the Northern Ireland conflict. In Chile, the Rettig Committee found that 2,279 people had died for 'political reasons' and that 95% had been killed by state forces (Rettig, 1991). In Northern Ireland, it is the other way round. Only 20% of casualties were killed by security forces with the vast majority being victims of various paramilitary organisations (Fay, Morrissey and Smyth, 1999). The simple fact is that, while there are excellent reasons for particularly holding the state to account for human rights abuses, to do that and ignore the abuses of 'non-governmental entities' would be counter-productive in terms of reconciliation.

International law gives us little guidance in this situation. The main subjects of such law are, of course, states and those who act on their behalf. In a Protocol II situation, non-governmental entities waging internal war could be held to account for their actions (United Nations Treaty Series 609, 1978). Protocol 11 is a Geneva Convention that proscribes a protocol on what should happen between parties who have been involved in an internal 'war'. A consensus that a 'war' did take place between the opposing sides would be an essential prerequisite before the protocol could be applied. Northern Ireland, like many other countries with internal conflicts, has difficulty achieving such a consensus. However, most authorities do not accept that Northern Ireland fits into a concept of full-scale internal war where the non-state entities control territory and effectively establish mini-states. This is a complex area but in a conflict such as that in Northern Ireland, it seems as though the actions of paramilitary organisations fall below the horizon of international human rights and humanitarian law.

In these circumstances, it is clear that, while the Government has an obligation to ensure that past abuses by its agencies are investigated and remedied, international law is not adequate as a framework for an overall process that offers both justice and reconciliation. In general, it appears that formal, 'black letter' law fails to provide a framework within which to construct such a process. That does not necessarily mean, however, that we have to abandon the search for justice.

So if a legalistic approach, based solely on the paradigms established by international human rights and humanitarian law is not the best way in which to reach a resolution based on truth and reconciliation, then what is? Are there alternative forms of justice other than the criminal law and the human rights paradigms that are based upon it? Let me turn to the alternative model of restorative justice and examine the extent to which it addresses this issue.

The restorative justice model

Drawing inspiration from the practices of diverse aboriginal societies, restorative justice operates today as a powerful theoretical and practical critique of retributive criminal law. It is founded upon a number of principles that, together, amount to a transformed understanding about the relationship between the individual, the community, crime and the state (Theissen, 2001; Boraine, 2000; Mika and Zehr, 1997).

First, is the view that crime is fundamentally a violation of people and interpersonal relationships rather than simply a breach of the criminal code. The focus of intervention is the relationship affected by crime, and restoration involves a continuum of responses to the needs and harms experienced by victims, offenders and the community.

Second, restorative justice maintains that crime and antisocial behaviour create obligations and liabilities. Offenders are encouraged to understand the harm committed and obligated to make things right, as much as possible. Victims must have every opportunity to participate in defining these obligations. Since local communities bear a responsibility for the welfare of all of their members, communities are encouraged to support victims but also to integrate offenders into community life and to ensure that they have the opportunities to make amends to their victims.

Third, restorative justice seeks to heal and put right the wrongs committed. This means meeting the needs of victims for information, validation, restitution, testimony, safety and support, a recognition that offenders themselves may have been harmed and a need for monitoring and follow-through in order to maximise healing, recovery, accountability and change.

How can we apply these three principles to the violent political conflict that Northern Ireland has endured? First, we might say that the violence – state or non-state, legal or not – represented a complete breakdown of the social contract, a violation of the basic understanding of how we should live together. Something was torn apart that needs to be put back together.

Second, we could legitimately say that the use of violence creates an obligation to the victims. Whether or not someone considers their use of violence justified, their actions harmed someone else, usually including people other than the actual target. It is right for people to take personal and individual responsibility for the exercise of violence even if it was legitimated by the law or a 'just cause'.

Third, the interests and needs of victims are emphasised. Compensation and practical support is important, but so is the opportunity to tell their story and to be taken seriously. It may or may not be possible to effect a reconciliation between individual perpetrators and victims, but the opportunity to vent feelings and then to make a common, if separate, commitment to a new social contract may be sufficient.

The 'justice' in restorative justice does not lie fundamentally in the sufficiency of reparation or the mechanisms of reintegration. It lies in the re-commitment of all concerned to a fair and just society, the active re-building of right relations and the taking of common responsibility for the future. The applicability of these concepts to a post-conflict reconciliation process hardly needs labouring (Bloomfield, Barnes and Huyse, 2003). What might need emphasis is the forward-looking character of the justice involved. Certainly, restorative justice requires a person to take responsibility for his or her past actions – but only in terms of recognition of the harm done to someone else. Whether the action was legally a crime, or an abuse of human rights, or indeed 'right' or 'wrong', is not in itself significant. What counts is to understand and recognise the damage caused to other human beings and to make a commitment that it will not happen again. In other words, a sincere and demonstrable commitment to a peaceful and just future replaces an adjudication on past misdeeds (Bowen and Consedine, 1999).

To make the potential consequences of this approach explicit, we might say that open disclosure of responsibility for past acts and an effective dismantling of military capability might replace the need or desire for prosecution of paramilitaries. By the same token, disclosure of past actions by state agencies and foolproof systems to prevent any future abuses might replace the need for individual enquiries into the past. We also ought to note that, while restorative justice can be complementary to criminal or human rights law, the boundaries must be clear. So, for example, it would probably be necessary to guarantee immunity from prosecution for those taking part in such a restorative process, at least in respect of any statements or admissions made in the proceedings.

In fact, in our circumstances, it might make sense to propose a restorative process as a complete alternative to any traditional legal process. This would be contrary to the South African experience, for example, where the threat of prosecution was one of the main incentives for people to make disclosure to the Truth and Reconciliation Commission (James and Van De Vijver, 2000). In Northern Ireland, however, the threat of prosecution simply lacks credibility. As far as alleged perpetrators from state forces are concerned, it is generally accepted that only special enquiries will discover anything close to the truth and will likely have to offer immunity to participants. For other perpetrators, if the criminal investigation and prosecution processes have not caught them yet, it is unlikely they will in the future, even if anyone would think the pursuit worthwhile with early prison release in operation. The Chief Constable of the Police Service in Northern Ireland has admitted that about two thousand outstanding cases will never come to trial (Orde, 2004). The political negotiations have also been dealing with a group referred to as ‘on the runs’, people who have been pursued but not finally prosecuted for crimes or others who went ‘on the run’ during their trials or absconded from prison. It is most likely that the outcome of these negotiations will involve some form of immunity from prosecution.

The consequences of this are that any proposed process will have to be voluntary, or at least without any legal compulsion. That is, in fact, a logical result of recognising the inadequacy of traditional legal frameworks for a reconciliation process and accepting the restorative justice approach. Restorative justice is most effective when participation is voluntary and involves an informed decision to be reconciled to the community at large.

On the other hand, this voluntary character does not necessarily imply that the process would have no consequences in the formal legal sphere. It might be feasible to offer amnesty, that is, the expunging of the criminal record, for those perpetrators who participated in the process. The offer of immunity from civil proceedings might also be significant in some circumstances such as cases where a group of victims agree to work with the restorative process and the threat of civil proceedings is withdrawn.

A possible process

It may be helpful to work through a scenario using a possible structure that would utilise restorative methods. A possible process would involve the appointment of a number of commissioners who might or might not be lawyers but would be experienced in mediation processes and acceptable to all sections of the community. The basic idea is that the victim would make a statement, after which the question would be put: 'does anyone wish to contest this account, explain or take responsibility for the acts described?' If no-one responds, the victim's statement would stand as the formal record of the incident. If the perpetrator (the responsible person) brought the case then the order of statements would be reversed. If a responsible person was prepared to engage, then the commissioner would initiate one or more mediation sessions. Over the past few years, in my role as a political representative involved in the peace negotiations, I have been asked by victims to approach various combatants on their behalf. For example, one woman who came to my office simply wanted to know the last words of her husband who was murdered in a case of mistaken identity by the IRA. She was subsequently introduced to the political spokesperson for the IRA, the armed wing of the Republican movement. Although this person could not identify the perpetrator, he was able to talk to her and issue a further apology on behalf of the organisation. Clearly, there is the possibility that this case could be taken much further through a more structured process. Other eligible cases might include:

- Where the victimisation involved death or serious injury to some person (some criterion of seriousness would be necessary);
- Where there had been no, or a plainly inadequate, investigation;
- Where there had been no criminal trial;
- Where the trial was 'incomplete' (i.e. where only some perpetrators were involved);
- Where the results of a trial are contested (by any party).

Those with standing to initiate a case would include:

- Next of kin of any person killed in connection with the conflict;[3]
- Any person seriously injured in connection with the conflict or their next of kin if since deceased;
- Any person prepared to take responsibility for an act of violence leading to death or serious injury, whether it appeared to be, or was adjudicated to be, legal or illegal.

Pros and cons of the restorative model

It is also important to highlight the pros and cons for potential participants. For victims, whoever the perpetrators, the major incentive would be to 'have their say', publicly ascribe responsibility and gain recognition for their hurt. Where no perpetrator had been brought to account, it would allow them to issue the challenge to take responsibility and, if it were not met, their account would stand on the record.

Some victims might, however, see this process as a sell-out, denying them the opportunity, however remote, of seeing retribution meted out to perpetrators. This would include those who insist on the total investigation of all alleged state abuses as well as those who insist that punishment by the criminal law is the only form of justice. The only way of overcoming these attitudes would be by convincing those that hold them that restorative justice is an appropriate paradigm within which to seek for truth, justice and reconciliation. It might be argued that the extent of the success of that project would be the extent of the acceptance of the concept of reconciliation itself.

For perpetrators or 'responsible persons', the pros and cons would vary depending on their status. For ex-prisoners, the offer of amnesty would be an incentive as the possession of a criminal record leads to serious negative economic and social consequences. For those who would contest the verdict handed down to them by a criminal court, this process would offer an opportunity to publicly oppose it, if not change it. For those not convicted nor sought for any crime the only incentive for co-operation would be the desire to contribute to the process of reconciliation. Clearly, if victims were allowed to identify alleged perpetrators, such people would, as we have noted, have an incentive to contest or explain the allegation.

It may be objected that those with the least incentive to participate are serving or former security force members who might have been guilty of crimes or human rights abuses. Very few have been made amenable to the criminal law and some of those have been protected and cosseted by their former employers. They are not in any practical danger of prosecution.

There are a number of points to be made in response to this argument. First, we have noted that there is an obligation on government to ensure adequate investigation of possible past abuses as well as future safeguards. In so far as it is practical and reasonable, possible gross abuses should be followed up by formal investigative processes. Second, there will be political pressure on the government and its employees to participate both in order to support reconciliation and to avoid public humiliation. After all, if an allegation was made by a victim that their loved one was illegally killed by security forces in a particular place at a particular time, unless someone came forward to contest that view, it would stand on the record. Third, the fact that many members of paramilitary organisations were convicted and imprisoned does not wipe the slate clean for those organisations. There were many actions for which no-one was held responsible and for many people these are just as much a running sore as unresolved state abuses.

The major disincentive for anyone participating in such a process may be identified as the perception of risk. Some may think that they will be at risk from opposing paramilitaries or perhaps state forces if they are identified as the perpetrators of certain deeds. Certainly the demands of security force witnesses for anonymity and secrecy at the Bloody Sunday Enquiry have emphasised that (www.bloody-sunday-enquiry.org). There is nothing to be done about this except to hope that time will decrease its impact. It might be possible to allow anonymity in public hearings, but secrecy and talking from behind screens are not appropriate for mediation sessions.

We should also remember that the process of making a success out of a restorative justice initiative would, in itself, be a major contribution to making reconciliation a reality. If everyone were ready and willing to take part in an inclusive reconciliatory process, it would not be hard to devise an appropriate structure. It is the fact that some countries are not at that stage that creates so many objections to whatever is proposed. Northern Ireland is still wavering on the edge – ex-prisoners and some victims groups have entered the process but the status quo still needs much convincing. What this tells us is that adopting a restorative justice paradigm is to adopt the belief that leopards really can change their spots. In that sense, the success or failure of a specific institution or structure is the success or failure not of the structure but of reconciliation itself.

A gender perspective

It is important to include a gender perspective in the context of restorative justice. Armed conflict can encourage a 'warrior identity' in which men bond together in their subjugation of women. The connections need to be made between aggressive forms of masculinity and militarism, the occupation of space and community control and the ways in which men also bond around these both in and out of war (Kelly and Radford, 1998; McWilliams, 1998). Making these connections requires full recognition of how a particular conflict has involved and affected men and women in different ways.

Restorative justice projects in Northern Ireland are receiving training from groups like Women's Aid particularly on the distinctive nature of abusive behaviour perpetrated on women in both domestic and political situations. Interestingly, one of the groups of victims still to come forward in Northern Ireland are the women from Republican communities who, in the early days of the conflict, were 'tarred and feathered' and left tied to a lamppost as a result of being caught socialising with British soldiers. When the men perpetrating these acts were challenged by feminist activists, they would not identify such behaviour as a violation of the women's human rights. At the same time, these men were demanding that the infringement of their rights by the British army be recognised internationally (McWilliams, 1997).

Those working with abused women understood the principles of restorative justice many years before they were applied as a tool to challenge anti-social or other criminal behaviour. The need for apology, taking responsibility for past behaviour and making a commitment not to do it again were all the demands made by women in abusive relationships. An abused woman judged the difference in her partner's behaviour not alone by deeds but by changed attitudes. So it is beneficial to apply what we know from work on domestic violence to violent conflict. Abused women know that examining the painful past, acknowledging it and understanding it, and above all transcending it, is the best way to guarantee that it does not – and cannot – happen again. They also know when it is important to protect women and children through the courts and when room can be left for the restorative model particularly where relationships can be mended. But far too often, female victims of conflict are forced to challenge models of justice that reproduce power inequalities or create a sense of re-victimisation. This must not be allowed to happen in restorative projects (McElrea, 1995).

Closing a conflict

As in the case of the coercive control of women in sexual or physical abuse, restorative justice is unlikely to be able to bring solutions to all circumstances. Formal law-based justice, especially in the human rights field, is likely to be needed in some cases. In particular, the state needs to be held to account where it appears that it has participated in flagrant abuses of human rights. It is much more dangerous for a society when the state – the supposed guardian of justice – abuses human rights than when similar abuses are perpetrated by groupings of individuals. It may not matter to the victims whether it is a policeman or a terrorist who wrongly shoots them, but it matters a great deal to society and the rule of law that it relies on. Different forms of justice should be considered when attempting to bring a conflict to a permanent close – but the more prescriptive formal human rights enquiries and domestic trials clearly have their limitations – political and legal risks, restoring the judicial infrastructure, financial obstacles and many more shortcomings. As we have discovered in Northern Ireland, keeping prosecution as an option in transitional justice is only justified if there is a simultaneous reorganisation of the justice system.

And just as important, Desmond Tutu, the Chair of the Truth and Reconciliation Commission in South Africa, makes the point that retributive justice is too impersonal and has too little consideration of victims. He argues for the African view of justice which is aimed at 'the redressing of imbalances and the restoration of broken relationships' which will lead to 'the healing of a traumatised and wounded nation' (Tutu, 2002: 115). Writing on the legacy of the civil war in Biafra, 1967–1970, when three million people died, Ifi Amadiume explains that 'the evil is in the social system [...] the guilt is collective. [...] It is a modern arrogance to assume the courts are instruments of healing' (in Bloomfield, Barnes, Huyse, 2003: 105). Similar arguments have been developed with respect to the Asian vision of dealing with victims and perpetrators, exemplified by the hesitation of the Cambodian people about instituting a retributive reaction to the crimes of the Khmer Rouge.

There can be no blueprint for societies in transition from conflict, but a careful mixture of the principles of human rights, equality and restorative justice should be brought to the particular circumstances of conflict resolution. Restorative justice, concentrating on making good the harm done rather than on the punishment of the guilty, has a part to play. The gacaca tribunals in Rwanda, the projects in Burundi and Bougainville illustrate current examples where restorative justice projects are working at different levels (Van Eck, 2000). In Rwanda, gacaca tribunals have been created, composed of persons of integrity elected by the inhabitants of cells, sectors, districts and provinces. Each prisoner (except those accused of the most serious crimes of genocide and rape) will be brought before the tribunal in the community where he or she is alleged to have committed a crime. The entire community will be present and act as a general assembly discussing the alleged act/s, providing testimony and counter-testimony, argument and counter-argument. Each level above the cell will have competence to judge appeals from the level below. Prisoners who ask for forgiveness can receive dramatic reductions in penalties. Reductions are less for those who only confess during the gacaca procedure, while penalties are unchanged for those who do not confess at all but are found guilty. Half of the sentence of all convicted can be transmuted into community service and to benefit from this, the accused have to ask for forgiveness publicly. When the gacaca procedure is completed, the claimant or survivor will receive a statement of their losses and can use this to receive reparations from a public fund. In Bougainville and Burundu, the restorative process relies on tribal elders who are experienced in mediation. The parties express their grievances against one another and the mediators then agree on the principles for resolving the conflict and living together. Rituals of reconciliation are then performed and the conflict is declared formally resolved.

Each initiative will have to take an uncharted path. Because of this, there is still a tendency in the international community to favour the retributive approach – ad hoc tribunals, the international criminal court, universal jurisdiction. Past experiences suggest that the best practice is to balance all costs and benefits of a given policy against each other, above all taking into account the particular conjunction of political, cultural and historical forces in a transitional society. What I have tried to show in this chapter is that the potential for involving victims, perpetrators and the wider community in a mediated process of establishing truth, taking responsibility and pledging peaceful intentions is immense.

In peace-building then, it is necessary to have a culture of human rights sitting alongside a process of conflict resolution. It is pointless to 'do' human rights first and then move on to reconciliation. It must be done not before, not after, but at the same time. Unreconciled people, still driven by fear or suspicion, do not afford each other's human rights the same respect. Put bluntly, good democratic politics only works when relationships between the various actors are positive enough to permit basic trust, respect and cooperation. So the crucial actors, both victims and offenders, must be understood. The crucial procedures – healing, justice, truth – must be undergone. And the habits and patterns of the past must be undone. So to end where we started, we cannot activate human rights without building new relationships. Human rights and conflict resolution are mutually dependent. And when they work together, we know that communities begin to move together with confidence from a divided past to a shared future.

Endnotes

1 I co-founded a political party centred on human rights in the mid-1990s in Northern Ireland. The political party, made up predominantly of women members from both sides of the political divide, started out in April 1996 with the intention of getting to the peace talks. Six weeks later the political party was elected and a group of women, known as the Northern Ireland Women's Coalition, seated its political representatives at the negotiating table alongside nine other political parties. These peace negotiations led to a successful conclusion in Belfast, Northern Ireland and on April 10th 1998, each of the political party leaders, including myself, became signatories to the Good Friday Agreement (HMSO, 1998).

2 These views were recorded during discussions with the 'Justice for the Forgotten' group which took place in Parliament Buildings, Stormont in April 2004 following my agreement as a Member of the Legislative Assembly to place a motion to the Assembly to have the Northern Ireland Secretary of State release further information to the Dublin/Monaghan Independent Enquiry.

3 It might be simplest to define 'in connection with the conflict' as where the act that caused the harm was a 'scheduled offence' (as defined in the Emergency Provisions Act 1991) or would have been if someone had been tried for it. In any event, a decision on political motivation is not necessary in our circumstances; there are only a tiny number of 'grey area' cases.

References

Bloomfield, D., Barnes, T. and Huyse, L., 2003, *Reconciliation After Violent Conflict,* (Stockholm: IDEA).

Boraine, A., 2000, *A Country Unmasked: Inside South Africa's Truth and Reconciliation Commission,* (Oxford: Oxford University Press).

Bowen, H. and Consedine, J., 1999, *Restorative Justice: Contemporary Themes and Practice*, (Christchurch: Ploughshares Publications).

Fay, M. T., Morrissey, M. and Smyth, M., 1999, *Northern Ireland's Troubles: The Human Costs,* (London: Pluto Press).

Fearon, K., 1999, *Women's Work: The Story of the Women's Coalition*, (Belfast: Blackstaff Press), pp. 110–121.

Harkin, C. and Kilmurray, A., 1985, 'Working With Women In Derry' in M. Abbott and H. Fraser (Eds.), *Women and Community Work in Northern Ireland*, (Belfast: Farset Press), pp. 38–45.

Harvey, C. (Ed.), 2001, *Human Rights, Equality and Democratic Renewal in Northern Ireland,* (Oxford: Hart Publishing).

HMSO, 1998, 'The Agreement: an Agreement Reached in the Multi-party Negotiations in Northern Ireland', (Belfast: HMSO).

James, W. and Van De Vijver, L. (Eds.), 2000, *After the TRC: Reflections On Truth And Reconciliation In South Africa*, (Ohio: Ohio University Press).

Jarman, N. (Ed.), 2003, 'Human Rights and Community Relations: Competing or Complimentary Approaches in Response to Conflict?' Conference Papers, (Belfast: Institute of Conflict Research).

Kelly, L. and Radford, J., 1998, 'Sexual Violence Against Women and Girls: An Approach to an International Overview' in R. E. Dobash and R. P. Dobash (Eds.), *Rethinking Violence Against Women*, (Thousand Oaks: Sage Publications), pp. 53–76.

Lederach, J. P., 1997, *Building Peace: Sustainable Reconciliation in Divided Societies*, (Washington: US Institute of Peace).

Mageean, P., 1997, 'Human Rights and the Peace Process in Northern Ireland', *Critical Criminology*, 8(1): 31–48.

McElrea, F., 1995, 'Accountability in the Community: Taking Responsibility for Offending' in *Rethinking Justice*, Vol. 1, (Auckland: Legal Research Foundation).

McEvoy, K. and Gormally, B., 1997, 'Seeing Is Believing: Positivist Terrorology, Peacemaking Criminology and the Northern Ireland Peace Process', *Critical Criminology*, 8(1): 9–30.

McWilliams, M., 1997, 'Violence Against Women and Political Conflict: The Northern Ireland Experience', *Critical Criminology*, 8(1): 78–92.

——, 1998, 'Violence Against women in Societies Under Stress', in R. E. Dobash and R. P. Dobash (Eds.), *Rethinking Violence Against Women*, (Thousand Oaks: Sage Publications), pp. 111–140.

Mika, H. and Zehr, H., 1997, *Fundamental Concepts of Restorative Justice*, (Akron, Pennsylvania: Mennonite Central Committee).

Morrissey, M. and Smyth, M., 2000, *Northern Ireland After the Good Friday Agreement: Victims, Grievance and Blame*, (Belfast: Institute of Conflict Research).

Orde, H., 2004, 'Address to the Federation of Police Officers in Northern Ireland', (Belfast: PSNI).

Porter, N., 2003, *The Elusive Quest: Reconciliation in Northern Ireland*, (Belfast: Blackstaff Press).

Rettig, R., 1991, 'Report of the National Commission on Truth and Reconciliation: The Crimes of the Generals,' (www.purochile.org/rettig) accessed 10.11.2004.

Rigby, A., 2001, *Justice and Reconciliation After The Violence*, (London: Lynne Rienner).

Robinson, M., 2002, 'Making Right Relationships An Everyday Practice', Lecture by the UN High Commissioner for Human Rights, (Belfast: Human Rights Consortium).

Smyth, M., Fay, M. T., Brough, E. and Hamilton, J., 2004, *The Impact of Political Conflict on Children in Northern Ireland*, (Belfast: ICR).

Theissen, G., 2001, *Supporting Justice, Co-Existence and Reconciliation After Armed Conflict: Strategies For Dealing With The Past*, (Berlin: Berghof Research Centre for Constructive Conflict Management).

Tutu, D., 2002, quoted in W. James and L. Van De Vijver (Eds.), *After the TRC: Reflections On Truth And Reconciliation In South Africa*, (Ohio: Ohio University Press), p. 115.

UN Report, 1997, 'Revised Final Report: Question of the Impunity of Perpetrators of Human Rights Violations (Civil and Political)', Doc.E/CN.4/Sub.2/1997/20/Rev.1.

UN Report, 1999, 'Report of the independent expert on the right to restitution, compensation and rehabilitation for victims of grave violations of Human Rights and fundamental freedoms', Doc. E/CN.4/1999/65.

United Nations Treaty Series, 1978, Protocol II Additional to the Geneva Conventions of 12 August 1949, The Protection of Victims of Non-International Armed Conflicts, 1125 U.N.T.S. 609.

Van Eck, J., 2001, 'Reconciliation In Africa' in W. James and L. Van De Vijver (Eds.), *After the TRC: Reflections On Truth And Reconciliation In South Africa*, (Ohio: Ohio University Press).

Victims Unit, 2001, *Reshape, Rebuild, Achieve* (Belfast: Northern Ireland Office), (www.bloody-sunday-enquiry.org) accessed 10.06.04.

Part II
Organisational Defences of Human Rights

SAM GARKAWE

'Amnesty for Truth': A Violation of Human Rights by South Africa's Truth and Reconciliation Commission?

Introduction

The latter part of the twentieth century provided international human rights activists and advocates with many reasons for optimism. The world saw the end of many abusive military dictatorships throughout Latin America, the termination of the discredited Communist system in Eastern Europe and the former Yugoslavia, and the closing stages of centuries of colonialism in Africa with the dismantling of the apartheid regime in South Africa. In each of these situations governments changed from repressive regimes that consistently violated human rights, to more open, accountable and human rights based regimes. A new interdisciplinary academic discipline, 'transitional justice', has sprung up that examines a variety of issues relating to how these governments deal with past violations of human rights (Boraine, 2001). Given the number of transitional governments in the world and their fragility, the success of 'transitional justice' will be one of the most crucial issues for human rights in the twenty first century.

This chapter will focus on the specific issue of what arrangements transitional governments make with respect to their past perpetrators of human rights. The social, economic, political and cultural context of each nation 'in transition' will be different, and solutions that fit one nation or culture may not entirely, or even in part, be appropriate for another. The transitional justice 'western' model for dealing with past perpetrators has generally been the criminal trial (whether international, national or hybrid), with its formal rules of evidence and procedure and due process guarantees for defendants, including the need for proof beyond reasonable doubt (Bass, 2000). With many transitional nations coming from the developing world, other models have been established. For example, Eastern Europe has largely relied upon 'lustration' or purges of past perpetrators, together with some compensatory laws for victims, as its primary 'transitional justice' mechanism (Symposium, 1995). Although this model has been strongly criticised for not affording sufficient due process for alleged perpetrators, in the context of societies where the majority of the population was at least complicit in the maintenance of the repressive regimes, it is easy to see why this form of 'transitional justice' flourished following the collapse of communism.

This chapter will be concerned with what many writers see as a very promising form of transitional justice for past perpetrators and a real alternative to the western model – the truth or investigatory commission. Prior to the South African Truth and Reconciliation Commission (the 'TRC'), unconditional amnesties for past perpetrators seemed to accompany all previous truth commissions. These were granted either as part of the Truth Commission's establishment, or were provided subsequently (Hayner, 2001). This reinforced the perception of many international human rights advocates that truth commissions were primarily aimed at avoiding or weakening the prospects of bringing perpetrators to justice (Robertson, 2000: 263). However, the TRC was intended to be a different form of truth commission as amnesty would only be provided for perpetrators if they could satisfy certain conditions, the primary one being that they provide a 'full disclosure' of their actions. In other words, truth would be traded for amnesty. Given that the use of truth commissions is increasing as a transitional justice mechanism amongst developing nations, the success of the TRC, and the lessons that can be learned from it, are significant issues for the future of human rights.

There are other compelling reasons why an analysis of the TRC from an international human rights perspective is crucial. One needs to view the TRC, a new institution created in the wake of South Africa's transition, from the perspective of the effort, time and resources the international community placed on the dismantling of apartheid (The UN and Apartheid, 1994). It must also be remembered that South Africa was one of the few nations in 1948 to abstain from voting for the 'foundation' instrument of modern international human rights – the Universal Declaration of Human Rights (1948). The challenge that the apartheid system posed to the new international order and the very basic international human rights norm of non-discrimination was manifest. While other nations may have clearly abused human rights just as much, or even more, than South Africa, it is submitted that in reality the apartheid system placed South Africa in a very different qualitative category altogether in terms of the future of human rights. In the words of the former Secretary-General of the United Nations, Boutros Boutros-Ghali

> The struggle against apartheid extended far beyond South Africa's borders, and was one that helped to define the role that the United Nations could play in resolving seemingly intractable issues. It also helped to shape the conscience of the international community as a whole. (The UN and Apartheid, 1994: 3–4)

A final aspect of the importance of the TRC is its regional and African context. In a continent devastated by centuries of colonialism, numerous corrupt and repressive regimes after the formal end of the era of colonialism, civil wars, poverty and disease (including the AIDS pandemic), many nations look upon South Africa as a model for the rest of Africa. Despite its violent history, repressive past and not so perfect present, South Africa is still seen as a relatively wealthy nation that has much influence and moral authority throughout Africa following its transition. Thus the importance that its primary transitional justice mechanism – the TRC – will honour human rights norms is also underlined.

The main purpose of this chapter is to critically assess the major complaint about the TRC's amnesty process from an international human rights perspective. This was, in simple terms, that it gave official sanction for people who committed terrible human rights violations (such as murder and torture) to 'walk free'. Slye (2000) elaborates on this basic critique by referring to three derivative criticisms. Firstly, granting amnesty was a violation of South Africa's international legal obligations to prosecute international crimes. Secondly, the granting of amnesty undercut South Africa's efforts to install respect for the rule of law throughout South African society, and this thus continued, if not increased, the culture of impunity that had characterised the apartheid years. The final critique is that the amnesty violated the fundamental rights of the victims of the repression. Each of these arguments will be assessed in turn in this chapter. However, prior to a discussion of these arguments it is necessary to have a clear understanding of how the provisions for amnesty actually worked, and what were the consequences of amnesty.

A description of the TRC's Amnesty process

The concept that perpetrators of gross violations of human rights during the apartheid years would be granted amnesty was agreed to as part of a last minute compromise that paved the way for South Africa's transition to democracy. The provision for amnesty was first expressed in the epilogue to the negotiated Interim Constitution (1993), but the details of the procedures and conditions for amnesty were later clarified and given legislative expression in the *Promotion of National Unity and Reconciliation Act 1995* (the 'Act'). This legislation, which established the TRC, was debated at length by the South African public, and set the terms and the necessary procedures for amnesty applicants.

Under section 18 of the Act, each applicant for amnesty had to apply individually to the Amnesty Committee ('AC') of the TRC within a prescribed time period.[1] The AC required applicants to attend a public hearing in practically all cases where applicants admitted to having committed serious offences (the Act: s19(4)). The two main criteria for amnesty were whether the applicant had made a 'full disclosure' of their actions, and that they had acted with a 'political objective' when they committed the criminal act.[2] The Act gave no guidance as to the meaning of 'full disclosure', leaving it up to the AC to determine whether this prerequisite was fulfilled in each individual case based on the ordinary meaning of this term. On the other hand, the Act provided certain factors that the AC had to take into account in their determination of whether a person had acted with a 'political objective' (the Act: s20(3)).[3] The only decision open to the AC was either to grant amnesty or not; there was no provision for the AC to attach any conditions to a finding of amnesty. There was no express right of appeal by victims and/or perpetrators from an amnesty decision, although they and the TRC itself could apply to a Court to overturn a decision of the AC.[4] Furthermore, proceedings of the AC could not be used as evidence in later criminal trials of applicants who had failed in their amnesty applications (the Act: s31(3)).[5]

The legal consequences of amnesty were set out in s20 (7), (8) & (9) of the Act. A finding of amnesty meant that the applicant could not be prosecuted for their crimes (and would be released from custody if already convicted or awaiting trial).[6] The other major consequence was that victims were also precluded from civilly suing a successful amnesty applicant, as well as the state or other organisation in respect of the acts (or omissions) for which they had been granted amnesty. On the other hand, if amnesty was refused, this would leave applicants open to be prosecuted and/or being sued in civil courts.[7] For this reason, the amnesty process was often referred to as a 'carrot' (the allure of amnesty) and 'stick' (the threat of prosecutions) approach to inducing perpetrators to come forward.[8] There were thus very powerful legal consequences of a finding of amnesty for victims, applicants and the state. Not surprisingly, given what was at stake for applicants and victims, both were entitled to prior notification of an amnesty hearing, where they also had the right to be present, to testify and to adduce evidence (the Act: s19(4)).

Did Amnesty breach South Africa's international legal obligations?

There are strong arguments under international law that States are under a duty to investigate allegations of human rights violations that amount to international crimes, and if the evidence warrants, to then place on trial alleged perpetrators. In particular, widely ratified Treaties on genocide, torture and war crimes seem to place an obligation on State Parties to take this course of action. An influential article by international human rights academic Diane Orentlicher entitled 'Settling Accounts: The Duty to Prosecute Human Rights Violations of a Prior Regime' (1991: 2537) asserts that states have obligations to place perpetrators of these types of crimes on trial if the evidence warrants. She argues that criminal prosecution is justified because it accords with a principle aim of sentencing – general deterrence – designed to prevent future criminal activity. Other arguments are that prosecution affirms the rule of law and the supremacy of civilian institutions, and thus advances the transition to democracy. Finally, she refers to the dangers of not punishing, which she argues creates an atmosphere of impunity that undermines the new government and institutions connected with the rule of law (see below).

The first counter-argument to Orentlicher's thesis is that there is no consensus that there is an international duty to prosecute even the most outrageous international crimes. In light of the many instances of states where amnesties have been granted to perpetrators of such crimes, one authoritative text on international criminal law concludes: 'the practice of states and international organisations suggests any general duty to prosecute human rights abusers [...] has not yet solidified' (Ratner and Abrams, 2001: 153). In the case of South Africa it is particularly significant that given the amount of effort the UN placed in fighting apartheid, at no stage did the UN appear to voice any objection to any aspect of the South African amnesty process. This is related to another very important point – that unlike the amnesties provided by Latin American governments, the South African amnesty legislation was agreed to by their democratic parliament, with the terms of the Act being debated for some time both within and outside the South African parliament, and furthermore, it was a conditional amnesty based on the principle of 'truth for amnesty'.

Other counter-arguments are that many writers recognise that even if an international legal duty does exist, it can be overridden where the stability of a state would be threatened by conducting criminal trials, and/or where the criminal justice system of the state is unable to provide for fair criminal trials (van Zyl, 2000; Zalaquett, 1992). Both these counter-arguments were highly relevant to South Africa at the time of its transition. First, while it is difficult to access the actual threat right wing security forces posed to the transition, some evidence does suggest that it was not insubstantial. Secondly, the criminal justice system under apartheid was widely perceived as being unable to deliver fair trials. A further argument is that there is always, in any legal system, an overriding discretion granted to prosecution authorities whether to proceed with the prosecution. Often included in this discretionary process are public policy considerations that would include matters such as the likely threat to future stability of the society if the prosecution proceeds, the ability of the nation's criminal justice system to cope with the trial, and the high burden of proof required for a criminal conviction. In the case of South Africa, in many situations of repression by the security forces under apartheid, much of the evidence was hidden and solely in the hands of perpetrators, making a criminal trial approach most unlikely to result in convictions. In fact, the criminal trial approach had much potential to exonerate perpetrators, such as it did with the botched 1996 prosecution of the former Minister for Defence, Magnus Malan and 19 others, who were all acquitted and proclaimed their innocence immediately after the trial.

For all the above reasons, the writer would reject the argument that the amnesty process violated South Africa's international obligations.

Did Amnesty add to the climate of impunity in South Africa?

The second argument by Slye is that amnesty allowed violent people to walk free, and this sent a poor message to future South African society that is hoping to recover respect for the law and its institutions, which were clearly very damaged under apartheid. Thus the amnesty process sacrificed short term stability for long term instability in South Africa that will, in time, undercut efforts to establish democracy and the rule of law. Perhaps also the high rates of crimes throughout South Africa provide some evidence that respect for the law has broken down. However, in relation to this last point, it is difficult to attribute high crime rates to the TRC granting amnesty to many of apartheid's perpetrators. The causes of crime are complex and stem from a multitude of factors.

The main problem with the above arguments is that they equate amnesty with impunity (or a lack of accountability). The argument does not take into account the fact that the South African amnesty arrangement was a conditional one, which in the writer's opinion, did not amount to impunity for alleged perpetrators. In particular, applicants for amnesty faced the following forms of accountability:

- Within a given time frame each applicant for amnesty had to make an individual application to the AC.
- If the application revealed that a serious offence had been committed, the applicant was then normally required to appear in person in a public hearing of the AC, which was likely to involve the press being present, with some hearings being telecast on the television or the radio.
- Because one of the primary conditions for amnesty was that applicants had to make a 'full disclosure' of their actions, doing so in a public process meant they had to admit to their wrongdoing in the full glare of the public, press and their own families and friends.
- At the public hearing applicants were to be subject to cross-examination from both the AC and the victims' representative.

- If an applicant succeeded in their application, their name would permanently be printed in both the Government gazette and in the TRC's Final Report, a form of public shaming.
- If an applicant failed his or her application, they would then be subject to criminal and civil liability.

The writer's view is that the above processes and procedures did represent a form of accountability for perpetrators. The TRC itself referred to its amnesties as an 'accountable amnesty' in an effort to distinguish its approach from the 'blanket' amnesty approach of past Truth Commissions (TRC Final Report, 1998: Vol. 1: 118). The following views of well-known anti-apartheid lawyer, George Bizos, and certainly no friend of perpetrators, confirms this argument

> Let me […] reassure you on the basis of the interaction that I have had with perpetrators, that amnesty did not come cheap for them. In having to confess publicly to what they had done, however guarded and reluctantly many have been in doing, they have endangered and in some instances terminated their relationships with their partners, children and friends. […] public disclosure is no small thing. Public shame, personal alienation and familial rejection should not be dismissed as insignificant. […] This qualified amnesty is not with impunity. (Bizos, 2003; 6–7)

The writer concedes that it is a debatable point as to whether the TRC's above forms of accountability were sufficient to satisfy the demands of justice and the international human rights community. However, it is worthwhile to reiterate again that there has been no official condemnation of the amnesty process by the United Nations or any of its constituent bodies. This is highly significant given the substantial involvement of the United Nations in the struggle against apartheid (The UN and Apartheid, 1994). In assessing the South African approach to amnesty, one must also take into consideration the main advantages of amnesty. Firstly, the condition for amnesty that perpetrators make a 'full disclosure' of their actions recognised the significance of truth seeking for victims as part of their process of healing, and also directly benefited victims by making it more likely they would receive information concerning the relevant criminal offence. In cases where victims had been killed, in some instances perpetrator's testimony revealed to survivors what happened to their loved ones, possibly clearing their loved one's names[9] and/or allowing for the recovery of their remains. This in turn led to their loved ones finally receiving a proper funeral. Many psychologists and other mental health practitioners argue that the discovery of the truth is essential for victims to 'move on' and recover from traumatic events of the past. Some also believe that truth is a precondition to reconciliation (Hayner, 2001: 6). Others, who favour 'restorative' solutions to criminal justice problems, also consider such a truth-telling approach to be a restorative solution to victims' problems.

Furthermore, it should be noted that had South Africa adopted a criminal trial approach, in most cases perpetrators would never have been subject to any form of accountability because they would have had little incentive to come forward. This is due to the fact that much of the wrongdoing of the security forces would have remained hidden as often they were the only people present apart from the deceased victim(s), and there was a culture of deceit and avoidance pervading the system, which included the destruction of documents. In such circumstances, it is clear that a criminal trial approach provides no incentive for perpetrators to come forward, as the onus of proof is on the prosecution to prove its case beyond a reasonable doubt. This should be compared to the amnesty process, where it is in the interests of the perpetrator to make as complete disclosure as possible, as this would increase their chances of gaining amnesty. Even in cases where there would have been sufficient evidence to launch a criminal prosecution, a number of factors made it unlikely that actual convictions would have resulted. These included the lack of prosecution resources and the general poor state of the South African criminal justice system, the likelihood that defendants having access to high quality legal representation, and the high burden of proof required for a criminal conviction. The acquittal of former Minister of Defence, Magnas Malan (already mentioned above) is testimony to these realities.

Did Amnesty violate the rights of the victims of repression?

The final argument by Slye against the amnesty provisions of the TRC was that they violated the rights of victims. There are two distinct elements to this critique. First, victims would be denied their 'right' to retributive justice against those who had committed the violations against them or their loved ones. Secondly, once amnesty was granted victims were no longer able to sue either the State or the offender in respect of the acts or omissions for which amnesty was granted.

In relation to the first element, it assumes that victims actually have a choice of 'retribution' under a criminal justice approach. In adversarial criminal justice systems, such as that found in Australia, the United Kingdom and South Africa, it is up to the prosecution, as representatives of the state, to decide to prosecute a particular perpetrator (Emsley, 1987; Rude, 1985). This decision is generally guided by a multitude of factors, and it is quite possible for prosecutors to decide not to prosecute where victims wish to do so, and on the other hand, for prosecutors to decide to proceed where a victim may have reconciled with the perpetrator and thus strongly opposes their prosecution. Furthermore, even if the authorities decide to proceed, the success of their case often depends on factors outside the control of victims, and if a guilty verdict is obtained, the amount (if any) of 'retribution' is dependent on a decision of the judiciary, of which the opinions of victims are generally not a relevant factor.[10]

The criticism that the TRC removes victims' rights to retributive justice also assumes that the South African criminal justice system was up to the task of judging perpetrators fairly and consistently. The reality was that it had been so discredited during apartheid and was so dysfunctional that it could not have been relied upon to provide fairness or consistency for alleged perpetrators. The lack of criminal prosecutions and convictions, including the acquittal of the former Minister of Defence, Magnas Malan (see above), supports the argument that few South African victims, if any, would have found satisfaction under the prosecution option. While it is true to say that the TRC amnesty process did remove the possibility of retribution in those cases where an amnesty applicant was successful, in reality this was not a viable option for the overwhelming majority of victims anyway.

In relation to the second element of the removal of victims' rights, namely their rights to sue in a civil court (either the offender or the State), the following could be said. First, as stated above, only a small number of criminal convictions would have resulted from a prosecution approach, and the fact that perpetrators would have had difficulty satisfying any court ordered restitution order, clearly few victims would have achieved reparations as a result of the criminal process. Secondly, only a relatively small number of educated and resourceful victims would have been able to mount successful civil suits against perpetrators or the State (Jenkins, 2000: 474; AZAPO case, 1996). Thus the TRC's approach to reparations (that is, to award smaller amounts of reparation through a non-adversarial process) was fairer than a system where only those educated and resourceful victims could successfully sue and obtain (relatively) large sums of awards.

One must also keep in mind that the provision for amnesty was only one aspect, albeit a crucial one, of the TRC's work. If one is to assess the impact of amnesty on the rights of victims, one must also balance the work of the AC against the work of the TRC's other two Committees that were primarily devoted to benefit victims. The first was the Human Rights Violations Committee (the 'HRVC'), established under Chapter 3 of the Act. The main benefit of the HRVC was that it allowed many victims to tell the world in their own language, and often for the first time, of what happened to them, and how the gross human rights violations had caused hardship and suffering to themselves, their families and their communities. Many argued that, in particular, the public hearings of the HRCV were often a 'cathartic' experience for most victims. This was due to the fact that they were conducted in an informal, sympathetic and reassuring atmosphere, without formal rules of evidence applying, and in the main without the 'threat' of cross-examination.[11] Despite some counter-arguments[12] many psychologists and others assert that there is therapeutic value for victims of traumatic events being able to tell their story in such a supportive atmosphere and in such a publicly recognised process.

The other Committee of the TRC was the Committee on Reparation and Rehabilitation (the 'CRR') established pursuant to Chapter 5 of the Act. The CRR was charged with deciding on policies and making recommendations to the government in relation to the reparation and rehabilitation of victims. It also had to resolve who were genuinely victims and thus entitled to these benefits. The work and recommendations of the CRR stands forever as a 'blueprint' of the many different aspects of reparations for victims and as to what should be the response of society to the suffering of the victims of repression during the apartheid era. Even though the response of the South African government has been slow and to many an 'immense disappointment' (Jenkins, 2000: 477), the comprehensive and broad nature of the CRR recommendations does establish a strong benchmark for all future transitional governments. It should be noted that the main alternative approach to the TRC, criminal trials, are not well-suited to recommend the types of broad reparative measures alluded to by the CRR.

In conclusion, the writer would assert that the amnesty provisions did not violate victims' rights. In fact, it is argued that the TRC did a lot more for victims in the South African context than the criminal justice alternative would have done.

Conclusion

The above analysis of the three primary criticisms of the TRC's amnesty – that it was contrary to South Africa's international legal obligations, that it added to the climate of impunity and disrespect for the rule of law, and that it violated the rights of victims – indicates that each does not stand up to scrutiny. When viewed in the context of the political, economic and cultural situation that South Africa found itself in, amnesty in the form as provided by the Act was a far better mechanism that the criminal trial approach. The concept of 'amnesty for truth' also carried with it a number of advantages that were particularly relevant in the South African context.

What lessons can be learned in other transitional societies from this analysis of the amnesty provisions of the TRC? While stressing that each situation of a nation in transition is unique and must be assessed on its individual merits, it is asserted that 'amnesty for truth' can be an appropriate basis for a truth commission type mechanism in a wide variety of situations. However, local adaptations will often need to be made. For example, careful consideration could be given to providing any future Commission empowered to provide amnesty with the ability to include conditions to be attached to the amnesty. If such a future Commission could approve amnesty, say with the provisos that the applicant pay reparation directly to victims[13] or they will lose their employment and/or benefits,[14] then victims might get a greater sense of justice from the process.[15] Providing such a Commission with this power is bound to be a difficult drafting exercise, as the process must allow for the due process rights of applicants to be protected, and not remove too much the incentive for perpetrators to apply for amnesty.

Another possibility is to combine the criminal justice model with the Truth Commission model – crimes of a certain magnitude could only be dealt with by the criminal justice system, whereas 'lessor' crimes could be subject to a TRC style approach. This is precisely how the Commission for Reception, Truth and Reconciliation in East Timor has been constituted (Stahn, 2001). This type of approach suited East Timor because many of the major perpetrators of serious crimes were no longer living in East Timor, were unlikely to return, and thus the process saw no need to include inducements of amnesty to encourage them to return. This should be compared to the situation South Africa found itself in when former oppressors and the oppressed had to find a way of being able to live together in one nation.

In conclusion, there is little doubt from the above discussion that the TRC and its unique approach to amnesty have raised many new possibilities for future truth Commissions type bodies. While the TRC was far from perfect (Garkawe, 2003), it is argued that it represented an innovative way for developing nations 'in transition' to come to terms with their past. If the lessons can be learned from the strengths and failures of the TRC, transitional justice will be strengthened, and thus the future of human rights into the twenty first century will be made much more secure.

Endnotes

1 This was December 1995 to May 1997 (Boraine, 2000: p.148).

2 The other criteria were that the applicant had complied with the technical requirements of the Act. These included that they had applied during the specified time period, in the prescribed manner, and the act, omission or offence that was the subject of their application was in fact a 'gross violation of human rights' as defined in the Act.

3 These factors were based upon the 'Norgaard' principles for extradition, and were founded upon a survey of state practice in defining and applying the 'political offence' exception to extradition law. They included the motive of the applicant, the context and object of their act (or omission), the legal and factual nature and the gravity of the act, whether the act was executed in response to an order or with the approval of a political organisation, and the relationship between the act and the political objective pursued.

4 As in most common law legal systems, there was a standard and limited right to appeal to a court where a non-judicial body (such as the AC) makes decisions that can be shown to have violated the law. The TRC did exercise this power on at least one well-known occasion when it had the High Court overturn a controversial and much criticised decision of the AC to grant a general amnesty to 37 leaders of the ANC who had made one joint application (Coleman case, 1998). For a critical analysis of this decision, see McGregor (2001: 39–44).

5 However, the fact that the applicant had applied for amnesty clearly would have the effect of alerting the prosecution authorities to the wrongdoing of the applicant, perhaps making it more likely that the applicant would eventually be prosecuted.

6 Perpetrators granted amnesty also were entitled to have any criminal and/or civil trial that they were the defendant in aborted if they were already in progress.

7 Any suspension of civil or criminal proceedings against amnesty applicants could be resumed at the discretion of the relevant court, with no adverse inference to be drawn by that court (the Act: s21).

8 The 'carrot and stick' terminology was used by the then Minister of Justice, Dullah Omar, who was largely responsible for the establishment of the TRC (Hayner, 2001: p.99).

9 The security forces, in order to cover up their own crimes, had in some cases said that the victim was a collaborator that had been killed by the liberation forces.

10 The crucial factors are the nature of the crime, the nature of the offender and their response to the charges, and the effects of the proposed sanction, taking into account the various purposes and justifications for punishment and the principle of proportionality (Fox and Freiberg, 1999: 180–359).

11 This should be compared to the role of victims during criminal trials, where they are limited in their testimony by the formal rules of evidence and procedure, and may be subject to rigorous and often traumatic cross-examination by defence lawyers (Mertus, 2000; Henning & Bronitt, 1998).

12 Some argue, for example, that there is a strong danger of re-traumatisation and unless there is adequate support services available at the time and in the aftermath, finding out the 'truth' about what happened to their loved ones can be counter-therapeutic (Hayner, 2001: 141–144).

13 This also would have been more in line with the alleged 'restorative justice' dimensions of the TRC. Restorative justice generally encourages perpetrators of criminal offences to 'make amends' to their victims directly, or perhaps indirectly. However, under the TRC amnesty process, once a perpetrator had been granted amnesty, the only form of monetary reparations victims could obtain was from the South African government (see Part V), and not from 'their' perpetrator.

14 Such an approach would have allowed for the inclusion of the purges or 'lustration' mechanisms commonly used in the transition of many Eastern European states, and thus create a hybrid of approaches. For a detailed critical analysis of this form of accountability see Symposium (1995).

15 One South African human rights organisation, Lawyers for Human Rights, unsuccessfully suggested this possibility during the public debate over the legislation that established the TRC.

References

AZAPO case, 1996, *Azanian Peoples Organisation (AZAPO) and others v The President of the Republic of South Africa and others* (1996) 8 BCLR 1015 (CC).

Bass, G., 2000, *Stay the Hand of Vengeance: The Politics of War Crimes Tribunals*, (Princeton and Oxford: Princeton University Press).

Bizos, G., 2003, 'Why Prosecutions are Necessary', in C. Villa-Vicencio and E. Doxtader (Eds.), *The Provocations of Amnesty: Memory, Justice and Impunity* (Cape Town: Institute for Justice and Reconciliation & David Philip Publishers), pp. 5–9.

Boraine, A., 2000, 'Truth and Reconciliation in South Africa: The Third Way', in R. Rotberg and D. Thompson (Eds.), *Truth v Justice: The Morality of Truth Commissions*, (Princeton: Princeton University Press).

Boraine, A., 2001, 'A Project on Transitional Justice', *Commonwealth Legal Education Association Newsletter*, 1(87): 19–25.

Coleman case, 1998, *Truth & Reconciliation Commission v Coleman & 36 Others*, No. 3729/98 (Cape Town High Court, unreported).

Emsley, C., 1987, *Crime and Society in England 1750–1900*, (London & New York: Longman Publishers).

Fox, R. and Freiberg, A., 1999, *Sentencing: State and Federal Law in Victoria*, 2nd ed., (Melbourne: Oxford University Press).

Garkawe, S., 2003, 'The South African Truth and Reconciliation Commission – a suitable model to enhance the role and rights of the victims of gross violations of human rights?', *Melbourne University Law Review*, 27 (2): 334–380.

Hayner, P., 2001, *Unspeakable Truths: Confronting State Terror and Atrocity*, (New York: Routledge).

Henning, T. and Bronitt, S., 1998, 'Rape victims on trial: Regulating the use and abuse of sexual history evidence', in P. Easteal (Ed.), *Balancing the Scales: Rape, Law Reform and Australian Culture*, (Sydney: Federation Press), pp 76–93.

Interim Constitution, 1993 – *Constitution of the Republic of South Africa* 1993 (Act 200 of 1993). [Note that this was later replaced by the Final Constitution – *Constitution of the Republic of South Africa* 1996 (Act 108 of 1996)].

Jenkins, C., 2000, 'After the Dry White Season: The Dilemmas of Reparation and Reconstruction in South Africa', *South African Journal on Human Rights*, 16: 415–485.

McGregor, L., 2001, 'Individual Accountability in South Africa: Cultural Optimum or Political Façade?', *American Journal of International Law*, 95(1): 32–45.

Mertus, J., 2000, 'Truth in a Box: The Limits of Justice through Judicial Mechanisms', in I. Amadiume & A. An-Na'im (Eds.), *The Politics of Memory: Truth, Healing and Social Justice*, (London: Zed Books), pp. 142–161.

Orentlicher, D., 1991, 'Settling Accounts: The Duty to Prosecute Human Rights Violations of a Prior Regime', *Yale Law Journal*, 100(8): 2537–2615.

Ratner, S. and Abrams, J., 2001, *Accountability for Human Rights Atrocities in International Law: Beyond the Nuremberg Legacy*, 2nd ed., (Oxford: Oxford University Press).

Robertson, G., 2000, *Crimes against Humanity: The Struggle for Global Justice*, (London and New York: Penguin Books).

Rude, G., 1985, *Criminal and Victim: Crime and Society in early Nineteenth-Century England*, (Oxford: Oxford University Press).

Slye, R., 2000, 'Justice and amnesty', in C. Villa-Vicencio & W. Verwoerd (Eds.), *Looking Back Reaching Forward: Reflections on the Truth and Reconciliation Commission of South Africa*, (Cape Town: University of Cape Town Press), pp. 174–183.

Stahn, C., 2001, 'Accommodating Individual Criminal Responsibility and National Reconciliation: The UN Truth Commission for East Timor', *American Journal of International Law*, 95(4): 952–966.

Symposium, 1995, 'Symposium: Law and Lustration: Righting the Wrongs of the Past', *Law & Social Inquiry*, 20(1): 1–273.

TRC Final Report, 1998, Truth and Reconciliation Commission, *Truth and Reconciliation Commission of South Africa Report*, (Cape Town: Juta & Co.).

The UN and Apartheid, 1994, – United Nations Blue Books Series, Volume 1, *United Nations and Apartheid 1948–1994*, (New York: United Nations Department of Public Information).

Universal Declaration of Human Rights, 1948, General Assembly resolution 217A (III), 10 December 1948.

van Zyl, P., 2000, 'Justice without Punishment: Guaranteeing Human Rights in Transitional Societies', in C. Villa-Vicencio and W. Verwoerd (Eds.), *Looking Back Reaching Forward: Reflections on the Truth and Reconciliation Commission of South Africa*, (Cape Town: University of Cape Town Press), pp. 42–57.

Zalaquett, J., 1992, 'Balancing Ethical Imperatives and Political Constraints: The Dilemma of New Democracies Confronting Past Human Rights Violations', *Hastings Law Journal*, 43 (6): 1425–1438.

LARA FERGUS

Activating Women's Human Rights: Side Steps and Leaps Forward at Amnesty International

Amnesty International is one of the best-known and most influential human rights organisations in the world, yet for women's human rights activists it has long been strangely silent on the vast majority of abuses women suffer. Amnesty was founded in 1961, when interpretations of human rights focussed almost exclusively on 'civil and political' rights and overlooked most violence against women, particularly in the so-called 'private sphere'. Though such interpretations have been challenged over the past few decades by women's human rights activists, Amnesty has largely continued to reproduce and reflect this 'public-sphere' bias in its own work. However, policy changes within the organisation over the last decade have gone some way toward addressing this bias: specifically the 1997 decision to include abuses by non-state actors in activism addressing governments; and the 2001 mandate change which expanded work beyond the 'civil and political' framework to include all grave abuses of human rights. Three years after the latter mandate change, Amnesty took the unprecedented step of focussing on abuses taking place within the family, in its *Stop Violence Against Women* (SVAW) campaign (2004–2010). In this, Amnesty appears to be pioneering a new era for human rights activism, and one of greatly increased relevance for women's human rights.

However, despite significant *policy* advances, the research presented here shows that much of Amnesty's activist *practice* remains locked in traditional 'public-sphere' interpretations of human rights. In Amnesty's most widespread and famous form of activist practice, letter-writing appeals, 'private sphere' abuses (and therefore most abuses against women) are almost totally absent. Appeals for abuses against men outnumber those for abuses against women by a factor of 4.85 to one for the 'Worldwide Appeals', and 7.92 to one for the 'Urgent Actions'. No decrease in this gender imbalance has been observed with the successive policy changes. Two years following the mandate change, the continuing small number of appeals for women and absence of 'private sphere' abuses in the appeals demonstrates a chasm between policy and practice. Amnesty appears to be 'side-stepping' the messages of its own policy and campaigning, and therefore compounding the silence surrounding abuses of women's human rights. There is an urgent need for Amnesty to address the continuing and entrenched marginalisation of women's human rights concerns within the organisation, not only in its research and activist practice, but also in its organisational structure, resource allocation and strategy decisions.

This chapter will do the following: First, I will outline some of the historic and contemporary debates surrounding women's human rights, and show how traditional interpretations of human rights have been effectively challenged and expanded by women's rights activists. Second, the chapter traces the development of Amnesty International's own policy regarding women's human rights, in response to these challenges. Third, the chapter establishes in quantitative terms, the extent and nature of Amnesty's activist practice around women's human rights throughout this development, and examines the factors influencing this. Fourth, I consider how the *Stop Violence Against Women* campaign may represent a 'leap forward' for Amnesty's activism on human rights abuses against women. Fifth, I make recommendations on how to incorporate Amnesty's obvious policy commitment to women's human rights, and the positive messages of the SVAW campaign, into activist practice.

Making women's rights human rights

Amnesty International itself has recently noted that 'violence against women is the greatest human rights scandal of our times' (Amnesty International, 2004a: 1). The report *It's in Our Hands* (2004a), produced for the *Stop Violence Against Women* campaign, paints a grim picture of what the term 'human rights abuse' means for women.

> At least one out of every three women has been beaten, coerced into sex, or otherwise abused in her lifetime, according to a study based on 50 surveys from around the world. Usually, the abuser is a member of her own family or someone known to her. (Heise, Ellsberg and Gottemoeller, 1999: 1)
>
> The Council of Europe has stated that domestic violence is the major cause of death and disability for women aged 16 to 44 and accounts for more death and ill-health than cancer or traffic accidents. (Parliamentary Assembly of the Council of Europe, 2002)
>
> More than 60 million women are 'missing' from the world today as a result of sex-selective abortions and female infanticide, according to an estimate by Amartya Sen, the 1998 Nobel Laureate for Economics. (UN Population Fund, 1999: 6)
>
> The Russian government estimates that 14,000 women were killed by their partners or relatives in 1999, yet the country still has no law specifically addressing domestic violence. (Fifth Periodic Report of the Russian Federation)
>
> The World Health Organisation has reported that up to 70 per cent of female murder victims are killed by their male partners. (WHO, 2002: 118)

Yet despite the scale of such abuse, the above forms of violence have only recently come to be viewed as 'human rights abuse' at all. They remain commonly constructed as either isolated aberrations with no political significance, or, worse, as inevitable expressions of 'culture', off-limits to scrutiny. This apparent 'blindness' to the systematic and ubiquitous nature of violence against women can in part be attributed to the historical circumstances in which the human rights framework developed, and the contemporary context in which it is interpreted.

Human rights law, many feminist critics have argued, was not constructed with a view to promoting gender equality, but rather to protect men from what they feared most: the power of the state (Binion, 1995). The United Nations *Universal Declaration of Human Rights*, or UNDHR (United Nations, 1948), was largely influenced by earlier documents outlining the 'rights of man' or the 'rights of the citizen', such as those which emerged from the French Revolution of 1789. Such documents were never intended to apply to women, and at least one early feminist activist, Olympe de Gouges, was executed for suggesting that they should be (Gay Levy et al., 1979). Whilst the UNDHR translated and updated these earlier documents into more 'gender neutral' language, it still largely reflects the concerns of elite men. This is not to say that such concerns are never shared by women or non-elite men, but that women and non-elite men face additional concerns that are not addressed in the UNDHR. Such concerns are the result of structural inequalities that the UNDHR does not analyse, such as those based on sex discrimination or resulting from colonisation.

Judith Bessant and Sandy Cook are particularly critical of international human rights law, arguing that

> the Universal Declaration of Human Rights (1948) and the International Covenant on Civil and Political Rights (1966):
>
> - fail to recognise many forms of violence as violence, and are unable to address those forms of endemic violence against women;
> - operate with a masculinist distinction between public and private spheres;
> - assume universalising principles that cannot be transferred into action which secures basic entitlements and greater self-determination; and
> - fail to compel sovereign states to give effect to international law. (Bessant and Cook, 1998: 10)

They demand a conception of human rights that takes into account the nature of relationships many women live in and the forms of violence women in particular suffer.

Cook and Bessant (1998) demonstrate the major feminist criticism of the traditional human rights framework: that, in focussing on the potential of the state as abuser, it fails to take into account abuses in the so-called 'private sphere', where the vast majority of abuses against women occur. Gayle Binion points out the profound consequences for women that this entails: women are 'rendered subject to the control of patriarchal familial authorities – fathers, brothers and husbands – with the understanding that familial matters are "private", and therefore beyond the scope of governmental authority and intervention' (1995: 516).

However, women's rights activists (and, more recently, Amnesty International) have noted that 'the family' may only be considered separate or autonomous from government *at the sufferance of the state.* 'Governments worldwide have not endowed "family" with any significant degree of autonomy. The framework for the family is everywhere within a political arena' (Binion, 1995: 519). The fact that the crimes of battery, rape, imprisonment, and so forth are largely ignored by the state when perpetrated by a family member is a 'failure of official responsibility, not an inability to police the environment. In a feminist analysis, the state's choice to overlook such criminal acts is as abusive of human rights as a refusal to interfere with the slave trade' (Binion, 1995: 519).

Many feminists insist, therefore, that governments accept responsibility for policing human rights violations within the 'private' sphere. This involves a theoretical and practical acknowledgment that private actors can and do abuse human rights, and are subject to the same international conventions that bind governments. This may seem obvious, but it is frequently overlooked in many versions of traditional liberal theory which casts the state as the primary human rights violator (Kiss, 1995). In order to establish this accountability, activists have made use of existing human rights norms – such as discrimination, torture, due diligence, equality before the law, bodily integrity, and the right to health and life, to draw attention to the specific abuses women suffer. For example, similarities have been highlighted between the systematic abuse of bodily integrity that is domestic violence and traditional concepts of torture.

Ana Elena Obando (2004) notes the importance of using a human rights framework to address violence against women, in that the violence is officially recognised, not as an 'individual' or isolated problem, but as a structural one, based on discrimination, which governments have an international obligation to respond to. Importantly, human rights *theory* does not, in general, make any distinction between abuses perpetrated by state or non-state actors – everyone has a right to physical integrity, for instance, regardless of who might threaten that right. It is only through *interpretation* of this theory that more value is placed on public actions, which is why human rights *law* (and, usually, human rights organisations) respond more actively to forms of state violence and to the repression of actors within the public/political sphere.

The development of Amnesty International's work on women's human rights

When Amnesty International was founded in 1961 its mandate was relatively simple: to work for the liberation of 'prisoners of conscience' and to end torture. The mandate expanded somewhat over the next few decades to oppose the death penalty, extra-judicial executions and 'disappearances', but remained focused on 'civil and political' rights abuses and to one class of perpetrator: governments, their agents and opposition groups. At the same time, the organisation defended and promoted the universality and indivisibility of all human rights, which, alongside the self-imposed limitations of the mandate, meant that inconsistencies and contradictions inevitably emerged (Watson, 1997).

Amnesty began to focus on the issue of abuse against women in 1989, when it organised formal working groups to document women's rights violations. It concluded that women suffer more rights violations than any other group in the world, both in times of war and through traditional practices excused by culture (Bahar, 1996). This study culminated in the release of *Women in the Front Line* (Amnesty International, 1991), which focused on abuses perpetrated by the state and opposition groups. The report did not, therefore, detail abuses in the 'private' sphere, nor did it go any way towards a theorisation of the relationship between the 'private' and 'public' spheres. However, it did extensively cover the forms of abuses women suffer at the hands of the state, such as rape, sexual humiliation, and threats whilst in detention, along with other abuses that men also suffer.

As Saba Bahar notes in her article on Amnesty International and the institution of the family: 'To address the specific violence that women experience, the organisation had to reconsider not only the private/public division but also its own emphasis on state-related violence against women' (Bahar, 1996: 107). This, along with the decision to run a campaign on women's human rights coinciding with the United Nations (UN) Fourth World Conference on Women in Beijing, demanded from Amnesty a considerable rethink of its own position. In 1995, Amnesty released *Human Rights are Women's Rights*, which documented its resulting theoretical reorientation, drawing on the UN Declaration on the Elimination of Violence against Women (United Nations, 1993) and defining 'violence against women' as encompassing (in addition to violence perpetrated by the state)

> physical, sexual and psychological violence within the family, including battering, sexual abuse of female children in the household, dowry-related violence, marital rape, female genital mutilation and other traditional practices harmful to women, non-spousal violence and violence related to exploitation; physical, sexual and psychological violence occurring within the general community, including rape, sexual abuse, sexual harassment and intimidation at work, in educational institutions and elsewhere, trafficking in women and forced prostitution. The extent and severity of such practices must be recognised if we are fully to address the context in which human rights violations against women occur. (Amnesty International, 1995a, 8–9)

The report goes on to detail the 'extent and severity' of such abuses, therefore articulating Amnesty's obvious verbal commitment to opposing human rights abuses against women, wherever and by whomever they were perpetrated. Despite this, because of its mandate of the time, Amnesty could not act on the vast majority of such abuses: those that take place at the hands of 'non-state actors', such as family members, partners or acquaintances.

At the International Council Meeting (ICM) of 1997 this anomaly was partly addressed in a decision to increase parameters for action to include abuses perpetrated by non-state actors. It was decided 'that Amnesty will act when governments breach their duty to ensure respect for human rights by failing to take action against abuse of human rights by private actors' (Amnesty International, 1997a), meaning that governments would be addressed for complicity, condoning, acquiescence, lack of due diligence or negligence with regard to abuses by private actors. Although this decision did not change the mandate for the category of abuse (which remained focused on 'civil and political' rights), it did recognise that private individuals and groups abuse human rights in ways that are almost indistinguishable from abuses perpetrated by the state.

At first glance, this widening of work to include non-state actors would seem a positive step for work on women's human rights. However, the continued restriction of action to 'civil and political' abuses meant that most 'private sphere' abuses (such as domestic violence) would continue to be ignored, as they were not defined as 'civil or political'. In this and in other cases, the distinction served to reinforce the silence surrounding abuses of women as sexist assumptions were made as to what constituted a civil and political rights abuse by a non-state actor. For example, Amnesty introduced letter-writing appeals when landowners and private security guards 'disappeared' in indigenous villages in Guatemala (Amnesty International, 1997b), but took no action on cases of women who 'disappeared' into sexual slavery. It seemed an abuse was never of the 'civil and political' kind if the victims were mostly or exclusively women.

The 2001 ICM was much more promising for women's human rights. After a four-year mandate review, the existing statute was completely changed by unanimous vote. It was rightly noted that by limiting oppositional work to a particular set of civil and political rights, Amnesty was undermining the notion of indivisibility of all rights and damaging its own credibility. Therefore, a 'full-spectrum approach' was adopted, and the new 'mission' became 'to undertake research and action focused on preventing and ending grave abuses of the rights to physical and mental integrity, freedom of conscience and expression, and freedom from discrimination, within the context of its work to promote all human rights' (Amnesty International, 2004b).

Amnesty would now address 'governments, intergovernmental organisations, armed political groups, companies and other non-state actors' (Amnesty International, 2004b). Activism would be limited only according to the gravity of the abuse, and prioritise those abuses that fell within the current Integrated Strategic Plan.

It was this mandate change that opened the way for Amnesty to act on the majority of human rights abuses against women. For example, in 2001, Amnesty produced the report *Broken Bodies, Shattered Minds* (2001) on the torture of women, as part of its *Stop Torture* campaign. The report included detailed cases of domestic violence (among other abuses) and noted where governments had failed in their human rights obligations in not exercising 'due diligence' to prevent the abuse, or ensuring access to justice for victims. Without the mandate change, this would not have been possible, nor would the more recent *Stop Violence Against Women* campaign. Until the distinction between different categories of rights and that of state/non-state perpetrators was dropped, Amnesty could not begin to address violence against women within its parameters for action.

In the next section, I will question whether this new-found possibility of working on such abuses has been fully grasped by Amnesty in the years following the 2001 mandate change.

From policy to practice: quantifying Amnesty's action on human rights abuses against women

The above policy developments, and the book-length reports including *Human Rights are Women's Right* (1995a), *Broken Bodies, Shattered Minds* (2001) and the recent *It's In Our Hands* (2004a), show Amnesty's commitment to advancing women's human rights in the face of historical interpretations which have all but ignored them. To what extent, however, have these developments affected the organisation's activist practice on women's human rights, insofar as this can be measured?

Amnesty is famous for having invented a very powerful form of activism: mass letter-writing on behalf of victims of human rights abuse. This remains the principle form of activism for most members, and it is this form of activist practice which is analysed here. Letter-writing appeals are produced and distributed by the International Secretariat in London, and detail the names of particular victims of human rights abuse, the circumstances, and the addresses of government officials to which members are requested to write, fax or email, demanding action be taken to stop the abuse.

The idea for my research began in 1996, when I was coordinating the Women's Network at the Victorian branch office of AI Australia. This work involved distributing urgent letter-writing appeals on behalf of any women victims of abuse to members of the Network. I noticed that, of the ten or so appeals of this type sent by the International Secretariat every week, I would have only two or three appeals for women to send on to my network. This seemed strange at the time, following the hive of activity surrounding the UN Fourth World Conference on Women, for which Amnesty had published *Human Rights are Women's Right* (Amnesty International, 1995a). What is more, the lack of appeals for women seemed to directly contradict that report, which observed that: 'Women are in double jeopardy. Discriminated against as women, they are also as likely as men, if not more so, to become victims of human rights violations' (Amnesty International, 1995a: 5).

However, in 1996, Amnesty's mandate was still very much limited to opposing 'civil and political' abuses committed by state actors, and, as demonstrated earlier in this chapter, women's rights are generally abused in ways which do not fall into this framework. I hypothesised, at the time that the limitations of the mandate were responsible for the lack of letter-writing appeals for women. Later, following the 1997 policy change to include abuses by non-state actors, and the 2001 complete mandate change, I decided to undertake more comprehensive research to see what effect this theoretical widening of the organisation's work had on letter-writing appeals over the last decade. The methodology and findings are briefly summarised below.

I decided to analyse two forms of letter writing appeals: the 'Worldwide Appeals' and 'Urgent Actions'. Not only did these represent Amnesty's most famous, most widespread and most tangible form of activism, they also allowed for a quantitative analysis. The Worldwide Appeals are published internationally in the monthly newsletter received by every member (typically three appeals per month). These appeals undoubtedly form the 'backbone' of Amnesty's oppositional activism, having the potential to draw over a million letters, faxes or emails from all over the world to the governments, officials or opposition groups accountable for the abuse in question. The Urgent Actions are appeals on behalf of individuals or groups in 'grave peril', which are communicated to networks of members who have volunteered to respond immediately to such appeals. These networks, of which the Women's Network I coordinated was a part, can generate tens of thousands of appeals within a short time.

Two other forms of activism exist, which I did not include in my analysis: the 'Action Files' and the 'Regional Action Networks'. In these cases, different files are distributed to different groups worldwide, are released irregularly, and take a variety of forms, all of which would render a comparative analysis invalid. The final form of activism undertaken by the organisation is campaigning. Campaigns, whilst utilising substantial resources and involving a great number of activists, primarily analyse and denounce patterns of abuse, rather than specific cases. Therefore, although I have included discussion of this form of activism, particularly with regards to the *Stop Violence Against Women* campaign, a quantitative case-based study was not possible.

For the Worldwide Appeals, I analysed all the appeals over the last decade (1992–2003), representing a total of 673 individuals. As the Urgent Actions were a much larger sample (at least eight per week), the study was limited to three one-year periods: 1996/7, 1999, and 2002, covering appeals for 6,563 individuals. In collecting the data I went through each appeal in Amnesty's own records by hand, noting the date; the country in which the abuse took place; the number of females and the number of males for whom the appeal was being made (where the sex was specified); Amnesty's concern regarding the type of abuse (for example, torture, possible extrajudicial execution); and a summary of the details of the case. Here, for reasons of space, I have presented only the gender breakdown, in graph form.

Worldwide appeals

Over the 11-year period from 1992–2003, the number of Worldwide Appeals requesting action on behalf of men outnumbered those for women by an average ratio of 4.85 to one, meaning only 17 per cent involved abuses against women. Following is a breakdown of the results by year.

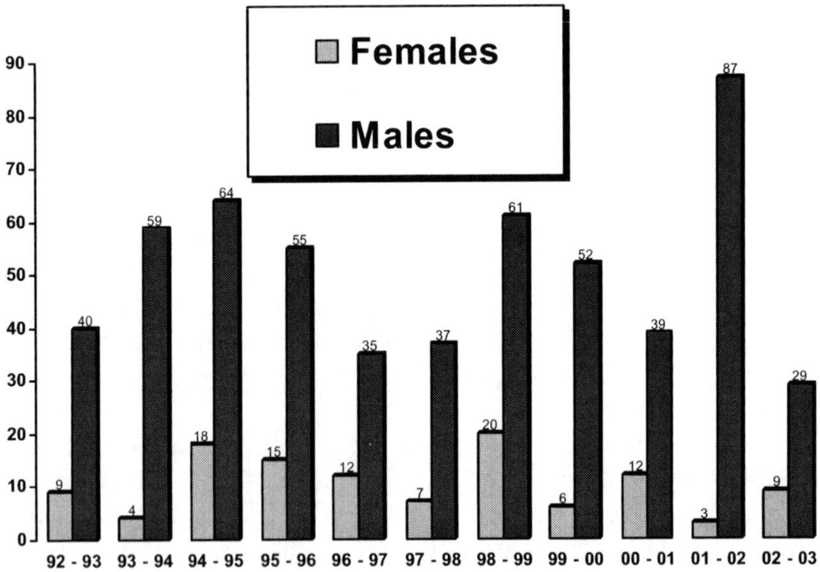

Urgent actions

For the Urgent Actions, the gender difference was even more pronounced. Here, the number of cases requesting action on behalf of men outnumbered those for women by an average ratio of 7.92 to one, only 11 per cent of appeals being for women.

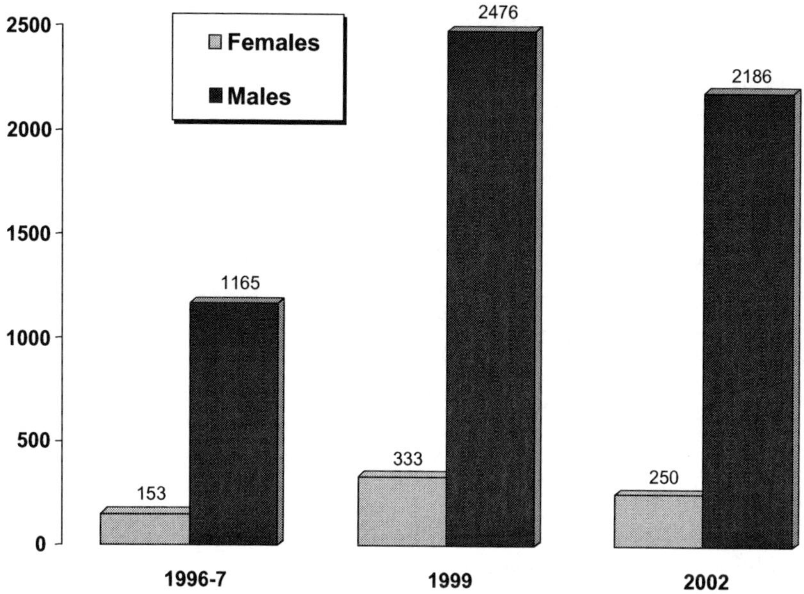

As noted, the pre-1997 limiting of Amnesty's work to abuses by government, opposition groups and their agents would go a long way toward explaining the demonstrated under-representation of women in the appeals of this time. However, following the 1997 non-state actor decision and, more importantly, the complete mandate change of 2001, when the 'civil and political' limitation was dropped, Amnesty could begin working on the vast majority of abuses against women which it had previously ignored. Over the last decade, then, we would have expected to see incremental narrowings of the gender gap in these appeals, with each relevant policy decision and widening of activism parameters at Amnesty (particularly in the periods following 1997 and 2001). We would expect this to culminate post-2001 in approximately equal numbers of appeals for women and men.

Yet, even two years after the mandate change, no difference in the gender ratio appeared in the Worldwide Appeals. The Urgent Actions showed an even higher gender inequality in the year following the mandate change (2002) than in the previous two samples, with appeals for men comprising nearly 90 per cent of all cases. Furthermore, the content of these appeals show a continuing focus on the same types of 'civil and political' rights abuses, mostly by government or opposition groups, as were found before the 'opening up' of the mandate. It appeared, in fact, that research and distribution of letter-writing appeals was continuing as if the old mandate were still in place.

By way of explanation, Amnesty has noted that changes to the organisation's research and practice resulting from the new mandate will be gradual, as there is a need to build expertise and contacts in new areas. However I believe the research which produced the books *Human Rights are Women's Right* (1995a), and *Broken Bodies, Shattered Minds* (2001) as well as many country-specific reports on abuses against women, such as on rape in Kenya, 'honour' crimes in Pakistan, and traffic in women to Israel (Amnesty International, 2002b, 2002a, 1999b, 1995e, 1995d, 1995b, 1995c), show that Amnesty does indeed have expertise and knowledge of specific cases of abuse against women falling within the new parameters for action. The research for these reports enabled Amnesty to make contacts with nongovernmental organisations working in these fields and to gain an in-depth knowledge of the abuses in question.

Another argument for the lack of appeals for women is based on issues of confidentiality and risk. A woman who has been raped, for example, and who is denied justice because of judicial negligence or discriminatory laws, may not, for various reasons, wish to have her case made public. This is entirely her prerogative, and although her case remains a human rights concern worthy of international attention, I would not suggest that Amnesty go against her wishes. In other cases, for example, that of a woman at risk of being killed to protect family 'honour', publicising her case could put her in even greater danger. Again, I am not suggesting that Amnesty take public action in such a case.

The problem with using 'confidentiality' or 'risk' as blanket explanations for not acting on human rights abuses against women, is that the same issues surround *all* forms of human rights activism, regardless of the sex of the victim or the type of abuse. Imprisoned or threatened political dissidents, for example, can be endangered further by the publicising of their cases: will appealing for their rights provoke a government into 'disappearing' them to 'rid themselves of the problem'? The fact is that Amnesty is constantly negotiating the usefulness of public action against the concerns that such action might be risky. Amnesty makes judgement calls every day when publicising an abuse, knowing the direct influence their actions can have on perpetrators, and that international attention is necessary as a deterrent to potential abusers. The letter-writing appeals are evidence of this, and there is no reason to assume that cases of abuse against women should be an exception. Why, for example, should domestic violence deaths and 'honour killings' not be acted on by Amnesty in the same way as it acts on other extrajudicial executions? If a government has not taken appropriate action to prevent them from occurring and to punish offenders (which is often the case), then that government is failing in its human rights obligations: there is no reason why such cases should not be part of Amnesty's letter-writing appeals. Yet no such appeals were found in the entire sample I studied.

A final possibility I considered for the male bias in the letter-writing appeals was that Amnesty was using sexist research methods. What information are the researchers looking for? What sources do they employ to find the information? How do they assess it? Upon what grounds do they decide to distribute it for action? One obvious problem in researching violence against women is that of the silence surrounding it. In the majority of the world's cultures, if women speak out about their abuse they either won't be believed or it won't be considered important. In some countries rape victims may even risk a punishment as severe as the death penalty if they cannot prove their case by producing male witnesses. Some abuses may not be considered as such by certain members of the dominant culture (often the most powerful members): domestic violence, female genital mutilation, *purdah*, dowry murders and widow immolation among them. This could easily lead to a self-censorship among women, compounding the silence. A further problem is that of 'proof'. As most human rights abuses against women, even when actually identified as such, take place in a 'private' context, they are unlikely to be accompanied by any form of documentation or to have any witnesses. These factors, along with many others, impact both on the initial 'inquiry' stages of the research and on this verification stage: who will corroborate the experience of women when women themselves may be unwilling to speak out about their abuse?

In 1999 Amnesty International released *Gender Sensitive Research Methodology Guidelines* (1999a) for researchers and activists. It provides detailed guidance on how to ensure that researchers gather information on abuses against those 'less visible' in any community. It notes that women, as a group, in most of the world's cultures do not have as 'loud a voice' in community decision-making, public institutions and the media as men do within the same culture. This means that when a researcher is seeking information about a particular group or community, informants are more likely to detail abuses against men, and, unless the researcher is actively using non-sexist research methods, the information gleaned is likely to have a strong male-bias as a result of women's relative 'silence'. The *Gender Sensitive Research Methodology Guidelines* go some way towards addressing the research problems mentioned in the previous paragraph. However, the existence of such a document renders the continuing gender inequality in the appeals even less explicable.

Finally, the existence of so few letter-writing appeals for abuses against women does not of itself mean that Amnesty is incapable of producing such appeals. Amnesty does have the resources and skills to produce research on individual cases of abuses against women, even in the 'private sphere', and can manage issues of confidentiality and risk. This is evidenced by the fact that detailed cases of abuses against women *have* been mentioned in reports (although without requesting member action). Also, two appeals for women who had been victims of domestic violence were released for a campaign on human rights abuses in Russia. The use of the appeals, however, was limited to the framework of that campaign: they were not widely distributed as general member actions. On other occasions, letter-writing appeals have been created from Amnesty research by women's networks in national offices, and distributed to members and groups who are 'interested in women's rights', as one activist put it. If women's rights are indeed human rights, then there is no reason why such appeals should not be coordinated by the International Secretariat and distributed internationally.

The *Stop Violence Against Women* campaign

The *Stop Violence Against Women* (STVAW) campaign (2004–2010) represents a leap forward in Amnesty's activism for women's human rights. Originally planned as a two-year campaign, it has been extended to a six-year period of international advocacy and action, and is the first campaign of such magnitude to be implemented since the organisation's mandate change in 2001. It will also be the first time that Amnesty has taken a clear-cut stand on violence against women in the 'private' sphere as a human rights violation under international law. Amnesty acknowledges that there will be gaps in its knowledge, understanding and methodologies and has specified that it will need to learn from others, particularly local service providers and activist organisations, with long-term experience in the field of violence against women. The campaign has a dual focus: first, on violence against women in the family, and second, on violence against women in conflict/post-conflict situations. The dual focus is not only a reflection of the sites of greatest danger for women, but is also symbolic of the organisation's new direction: 'private' and 'public' violence against women is recognised as a continuum. This 'violence is both rooted in discrimination and serves to reinforce discrimination [...] which denies women's equality with men in all areas of life' (Amnesty International, 2004a).

Interestingly, the campaign is *internal* as well as external, meaning that Amnesty is undertaking a review of how it incorporates the values and principles associated with women's human rights into its own organisational culture. In the campaign report *It's In Our Hands*, Amnesty notes that it 'has been slow to come to the defence of women' and that 'more has to be done to establish gender equity at the heart of Amnesty International's work' (2004:15). This acknowledgement is enormously promising, and Amnesty will be observed with interest over the next decade to see how it implements the promise of such statements into its work.

The campaign's approach will focus on addressing government responsibility for women's rights through the 'due diligence' approach. Governments must show a certain level of 'diligence' to prevent violations of women's human rights, to investigate and punish acts of violence, and to provide compensation where necessary. 'Due diligence' means that governments must respect, protect, fulfil and promote human rights. That is, first, the respect means they must not abuse or interfere with human rights. Second, the requirement to protect means that they must take measures to prevent third parties from interfering with human rights (and punish them when they do). Third, the need to fulfil rights means that they must adopt 'appropriate legislative, administrative, budgetary, judicial, and other measures towards the full realisation of the right' (Amnesty International, 2004b: 15). Fourth, the need to promote rights requires governments to develop specific promotional programs and measures to make women's right to freedom from violence a reality.

The development of a 'due diligence' model opens up new possibilities for Amnesty's activism, particularly with regards to women's human rights. Until now, the focus of Amnesty's letter-writing appeals has been exclusively on states failing to *respect* human rights (that is, themselves abusing human rights). Under the due diligence model, letter-writing actions could also encompass holding governments accountable for the protection, fulfilment and promotion of human rights. This has implications for law reform advocacy, funding of services, education and community-awareness raising. Addressing such issues is essential to the full achievement of all human rights, and is particularly necessary to counter sexist discrimination and oppression in which human rights abuses of women thrive.

The above quantitative analysis was completed the year before the launch of the campaign, and cannot claim to have taken into account the impact of the campaign on the letter-writing appeals since then. However, it should be noted that the research did cover two years beyond the last major policy change – the expansion of the mandate in 2001 – and during that time, despite Amnesty's amassing of evidence of human rights abuses of women, very few letter-writing appeals based on this evidence were produced. My hope is that the internal component of the SVAW campaign will succeed in getting women's human rights concerns into Amnesty's letter-writing appeals, where earlier policy decisions have so far failed.

Conclusion

The objective of this chapter has been to illuminate inconsistencies of practice between Amnesty's obvious policy commitment to women's human rights, particularly since the launch of the *Stop Violence Against Women* campaign, and the action actually taken by the organisation and its members to counter abuses. The findings of my quantitative analysis of letter-writing appeals show that, until 2003, policy and mandate changes were not reflected in the bulk of Amnesty's activist practice. The result of this is a situation where, despite positive public messages supporting women's human rights, most case-specific action taken by the Amnesty continues to focus on traditional 'public sphere' interpretations of human rights, and to be on behalf of men. The enormous numbers of abuses against women are allowed to pass in relative silence. It is likely that entrenched assumptions and practices within the organisation limit the new mandate's implementation.

I make the following recommendations conscious of the opportunity presented by Amnesty's current internal review of policy and practice regarding women's human rights for the SVAW campaign. Firstly, the release of the *Gender Sensitive Research Methodology*

Guidelines has not proven sufficient to ensure gender equality in research outcomes. There is an obvious need to ensure that all researchers receive extensive training in such methodologies, and apply them at the inquiry, validation and distribution stages of research into human rights abuses. The organisation needs to ensure that its research practices actively seek out 'less visible' cases of abuse, or else be complicit in the 'hiding' of them. Also essential are training sessions for other staff and volunteers on women's human rights in general.

Secondly, in recognising that non-state actors abuse human rights in ways that frequently are indistinguishable from the abuses perpetrated by the state, Amnesty has committed itself to addressing governments to uphold 'due diligence' on such cases. The strategy for the *Stop Violence Against Women* campaign notes that one such abuse, domestic violence, 'poses the single largest threat to all women' (Amnesty International, 2003: 6) and that 'government negligence establishes a tolerance of violence against women' (2003: 13). The necessity of taking oppositional action in such cases is self-evident: widespread letter-writing appeals must be produced immediately.

Thirdly, the recent expansion of the mandate to include work for economic, social and cultural rights means addressing government responsibility to create or encourage an environment where abuse is less likely to occur. The realisation of economic, social and political equality for women is a fundamental condition of this environment.

Fourthly, as with other areas where historical sexism has led to an under-representation of women, systems such as the application of quotas or prioritization of work on abuse against women should be considered to address the male bias in the letter-writing appeals.

Finally, there is a pressing need to establish systems and structures which serve to unify work on women throughout the national sections. The newly-established Gender Unit requires significant financial support and decision-making power. One problem already noted by campaign activists within the organisation has been that 'many cutting edge developments in [women's human rights] have been the result of personal commitment rather than institutional policy and may not be sustainable' (Amnesty International, 2003: 16).

It is therefore essential that fulltime, paid positions, responsible for women's rights activism, be created in sections to relay research and actions from the Gender Unit, coordinate women's network volunteers, and participate in strategy development.

The Secretary General of Amnesty, Irene Khan, noted in a press release in March 2004, that

> The international community has taken up the cases of some forms of violence against women but regularly fails to address others, turning a blind eye when international politics make it inconvenient, or the local situation makes it appear "too difficult". It highlights one of the greatest challenges facing women's rights activists today – the fleeting, tokenistic interest that governments take in women's human rights.

So why are negligent governments, whose action is fleeting and tokenistic on abuses such as domestic violence, not being addressed directly by Amnesty and its members? Amnesty must demonstrate its commitment to women's human rights by *acting* on this and other abuses of women in the same way as it acts on abuses of men's human rights – through research into cases of abuse and distribution of appeals for letter-writing campaigns. If Amnesty cannot give voice to women's human rights concerns in its most wide-spread form of activism, the aim of stopping violence against women will remain just a catch phrase.

References

Amnesty International, 1991, *Women in the Front Line*, (London: Amnesty International).

——, 1995a, *Human Rights are Women's Right*, (London: Amnesty International).

——, 1995b, *Women in Afghanistan: A human rights catastrophe*, (London: Amnesty International).

——, 1995c, *Women in Kenya: Repression and resistance*, (London: Amnesty International).

——, 1995d, *Women in China: Imprisoned and abused for dissent*, (London: Amnesty International).
——, 1995e, *Women in the Middle East: Human rights under attack*, (London: Amnesty International).
——, 1997a, *International Council Meeting Report – Part Three*, (unpublished document, distributed to Amnesty International members).
——, 1997b, *Urgent Action 30th January*, Guatemala (unpublished appeal case, distributed to Amnesty International members of Urgent Action network).
——, 1999a, *Gender Sensitive Research Methodology Guidelines*, (unpublished document, distributed to Amnesty International members).
——, 1999b, *Pakistan: Violence against Women in the Name of Honour*, (London: Amnesty International).
——, 2001, *Broken Bodies, Shattered Minds*, (London: Amnesty International).
——, 2002a, *Pakistan: insufficient Protection of Women*, (London: Amnesty International).
——, 2002b, *Kenya: Rape, the Invisible Crime*, (London: Amnesty International).
——, 2003, *Campaign Violence Against Women Global Strategy 2004–2006*, (unpublished document, distributed to Amnesty International members).
——, 2004a, *It's In Our Hands: Stop Violence Against Women*, (London: Amnesty International).
——, 2004b, *Statute of Amnesty International*, as amended by the 26th International Council meeting in Morelos, Mexico, 16 to 23 August 2003.
Bahar, S., 1996, 'Human Rights Are Women's Rights: Amnesty International and the Family', *Hypatia*, 11(1): 105–134.
Bessant, J. and Cook, S., 1998, 'The Sovereign State and Obligations to Protect Women Against Violence', *Just Policy*, June (13): 10–19.
Binion, G., 1995, 'Human Rights: A Feminist Perspective', *Human Rights Quarterly*, 17(3): 509–526.
Fifth Periodic Report of the Russian Federation, UN Doc. CEDAW/C/USR/5, para. 6.

Gay Levy, D., Branson Applewhite, H. and Durham Johnson, M., 1979, *Women in Revolutionary Paris 1789–1795: Selected Documents*, (Urbana, USA: University of Illinois Press).

Heise, L., Ellsberg, M. and Gottemoeller, M., 1999, 'Ending Violence Against Women', *Population Reports, Series L, No. 11*, (Baltimore: John Hopkins University School of Public Health), December.

Khan, I., 2004, Speech delivered at *Stop Violence Against Women* campaign launch and press conference, March 5, Amnesty International. (http://news.amnesty.org/index/ ENGAFR461900320044) accessed 13.8.2004.

Kiss, E., 1995, 'Alchemy or fool's gold? Assessing Feminist Doubts about Rights', *Dissent*, Summer: 342–347.

Obando, A. E., 2004, 'How Effective is a Human Rights Framework in Addressing Gender-Based Violence?', Women's Human Rights Net, (http://www.whrnet.org/) accessed 13.8.2004.

Parliamentary Assembly of the Council of Europe, 2002, 'Domestic Violence against Women', Recommendation 1582, adopted 27 September 2002.

United Nations, 1948, *Universal Declaration of Human Rights*, (New York: United Nations General Assembly).

——, 1966, *International Covenant on Civil and Political Rights*, (New York: United Nations General Assembly).

——, 1979, *Convention on the Elimination of All Forms of Discrimination against Women*, (New York: United Nations General Assembly).

——, 1993, *Declaration on the Elimination of Violence against Women*, (New York: United Nations General Assembly).

United Nations Population Fund, 1999, *Violence Against Girls and Women: A Public Health Priority*, (New York: UN Population Fund).

Watson, E. A., 1997, 'Amnesty International and Women's Human Rights: an Organisational Dilemma', *Australian Journal of Human Rights*, 4(1): 124–144.

World Health Organisation (WHO), 2002, *Violence Against Girls and Women: A Public Health Priority*, (Geneva: World Health Organisation).

MICHAEL MORISON

Democratisation and Capacity-Building: An Uncomfortable Alliance in the East Timor National Elections 2001–2002

Introduction

I had been in the village of Suai on the south-west coast of Timor Leste for only a few days. I had been assigned to the district as a civic education officer with the United Nations in the lead-up to the 30 August 2001 election. A week earlier I had met, for the first time, the four young university educated Timorese men and women with whom I would be working for the next seven months. In the windswept moonscape of the village of Fatumean on the tense border with Indonesia my local colleagues and I decided to start our first civic education session by asking 'What does democracy mean to you?'

One young man of about nineteen replied: 'Democracy is what people with guns and money say it is'. The crowd went quiet. Still reeling from this response I pointed to a young woman of about the same age who then stood up to ask a question. She said: 'voting in your country (Australia) is compulsory – how is being forced to vote democratic, especially if you don't like any of the candidates?'

Mistakenly, I had expected simple, perhaps even naïve answers to our question. But at that point, in this mountain village far from anywhere, I realised I was surrounded by one of the youngest and most politically aware populations in the developing world. An awareness no doubt forged by a twenty-five year struggle against an oppressive foreign power. At that moment, I also realised that my team and I were in for an interesting time over the next few months.

My job, as the district coordinator of the program, was to help a group of young Timorese students explain a democratic system to 50,000 people across the forty-four villages of our district. Our message was about the momentous constitutional and political transition underway in Timor Leste. On a personal level, as a political scientist and lawyer, I had a unique opportunity to experience a United Nations democratisation and peacekeeping mission at village level, amongst the extraordinary people of Timor Leste.

This paper is in part anecdotal and in part analytical. It is based on the writer's experiences in Timor Leste working with a group of young, educated and opinionated Timorese, but it is also informed by viewpoints on politics and the law. As such the focus will inevitably touch on political, legal and judicial developments, and on the rebuilding of political and legal infrastructure as a basis for development.

The focus of this paper is that UN peacekeeping, as a vehicle for democratisation, appears not to prioritise initiatives which seek to rebuild civil society groups from community level upwards over the long-term. Rather, 'transitional administrations', as they are known, appear to favour rapid and often inadequate deployment of personnel and resources seeking short-term results. Such short-term outcomes make good public relations stories but leave the communities they are supposed to benefit with little of any substance in the long-term.

A broader problem

Understandably, the decisions made by the UN administration commented upon in this paper took account of certain pragmatic factors at the time. As a fieldworker, I was not privy to these factors or the decision-making process. However, I could appreciate the effects of these decisions on my program and on the villagers it was designed to assist.

It is not my intention to criticise the United Nations organisation as a whole, or the good work done by many of its staff in Timor Leste.

Having worked within the organisation I know how difficult the job can be. All too often UN member states will publicly insist that 'something must be done' about a situation of grave human rights abuse, but when the time comes to commit real resources, they lack the political will to live up to the task. The UN and the NGO community are then left to make the best of the situation, often in an atmosphere of criticism emanating from those unwilling to provide resources in the first place.

In fact, for some time a similar debate has been occurring within the UN itself. The *Brahimi Report*, a comprehensive study of the past, present and future of all aspects of peacekeeping operations commissioned by the Secretary General Kofi Annan, noted that behind the challenge of each peacekeeping operation

> [...] lies the larger question of whether the United Nations should be in this business at all. [...] [I]ntra-state conflicts continue and future instability is hard to predict, so that despite evident ambivalence about civil administration among United Nations Member States and within the Secretariat, other such missions may indeed be established in the future and on an equally urgent basis. Thus, the Secretariat faces an unpleasant dilemma: to assume that transitional administration is a transitory responsibility, not prepare for additional missions and do badly if it is once again flung into the breach, or to prepare well and be asked to undertake them more often because it is well prepared. (General Assembly and Security Council, 2000)

Such a comment points to the flaw in the democratisation project: that it cannot be done effectively using short-term initiatives. If the international community is to engage in this process at all, it must be done appropriately and at a measured pace in order to produce effective, lasting and stable results. This means long-term commitments to rebuilding of civil societies, properly assessed for their relevance to local conditions, practicality of application and genuine ability to contribute real skills to the local population.

It is the conclusion of this paper that if much of the good work of the international community in Timor Leste begins to unravel over the next few years, it will be due to the types of factors discussed here. Too much of the change in Timor Leste has been imposed from the top down, based on decisions which appear to serve the interests of ideological and political pragmatism rather than the best interests of the people.

These observations begin with a look at some of the problems faced by our civic education initiative, the implications of decisions such as the imposition of the US dollar and the Portuguese language on the country along with issues surrounding the election, the legal system and human rights enforcement. Civic educators, human rights workers, electoral and development workers, and for that matter all of those involved in post-conflict capacity-building initiatives can learn a great deal from the experience of the international community in Timor Leste.

Some unexpected views

From the outset, my team had lively discussions in broken English on political topics. To say the least their views surprised me. They strongly believed that despite the efforts of the international community to create a multi-party democracy in Timor, the result would overwhelmingly be a victory for the members of one particular party and that these people would be drawn from a familiar group. They all agreed that the majority of those who would eventually come to occupy positions of power in Timor Leste would be an older Portuguese-speaking elite, despite stated UN policies to enfranchise women, the young and minorities.

Perhaps more controversially, their view was that although many of those amongst this group had been very active working for the liberation of Timor Leste from Lisbon, Luanda and Antananarivo, most of them had not been in the country during the difficult period of Indonesian rule. Some in fact had been absent for the majority of the occupation. Needless to say, they did not believe that this was a fair outcome.

In summary, they were extremely suspicious of the motives and commitment of the Portuguese-speaking elite in Timor Leste and believed that the international community through the UN was in the process of installing a pre-determined group who had not earned their positions of power. They were sure that young Timorese people would not be happy with the outcome and would make that clear in the coming years, if necessary by force. They also believed that the international community would come to forget Timor Leste when some new distraction came along. Needless to say these views seemed very cynical, somewhat puzzling and very disturbing to this idealistic young fieldworker.

Civic education misunderstood

From the early days, many of us felt that the importance of civic education was not fully understood by the UN administration. At best, we felt that it was seen as a minor offshoot of the electoral education process, little more than an explanation for the reason why a voting paper was to be placed in a box on election day. In fact, our task was to explain the whole landscape of multi-party democracy, the role of the Constitution and the parliament and the importance of a free and fair election.

Much of our frustration came from the fact that our project was hamstrung by lack of resources, despite clear evidence of great enthusiasm for what we had to discuss. Sadly, the resourcing processes moved excruciatingly slowly. The project was also hampered by certain ideological factors which are not within the ambit of this paper to analyse, but will be the subject of future writings.

At the outset, our unit was poorly housed and ill equipped. I was deployed into my allotted district in May 2001 for an election on 30 August, in many ways already too late to do a fully effective job, with no budget, no staff, no vehicle or equipment. In early July, tired of borrowing scarce vehicles from other projects I went to Dili to pick up a vehicle. Over the next month, due to the hard work of the exhausted staff in the national office, resources trickled into the project. Generators and televisions with which to show video presentations, much later the videos themselves and eventually the printed material and banners arrived. Finally an Indonesian speaking international colleague and another vehicle for her to drive also came. By 30 June 2001, one month before the election, we were fully resourced to do the job we were assigned. This meant achieving the majority of the task in one month amidst the chaos of the political party campaigning period.

The civic education micro-grant scheme, a well devised but poorly implemented program to identify and provide civil society groups with funding to conduct civic education initiatives, was finally implemented during late July 2001. These groups needed help to be guided through the application process and provided with funds within a one month time frame, all in the face of frightening bureaucracy. Our six groups were finally up and running in the dying days of the campaigning period, just prior to the election.

The late deployment of materials and finance worried many of us at district level, including our Timorese colleagues. We speculated that 'Dili' misunderstood the aim of our program which was to strengthen civil society groups so that when the mission was complete and the UN finally withdrew, a strong foundation would be left behind to carry on our work.

Rather, the system seemed to be geared towards a primary goal of 'staging an election', like a theatre production, followed by a quick and cost-effective withdrawal by the international community. In many ways we felt that the civic education program was being treated as though as it should operate like the UN sponsored Independent Electoral Commission (IEC). That is, the rapid deployment of international electoral staff *en masse* to conduct an election followed by a similarly rapid *en masse* repatriation once the election was complete.

Our conclusion was that effective democratisation requires longer term commitment to genuine civil society reconstruction. In hindsight, the civic education process should start as early as practically possible. It should also occupy a significant place in the order of funding priority. In order for it to be effective, future civic education initiatives should be fully resourced well in advance, at least twelve months prior to election day depending on the size of the district. As the anecdote at the beginning of this paper demonstrates, civic education plays a vital role in allaying fears, correcting misinformation and quelling the inevitable suspicion of the motives of the international community.

Civic education should be initiated as a 'ground-up' strategy in which civil society groups are chosen, trained and funded to conduct the entire civic education project over a long term lead up to the election period. This would serve to strengthen the groups themselves, feed vital information into the community at grassroots level while leaving a lasting legacy and strong foundation upon which to build the new democracy.

Strange bedfellows: the US dollar and the Portuguese language

Several months out from election day, the rumours that the US dollar was going to be made the official national currency were proven to be correct. This seemed an extraordinary move and was the first in a series of decisions that dismayed my young friends. The majority of villagers were happy to use the familiar Indonesian currency with its small workable denominations. These were useful for buying food and other everyday items in the markets. In the districts, the dollar was seen as the currency of the 'internationals' and, although widely desired, was rarely seen. Everyone seemed happy with the existing arrangement and certainly did not see the Indonesian rupiah as a remnant symbol of the former oppressor.

In Dili, the dollar had served to over-inflate the price of food, accommodation and most other necessities for both international staff and locals. This in turn only made the obvious differences between international staff and locals more marked. The dollar is now in wide use in the districts with similar effects. Many Timorese still do not understand why the Indonesian rupiah was not retained until a national currency could be developed and implemented.

The decision, seemingly ideologically motivated, to make Portuguese the national language was another factor which served to reinforce the strong belief, especially amongst the young, that the international community aimed to reinstall a foreign elite; an elite whom some believed had abandoned them in their time of greatest need. Portuguese was considered by many young people to be the language of that elite. It was also seen, to a certain extent, as the language of the oppressor. On a more basic level, many people, especially the younger Timorese raised during the time of the Indonesian occupation, simply do not understand the language (The Law Report, 2003).

Historical factors have contributed to the creation of a large population of young, under-employed men and women who experienced the full horror of the Indonesian occupation. This group expected that independence would bring wealth and comfort quickly and easily. They saw the wealth of UN and NGO workers and now see the wealth of the new ruling class, while seeing little change to their own position. Their situation is not helped by the fact that the members of the National Assembly, many of whom spent the occupation in Portugal, Angola or Mozambique, have made Portuguese the official language and therefore the language of the public service. Very few government jobs are open to people who do not speak the language. As one journalist noted in the aftermath of the Dili riots in early 2002: 'to the poor job-seeking youth, whose first language is Bahasa Indonesia, (Portuguese) is an insult' (Dodd, 2002).

Recent reports have indicated that the problem of language is particularly acute in the nascent court system of Timor Leste. At times four languages – Portuguese, Bahasa, Tetum and English – are in use in the court, which contributes to serious delays in the equitable administration of justice. The proceedings are however mostly conducted in Portuguese. Many of those coming before the court on an unrepresented basis cannot speak Portuguese and therefore are not able to understand anything of what is happening to them. Having representation does not guarantee justice either. Many of the legal representatives are themselves unable to speak or understand Portuguese (Dodd, 2002).

A ruling on 15 July 2003 by Chief Judge Claudio Ximenes of the Supreme Court of Timor Leste highlighted the schizophrenia of the situation. In a verdict on the appeal of Armando Dos Santos, Judge Ximenes ruled that because the Indonesian occupation of Timor Leste was unlawful under international law, any Indonesian law imposed as a result of the occupation was therefore invalid (Jolliffe, 2003). By extension, therefore, the validity of UN Regulation 1999/1, which states that the Indonesian penal code in force prior to 25 October 1999 should continue, has also been called into question. As a result the only applicable, or subsidiary, law left to apply in Timor Leste can be Portuguese law. The ruling has created the absurd and untenable situation that Armando dos Santos was convicted under Portuguese law rather than, as charged, under Indonesian law. The ruling also brought into question all previous rulings by the court under the Indonesian penal code (Judicial System Monitoring Program, 2003).

An application on 23 July 2003 to the Supreme Court sought a declaration of clarification on the issue of subsidiary applicable law in Timor Leste. The position of the Prosecutor General is that under UNTAET (UN Transitional Administration in East Timor) regulations and the Constitution of Timor Leste, Indonesian law is the subsidiary applicable law in Timor Leste (Office of the Deputy General Prosecutor for Serious Crimes, 2003).

'A government of national unity'

The eleventh hour decision by the transitional administration to create a 'government of national unity' was a difficult thing to explain to villagers. On Friday, 24 August 2001 the UN administrator of Timor Leste, Sergio Vieira de Mello, sadly later killed in Baghdad, told the Portuguese daily *Publico* that

> the government will be comprised of members of the two or three parties that garner the greatest number of votes, of independent candidates, if elected, and of independent figures who are not participating in the elections but have recognised competence. (Agence France Presse, 2001)

We took this to mean that the composition of the National Assembly would not be determined solely by the outcome of the election but by political sensitivities on the ground in Dili. One of those sensitivities was UN concern that the elected government would be overwhelmingly dominated by the Fretilin party (Baker, 2002). Fretilin (Frente Revolucionario de Leste Timor Independent), originally formed to fight the Portugese, became the main Timorese independence movement through the struggle against Indonesian occupation.

At the time, having spent many weeks explaining to the people of our district the benefits of a freely elected pluralistic government, there were many questions from both colleagues and villagers. My colleagues were very suspicious of this and held it as further evidence that the process as watched over by the UN was going to be neither free nor fair. At the same time, many younger Timorese we met believed that despite the historical and cultural importance of Fretilin, the domination of Timor's first parliament by an elite Portuguese-speaking majority was not a good outcome. As a result, it seems very few young and capable Timorese women and men have been incorporated into positions of power in the new Timor Leste.

To an extent this problem may have been caused by the dual voting system adopted as the model for the election by the IEC. Under this model, the Constituent Assembly is made up of 88 members. One representative was selected for each of the 13 districts Timor Leste, elected on a majority basis, meaning that the candidate with the highest number of votes in the district will be the district representative. A further, and very considerable, 75 representatives were elected on a nation-wide proportional representation system, meaning that individual political parties won seats in the assembly in proportion to the share of votes they received in the election for national representatives.

In the final instance, 12 of the 13 district representatives came from the Fretilin party. Of the 24 members of the Second Transitional Government of Timor Leste, 10 are officially members of the party while at least five more are likely to vote with the party. The outcome therefore is that Fretilin overwhelmingly controls the decisions made by the Assembly. One could justly ask, as my young friends foreshadowed, whether this is the truly democratic government promised to Timor Leste by the international community?

As the name suggests, the Constituent Assembly Election was staged to appoint a group of representatives to determine the text of the Constitution of Timor Leste. If allowed, or required by the interim Constitution, the Constituent Assembly would then become the Legislative Assembly of Timor Leste. The Assembly then did what the majority of my young colleagues said it would do: namely write the Constitution so as to make the first Assembly the first government of Timor Leste.

While one could suggest that the Assembly is therefore no more or less democratic than the Australian Upper House or Senate, and indeed there is widespread debate on this issue in Australia, in practice this means that the Assembly is made up of members drawn heavily from Fretilin. The 'government of national unity' may well have been early recognition that the election was never going to be truly democratic due to the extraordinary influence of Fretilin, an influence which stems in apart from its well deserved role in the struggle.

On 5 December 2002 rioting in central Dili resulted in the destruction of several shops and buildings, including the house of Prime Minister Mari Alkatiri and the fondly remembered 'Hello Mister' supermarket. Observers have commented that the violence was partly fuelled by a perception amongst the young that justice is not being done in regards to the alleged perpetrators of the 1999 militia atrocities (The Law Report, 2003). Linked also to the violence is the disillusionment, again particularly acute amongst the young, at the performance of the Prime Minister, along with what one journalist described as 'his clique of old Fretilin leftists, who have learned nothing and forgotten nothing since their days in Mozambique's failed socialist state more than 30 years ago' (Barker, 2002).

Aggravating the situation is the sudden deflation of the bubble economy created by the withdrawal of UNTAET and it is well-paid international staff. Unemployment is estimated at 65 per cent and 40 per cent of Timor Leste's 800,000 people earn less than A $1 a day (Barker, 2002).

Geoffrey Barker summarised the situation well in an article in *The Australian Financial Review* in late 2002:

> Opposition MPs contest the legitimacy of a government that was shoe-horned into power by a UN administration determined to force a rapid political transition after the historic 1999 referendum voted overwhelmingly for the country to break away from Indonesia. They point out that the 88-member assembly elected in August, 2001, was chosen only to draft a new constitution and that Fretilin used its numbers to extend its rule for five years – while reneging, with the UN's acquiescence, on a pledge to form a national unity government. (Barker, 2002)

M. Baker also wrote in *The Age*:

> The government is dominated by exiles who fled the country after the Indonesian invasion in 1975 and only returned when the peace was won. Many of them, like Alkatiri, led relatively comfortable lives in Mozambique, another former Portuguese colony. They are bitterly resented by the Fretilin veterans and members of the urban resistance who stayed behind to fight and now feel marginalised and estranged. (Baker, 2002)

A former aid worker interviewed for this paper described how she returned to her village in central Timor for the Presidential election of 2002 to find that the majority of her friends had not seen the local National Assembly member in the village since they elected him the year before (Interview with Penelope Beaumont, 2003). Recent violence caused by infiltrators from West Timor and stories of disaffected Falintil fighters forming militia groups have also begun to filter out (Toohey, 2003). These stories suggest that all may not be well for the future government of Timor Leste. One can only hope that they come to nothing.

Access to Justice: Human Rights and the Serious Crimes Unit

A 2003 report of the Office of the High Commissioner for Human Rights (OHCHR) indicated that access to justice continues to be one of the greatest obstacles to the promotion and protection of human rights in Timor Leste. The report further indicated that delays in the judicial system caused by the operation of only three district courts have had a ripple effect on case management. Prolonged pre-trial detention is causing overcrowding and violence in the jails, which affects morale in the police force and prison service. At the time of writing, the report indicated that there was a backlog of 70 appeals pending before the Court of Appeal (OHCHR, 2003: 38).

Where internationally imposed justice fails to perform, the traditional justice system steps into the breach. It is essential that traditional methods of dispute resolution be incorporated and integrated into any externally imposed system. However, UN Human Rights reports have indicated that exclusive use of traditional dispute resolution methods can result in significant injustices for vulnerable groups and women (OHCHR, 2003: 35).

Reports from the OHCHR in late 2004 indicate that the three district courts in Baucau, Suai and Oecussi continue to be 'largely non-functional' and, when sitting, are hampered by continuing long delays and absences of judicial officers (OHCHR, 2004: 25). Detainees are also continuing to be kept in pre-trial detention for unacceptably long periods of time. As noted above, disputing parties are increasingly turning to the male-dominated traditional justice system, which is particularly troubling for women victims of gender-based violence (OHCHR, 2004). The traditional system performs an important function which must be respected and encouraged, but which must also strive to provide justice for all regardless of gender or social status.

The budget for the United Nations Assistance Mission in East Timor (UNAMET) Human Rights Unit for the period October 2002–2004 appears to be US$800,000 (OHCHR, 2003). That budget is to support implementation of the principal international human rights instruments, to provide support for the functioning of the Commission on Reception, Truth and Reconciliation, to provide human rights training and skills building for the administration of justice professionals, to provide human rights training and skills building for civil society, to support the establishment and functioning of a local agency for justice and human rights and to support the development of legislation to ensure conformity with international human rights standards (OHCHR, 2003). This is clearly inadequate funding for so many vital projects.

The Serious Crimes Unit (SCU) was set up to investigate and prosecute all serious crimes (including genocide, war crimes and crimes against humanity, murder, sexual offences and torture) which occurred between the beginning of 1999 and October 25 of that year.

As of mid-2003, 65 indictments had been filed with the Special Panel for Serious Crimes (SPSC) at Dili District Court. In the indictments, there are charges filed against 326 indictees. The accused in the 65 indictments include 32 Indonesian military Commanders and Officers, 4 Indonesian Chiefs of Police, 49 Timorese Indonesian military officers and soldiers, the former Governor of Timor Leste and 5 former District Administrators. More than 25% of those individuals indicted by SCU were members of the Indonesian security forces in 1999 and charged with Crimes against Humanity. As of mid-2003, 221 of those accused persons, over 70% indicted by SCU, remain at large in Indonesia (Office of the Deputy General Prosecutor, 2003).

A number of indictments were issued at the beginning of 2003 charging senior Indonesian military and police officers as well as militia leaders with having had command responsibility for the widespread attack against the population. It is thought that up to 169 people who have been indicted in the Special Panel are currently at large in Indonesia. A further problem is that Indonesia has not yet ratified the Memorandum of Understanding regarding co-operation in legal, judicial and human rights-related matters signed in April 2000 by UNTAET and Indonesia (Office of the Deputy General Prosecutor, 2003).

During 2003, extensive delays occurred in the prosecution of serious crimes due to the fact that not enough international judges had been recruited to enable both the Special Panel and the Court of Appeal to function simultaneously. This occurred in part because the Timorese President and Parliament delayed the appointment of a President of the Court of Appeal. Although many serious crimes cases have already been finalised, it is unlikely that hearings for all indicted cases will take place before May 2004 (Office of the Deputy General Prosecutor, 2003).

There are also concerns that the government itself has been less than firm in its support both for the SCU and the justice process itself. Statements by Xanana Gusmao and Jose Ramos Horta in March,

2003, after the SCU issued a round of indictments against Indonesian military and local government figures (including one against former Indonesian Minister of Defence General Wiranto), suggest that good relations with Indonesia are more highly prized than the pursuit of justice (Bhuta, 2003; Pace and Rimmer, 2003; Plunkett, 2001). Despite strong demand at village level for a formal justice process, the new government is faced with many competing priorities, particularly the lucrative Timor Sea oil and gas negotiations. Those priorities also include securing Timor Leste's vulnerable position in the region by gaining the approval and patronage of Jakarta. For similar reasons the justice process is unlikely to be given special attention by Australia or the United States. Australia is keen to repair its relationship with Indonesia after the intervention of the Australian military in the violence of September 1999 and the US is keen to make Indonesia, the world's most populous Muslim country, an ally in the war against terrorism.

By the end of 2003, the SCU had filed 81 indictments against 369 accused filed with the SPSC. From these, there have been 46 convictions, one acquittal and two dismissals. SCU staff continues to investigate alleged serious crimes and at the time of writing, around 16 trials were in progress at the Special Panel for Serious Crimes (JSMP, 2004a: 3).

In early May, 2004 the UN Secretary General recommended the winding up of investigations of the Serious Crimes Unit (SCU) and the reallocation of SCU resources from investigation to trials and appeals in order to accelerate the completion of any pending litigation. The SCU needed to finish all its investigations by September 2004. All trials were to be completed by May 2005 (JSMP, 2004b).

NGO estimates as at May, 2004, are that approximately 40–50% of the estimated 1400 murder cases from the militia violence of 1999 remain uninvestigated, 18 cases are at hearing stage and a further 30 are awaiting trial (JSMP, 2004a). The closure of the SCU means that there will be large areas of Timor Leste where Crimes against Humanity remain uninvestigated and therefore untried. In Bobonaro, for example, according to the Deputy Prosecutor for Serious Crimes, there are well over 100 cases of murder which occurred in 1999 which have not yet been investigated (JSMP, 2004c). NGOs fear that the end of the judicial process in Dili will result in victims 'taking justice into their own hands'. The return of militia members from West Timor into communities in Timor Leste will also compound this problem (JSMP, 2004c).

That justice is done and seen to be done is critical in an environment where impunity for human rights abuses and violence is taken for granted. The Indonesian security forces acted with impunity, as did the militias responsible for the terror and destruction of 1999. For the people of Timor Leste to move forward it is vital that a society be created where the rule of law is respected and in which violence is not tolerated.

UNTAET and its successor missions should have made the SCU process and its accompanying embryonic Truth and Reconciliation Commission a higher priority than the election process itself. The foundation of a correctly functioning democracy is a respect for the rule of law by all arms of government. The rebuilding of all legal and human rights infrastructure should be of the highest priority in any post-conflict situation.

Conclusion

At village level our project, like many coordinated by the international community, succeeded in emphasising the role of all Timorese people in the democratisation process. However, at a national level, the legacies of many of the decisions taken during and after the independence process may well come to undermine the good work done at village level. The goal of such a process should be primarily to enhance the skills and abilities of the people at community level to manage their own affairs. If such initiatives operate from the grassroots level upwards, a solid foundation will be established upon which to build the institutions of the new state.

This paper has touched upon the short-term and somewhat *ad-hoc* approach taken to Civic Education during the electoral processes of 2001–2. It has also looked at several unpopular policy decisions relating to currency, language and the composition of the National Assembly. In addition, the short-sighted approach taken to important agencies dealing with human rights and serious crimes will have an effect on Timorese society for generations to come.

These problems, unless remedied, will continue to undermine the capacity of the newly independent state of Timor Leste to progress towards the rebuilding of the basic institutions of civil society, a respect for the rule of law and a concomitant respect for human rights.

These problems not only apply to this particular UN mission, but to all democratisation efforts undertaken by the international community. To serve the interests of true self-determination, democratisation must aim towards a 'ground up' approach. This means genuine long-term capacity-building by supporting existing civil society groups from village level upwards, as opposed to the rapid imposition of 'government' from the top down.

It also means long-term commitments to justice and reconciliation, to encouraging civil society groups, to recreating an understanding and respect for the rule of law, to rebuilding legal infrastructure and ultimately to engendering a respect for the diversity of opinions that go to make up a genuine democracy. Looking at Timor Leste today, many of the things my young colleagues predicted have indeed come to pass. Let us hope they do not prove to be insurmountable obstacles to the success of the world's newest democracy.

References

Agence France Presse, 2001, 'UN Administrator for East Timor plans broad-based Government', East Timor Action Network, (www.etan.org) accessed 27.08.2003.

Baker, M., 2002, 'East Timor: Inside The Tinderbox', *The Age*, 14 December.

Barker, G., 2002, 'Gusmao must take control', *The Australian Financial Review*, 9 December.

Bhuta, N., 2003, 'Justice delayed', *Alternative Law Journal*, 28(3): 141–2.

Dodd, T., 2002, 'Wealth divide behind Timor Violence', *The Australian Financial Review*, 6 December.

General Assembly Security Council, Fifty-fifth session Fifty-fifth year, Item 87 of the provisional agenda, *Comprehensive review of the whole question of peacekeeping operations in all their aspects*, 21 August 2000, A/55/305–S/2000/809, (www.un.org) accessed 01.02.2003.

Interview with Penelope Beaumont, former District Electoral Officer, Independent Electoral Commission (IEC), East Timor 29 June, 2003.

Jolliffe, J., 2003, 'Old European Tongue brings Chaos to newest Asian Nation', *Sydney Morning Herald,* July 26–27.

Judicial System Monitoring Program (JSMP), 2003, Press Release, 17 July 2003, (www.jsmp.minihub.org) accessed 25.07.2003.

JSMP, 2004a, 'The Future of the Serious Crimes Unit', Issue Report, Dili, East Timor, January 2004, (www.jsmp.minihub.org) accessed 20.11.2004.

——, 2004b, 'Limited Progress in the work of the Special Panel for Serious Crimes', Press Release, 12 July 2004, (www.jsmp.minihub.org) accessed 20.11.2004.

——, 2004c, 'UN Sacrifices Justice For Dollars, Thousands of Victims Left Without Justice as UN Winds Down Investigations into Crimes Against Humanity', Press Release, 6 May 2004, (www.jsmp.minihub.org) accessed 20.11.2004.

Office of The Deputy General Prosecutor For Serious Crimes, 2003, Timor Leste, Serious Crimes Unit (SCU) Update VII/03, 5 August 2003, (http://www.jsmp.minihub.org/News/5_08-03.htm) accessed 25.08.2003.

Office of the High Commissioner for Human Rights (OHCHR), 2003, Mission of Support in Timor-Leste (UNMISET), TIMOR-LESTE, *Quarterly Report*, 3 June 2003, (http://ap.ohchr.org/documents/dpage_e.aspx?c=184&su=182) accessed 20.11.2004.

Office of the High Commissioner for Human Rights (OHCHR), 2004, Asian and Pacific region, *Quarterly Reports Of Field Offices*, 21 September 2004, UN Mission of Support in Timor-Leste (UNMISET), Quarterly Report, (Third quarter of 2004), (ttp://ap.ohchr.org/documents/dpage_e.aspx?c=184&su=182) accessed 20.11.2004.

Pace, J. and Rimmer, S., 'Hamstrung justice', *Alternative Law Journal*, 28(3): 143.

Plunkett, M., 2001, 'Re-Establishing the Rule of Law in Peace Operations – the East Timor Experience', *The International Society for the Reform of the Criminal Law,* 15th International Conference, Politics, Crime and Criminal Justice, 26–30 August 2001, Canberra, Australia.

The Law Report, 2003, *East Timor's Struggling Legal System*, ABC Radio National, Transcript 22/04/2003, (www.abc.net.au) accessed 22.04.2003.

Toohey, P., 2003, 'Trouble Comes Closer to Home', *The Australian*, 25–26 January.

Part III
Human Rights in International Contexts

CHEE SOON JUAN

Human Rights: Dirty Words in Singapore

'I didn't know it was that bad' is the typical response I get from foreigners after they hear about the political situation in Singapore. When one talks about Singapore, repression and fear are not the mental images that readily come to mind. Anyone having the pleasure of traipsing through the world's most beautiful airport – showcasing all that is clean and efficient on the island – would find it hard to believe the extent of authoritarian control in this country.

And yet the city-state, sandwiched tightly between the Indonesian archipelago to the south and the Malaysian peninsular to the north, is one of the most democratically challenged societies in Asia. The methods of control and intimidation that the ruling People's Action Party (PAP) employs is the subject of discussion in this chapter.

Getting rid of the opposition

Let us begin with the Internal Security Act (ISA). Introduced by the British during the colonial years, the ISA, or the Preservation of Public Security Ordinance as it was then called, allows the government to arbitrarily arrest and indefinitely detain citizens it suspects of endangering public security.

Armed with such immense powers, governments would be sorely tempted to apply them on the opposition. The PAP, of course, found the temptation too hard to resist and in February 1963, ordered the arrest of more than 150 opposition members of parliament, newspaper editors, labour leaders and other political activists. Many, if not all of those arrested were never charged of a crime but were nevertheless consigned to serve prison sentences, some of which lasted up to two decades.

The longest serving-detainee was Chia Thye Poh. On one fateful day in 1966, security agents visited Chia and told him that he was being arrested under the ISA (Chee 1997, pers. comm.). With that, the opposition MP was led away and locked up for the next 23 years. After his release, he was banished to an island south of Singapore for another nine years, allowed to come to the mainland only during daylight hours.

The use of the ISA continued throughout the 1960s and 1970s. One of the detainees arrested in 1963, Poh Soo Kai, was released in 1972 whereupon he embarked on a campaign to call attention to the ISA. As a result, the Socialist International, of which the PAP was a member, moved to expel the party from its ranks. Pre-empting the unceremonious boot it was about to receive, the PAP quit the organisation in 1976. One week after the episode, Poh was re-arrested. He was released six years later, during which he spent two years in solitary confinement (Chee, 1998).

In 1987, the government announced that it had arrested and detained 22 individuals for conspiring to 'violently overthrow' the government and establish a Marxist state. It turned out that some of those arrested had been helping an opposition party while others were Catholic Church workers helping the poor and still others who were lawyers assisting abused foreign maids working in Singapore. After more than a year of imprisonment during which punches, slaps, sleep deprivation and other forms of torture were dished out in liberal helpings, the detainees were forced to confess to their waywardness (*Asia Watch*, 1990).

Upon their release, some of the detainees got together and issued a press statement to proclaim their innocence and to reject the government's claim that they were not subjected to torture and abuse. They were promptly re-arrested and made to swear statutory declarations to repudiate their press statement in order to regain their freedom. Any attempt to refute the government again would result in the detainees being prosecuted in a court of law for making false statutory declarations.

More recently, 37 persons have been imprisoned under the ISA for allegedly being involved in terrorist networks and plotting to attack US interests in Singapore, following the September 11 tragedy. A few have since been released but the majority remain in custody without trial (Amnesty International, 2004).

The media problem

Of course, none of the above would have been possible without the concomitant subjugation of the media. Soon after it came into power in 1959, the PAP started its campaign to rid Singapore of a free media.

One of the first victims was the *Straits Times*, the country's only morning broadsheet. Then-editor Lesley Hoffman had been critical of the PAP and knew that his days as a journalist in Singapore were numbered when Lee Kuan Yew became the Prime Minister. For his own safety, Hoffman eventually left the country, after which the newspaper was reconstituted (George, 1974). Today, the publication functions primarily to echo the government's stance.

In 2004, a US citizen employed by the newspaper as its global affairs columnist, had this to say when he resigned from the newspaper company

> The *Straits Times* has no competition in Singapore. It's owned wholly by a company called Singapore Press Holdings, whose stock is sold publicly but whose affairs are closely monitored by the government of Prime Minister Lee Hsien Loong, son of Singapore's founding father, former Prime Minister Lee Kuan Yew. The paper is run by editors with virtually no background in journalism. For example, my direct editor was Ms Chua Lee Hoong, a woman in her mid 30s. She was an intelligence officer. Other key editors are drawn from Singapore's bureaucracies and state security services. They all retain connections to the state's intelligence services, which track everyone and everything. (Gupte, 2004)

After the take over of the *Straits Times,* another daily, the Malay-language *Utusan Melayu*, also ceased publication because of threats from the government. In 1971, four of the most senior staff members of the *Nanyang Siang Pau*, a Chinese-language newspaper, went straight to prison for 'glamorising Communism' and for being involved in a 'black operation'. It was closed down. In one year, the wrecking ball swung from the communist left to the American right. This time, the *Singapore Herald*, a vivacious tabloid, was also accused of being involved in a 'black operation', this time with the U.S. intelligence. It was also closed down. In between, another independent daily, the *Eastern Sun*, was just as unceremoniously and brutally shut down, again because the newspaper was accused of being involved in some 'black operation'.

Presently Singapore's local print media is run by the Singapore Press Holdings and MediaCorp, two companies under the directly control of the state. The broadcast media's history is less eventful – it came firmly under government control from the outset.

Having successfully dragged the local media through obedience school, the Singapore Government started work on the foreign press. One by one, regional and international publications which commented unfavourably of the PAP and its politics were taken to court in expensive defamation suits or criminally prosecuted. *Asiaweek*, *Far Eastern Economic Review (both defunct)*, *Asian Wall Street Journal*, *Time*, *International Herald Tribune*, *The Economist*, and *Newsweek* all met with such a fate. Other punitive actions taken against the offending publications included restriction of their circulation in Singapore.

In the run-ins with the Singapore Government, the foreign press was repeatedly the one to capitulate. In some cases, the battle was protracted, while in others the resolve to stand up for their rights was as firm as warm butter. The end result was that even the foreign media seemed to have compromised its integrity as noted by the late Mr Derek Davies, former editor of the *Far Eastern Economic Review*:

> Lee [Kuan Yew], having failed to stop the foreign media from 'meddling in Singapore's domestic affairs', told me that instead of attempting to control editors and journalists, he would target the pockets of owners and publishers. 'I will hit you where it hurts. Then we will see your commitment to a free press.' Anyway, he enjoyed a confrontation with the media. 'Don't forget, I can hurt you more than you can hurt me.' A bill was then being prepared with the aim of giving the government powers to limit the sales of foreign publications in

> Singapore, thereby reducing their revenues from circulation and advertisements. That would bring direct and more effective pressure to bear on editors. Privately, I felt that foreign publications would hardly submit to such pressure, but I was wholly wrong and Lee was largely right. (Haas, 1999: 78)

In 1999, I did a few interviews with broadcasters such as CNBC, CNN and Reuters. Shortly after these interviews, the Government issued a warning that foreign TV stations that broadcast from Singapore had to abide by the same rules and standards that governed the Singapore station. Mr George Yeo, the Minister for Information and the Arts announced in Parliament: 'Just look at the way foreign channels have become part of the domestic politics in Malaysia and Indonesia. We should worry for ourselves' (*Straits Times*, 13 March 1999). A backbencher then stood up and railed: 'Indeed, we have witnessed many interviews on CNBC and BBC with some populist politicians in Singapore of late for frivolous causes' (*ibid*). This was, of course, a reference to my speaking in public without government approval, a matter which I will discuss at length below.

Shortly thereafter, the government amended the Singapore Broadcasting Act to enable it to prosecute foreign broadcasters, as it does with the international press, for 'engaging in the domestic politics of Singapore' (Chuang, 2001).

Since then, there have been almost no interviews with Singapore's pro-democracy activists or reports on Singapore's politics from foreign broadcasting stations.

The actions against the media in Singapore has resulted in international media watch groups criticising the PAP for its continued suppression of the media. Reporters Without Borders (RWB) placed Singapore 147th out of 167 countries in its annual survey measuring governments on their respect for press freedom, which is 'by far the lowest ranking of any developed country in the annual ranking – and just one notch above Iraq and 18 above Myanmar' ('Singapore Responds to', 2004).

In fact, RWB gave the former Prime Minister, Goh Chok Tong, the 'Predator of Press Freedom' award for his role in the government's continued suppression of press freedom together with the likes of Muammar Gaddafi, Robert Mugabe, Kim Jong-II, and Fidel Castro

(Reporters Without Borders). Another media group, the Committee to Protect Journalists, wrote

> State control of the media in Singapore is so complete that few dare to challenge the system and there is no longer much need to arrest or even harass journalists. Even foreign correspondents have learned to be cautious when reporting on Singapore, since the government has frequently hauled the international press into court to face lengthy and expensive libel suits. (Committee to Protect, 2000)

Voting for autocracy?

The PAP has won every election since it first came into power in 1959. When the opposition boycotted parliament in 1968 because the government refused to hold parliamentary sittings for more than a year, the ruling party seized the opportunity and engineered elections such that for the whole of the 1970s there was no opposition in the house. Presently there are only two opposition MPs in a house of 84.

Elections in Singapore have been given such a makeover that no one expects the PAP to lose a significant number of seats, much less the election itself. Because of the climate of fear combined with an entrenched sense of helplessness, few dare to volunteer their help for the opposition. Fewer still dare to offer themselves as opposition candidates.

There is no independent elections commission; the Elections Department works from under the Prime Minister's Office. The campaign period lasts for all of nine days. Electoral boundaries were announced one day before the elections were called in 1997. In 2001, voters were given stock-market shares by the government which they could convert to cash – on the eve of polling.

All this has resulted in the fact that in the past few elections, the opposition has not been able to field candidates in more than half of the seats, thereby allowing the PAP to return to power even before the first vote is cast. Freedom House summed it up best when it wrote:

'Citizens of Singapore cannot change their government democratically' (Freedom House, 2004).

Several years ago, a candidate's wife called me up on the eve of nomination day and begged me not to allow her husband to stand as a candidate. She threatened to jump from her flat if her husband took part in the elections and threatened to take her children with her. As it was too late to back off, the candidate went ahead with his plans but stayed home the entire campaign to ensure that nothing untoward happened.

One factor that makes Singaporeans so fearful of taking part in elections is the use of libel laws by the PAP. The judiciary is seen by many to be partial to the ruling party. Several opposition leaders have been rendered bankrupt when they have been unable to pay the millions of dollars in damages following defamation lawsuits taken out by PAP leaders.

Veteran oppositionist, Joshua B. Jeyaretnam, has paid more than a million dollars to Lee Kuan Yew and other PAP litigants. A former judge, Jeyaretnam had to sell his houses and almost all his possessions to make good on the payments. In January 2001, he was declared bankrupt because he could not pay the hundreds of thousands of dollars he still owed his opponents ('Jeyaretnam Declared Bankrupt', 2000). Under the law he will lose his seat in parliament and be barred from future elections.

Tang Liang Hong, a successful corporate lawyer and an opposition candidate in the 1997 elections, was sued for defamation for remarks he made about PAP leaders during a public rally. Following the elections, Tang fled the country. His wife's passport was quickly impounded and she was made a co-defendant in the lawsuit. Their assets were seized. Months later, a high court judge awarded the 11 PAP plaintiffs US$4.7 million, later reduced to US$2.1 million (*Straits Times,* 7 February 1998). Tang was subsequently declared bankrupt when he failed to pay the money. He and his wife lost everything they owned in Singapore. The story would have been less wretched had it ended there. During his exile, the government charged him with 33 counts of tax evasion. There is presently an outstanding warrant for his arrest.

In 2001, Lee Kuan Yew and Goh Chok Tong sued me for defamation for raising questions about Singapore's secretive loan to the Suharto regime in 1997 just before he was toppled. The courts then refused to allow me to engage foreign lawyers in the form of Queen's Counsels (QC), even though I had indicated that I could not find a local lawyer to represent me and that Lee and Goh had engaged a Senior Counsel (Singapore's equivalent of the QC) to act for them. The case was subsequently awarded to the plaintiffs in a summary judgment which meant that I was not given an open trial to defend myself and call for witnesses. At the time of writing this chapter, the plaintiffs have asked for no less than US$500,000 in damages.

This was not the first suit brought against me. In 1993 when I was sacked from the National University of Singapore three months after I joined the opposition and contested an election, I was also sued for defamation by my head of department, who was a PAP MP, for saying that my dismissal was politically motivated. The amount of costs and damages awarded was approximately US$300,000.

Such a scenario has prompted the international legal community to remark about the judiciary in Singapore:

> Civil defamation suits are being misused by the Executive to intimidate and deter those Singaporeans holding dissenting views. (Amnesty International, 1997)
>
> [Defamation lawsuits have] done little to overcome the courts' reputation as improperly compliant to the interests of the country's ruling People's Action Party. (International Commission of Jurists, 1997)
>
> What emerges…is a government that has been willing to decimate the rule of law for the benefit of its political interests. Lawyers have been cowed to passivity, judges are kept on a short leash, and the law has been manipulated so that gaping holes exist in the system of restraints on government action toward the individual. (McKay, 1990)

Labour pains

Since the 1960s when the government used the ISA to imprison labour activists, the PAP has launched a relentless campaign against trade unions. In 1966, the government passed the Trade Unions (Amendment) Act, making strikes and other industrial action illegal unless approved through secret ballot by a majority of a union's members. Sympathy strikes were also outlawed, as was the formation of a federation of unions for workers in essential services (Rodan, 1989).

The National Trade Unions Congress (NTUC) was formed to act as an umbrella labour organisation in Singapore. In the late 1970s, the Government rewrote the NTUC's charter to enable non-members to assume key posts in the organisation. Half of the union's governing body and one-third of its delegates could now be filled by Government appointees. Presently, the Union's secretary-general is a Cabinet Minister and the six assistant secretary-generals are all PAP MPs.

This 'concern' was amply demonstrated in January 1986, when Ong Teng Cheong, then deputy Prime Minister and NTUC secretary-general, sanctioned a strike in the shipping industry. Ong said that he did not tell the Cabinet about his decision, which incurred the wrath of some of the Ministers in the process. 'The Minister for trade and industry was very angry,' he revealed, 'his officers were very upset. They had calls from America, asking what happened to Singapore? We are non-strike. I said: if I were to inform the Cabinet or the Government they would probably stop me from going ahead with the strike' (*Asiaweek*, 10 March 2000). There have been no strikes since.

The PAP-NTUC nexus has been strengthened through the years. Union officials who ran in elections as part of an opposition party were asked to step down. The NTUC leadership has made it very clear that it shares 'the same political ideology as the PAP and maintains a symbiotic relationship with the party' (*ibid*).

Not surprisingly, the Singapore workers grew increasingly sceptical of the role of the NTUC. More and more workers started to disassociate themselves with the union. Given that there were no alternatives, they became more and more vulnerable often at the mercy of employers who had the power to terminate the services of an employee by reason of redundancy or reorganisation.

One union that did not come under the control of the NTUC tried to exert its independence. In 1980, the Singapore Airlines Pilots' Association called for a members' work-to-rule action and, in doing so, disrupted the schedules of several Singapore Airlines' (SIA) flights. Lee Kuan Yew personally confronted the pilots. As a consequence, the association was deregistered and the officials of the union prosecuted (Leggett, 1993: 125).

State intervention may have closed down the pilots' union but disputes between SIA's management and its pilots popped up from time to time. It happened again in 2003 when the another pilots' union the Airline Pilots' Association-Singapore (ALPA-S) accused its leadership of being weak in negotiations with the management over retrenchments the airline made several months earlier.

At one of its meetings, members called for the leadership to resign and for union elections to be held to elect new leaders who would be take a stronger stance in negotiations. Again Lee Kuan Yew stepped in. He singled out pilot Ryan Goh for campaigning for a new and more assertive ALPA-S leadership. Lee accused Ryan Goh of not having any loyalties to Singapore (the pilot was a Malaysian who was a permanent resident in Singapore for many years). Goh's permanent residency status was revoked and he had to leave Singapore.

The government subsequently amended the Trade Unions Act to allow leaders of labour unions to arrive at agreements with management without having to seek the consent of union members ('Singapore Toughens Trade', 2004).

There is no legislation requiring minimum wage in Singapore and retrenchment entitlements for laid-off workers. As a result Singaporean workers, especially those employed in manual labour, are relatively among the worst paid in the world. The median wage of an office cleaner or driver, adjusted for productivity, 'is among the lowest in 59 countries worldwide.' Only Russia, the Ukraine, and Ecuador are paid less (*Singapore Workers Relatively*, 1999). Secretaries do not do much better; their wages rank 50th among the 59 countries (*ibid*).

All this takes place in country where Ministers help themselves to salaries that are the highest in the world – a Cabinet Minister earns more than the President of the United States, and the Prime Minister of Singapore's salary is higher than that of the President of the US, Prime Minister of the UK, President of France, Prime Minister of Italy, and Chancellor of Germany combined!

Curtailing freedoms

It may come as a shock to some that despite the authoritarian control there exists a Speakers' Corner in Singapore, one that takes after London's famous Hyde Park. Apart from the fact that both versions are located in a botanical setting, however, little else is similar. The Singapore version stipulates that all speakers must first register themselves at the police station situated right on the green. No loud hailers, microphones or any voice enhancement instrument are allowed. Topics regarding sensitive matters such as religion are banned. Police personnel, including intelligence officers, mingle with the listeners and keep a close eye – and ear – to all that happens. 'If a person says something that is against the law, if he libels, if he says something that intimidates people, then of course there must be an investigation,' the Minister of State for home affairs warned ('Singapore to Keep', 2000). (Some wit in Singapore suggested that the more appropriate name for the place is 'Speakers Cornered'.)

On 10 December 2000, a marathon run was organised to commemorate International Human Rights Day as well as to protest against the ISA. Participants would run through neighbourhoods throughout the island wearing 'Abolish ISA!' T-shirts and finish at Speakers' Corner, where speeches and songs were planned. The run was, of course, banned. Under the law, a permit would be needed because five or more persons walking or running together with common intent constitutes a public procession. I proceeded to run the marathon myself, accompanied by one other runner for moral support.

At the end of my run, a group of activists and supporters gathered at the venue where the speeches were to be made. Before the program started, however, some of the activists raised their clenched fists and, in unison, shouted 'Abolish ISA!' This act of defiance was repeated following the conclusion of the speeches. A few days later, a letter was published in the local newspaper demanding that the police take action against the protesters for raising their fists and chanting slogans (*Today*, 14 December 2000). The police complied, and called two activists who participated in the event in for questioning. They also issued a warning that the Speakers' Corner must not be used for marches, demonstrations, or 'disorderly behaviour', specifying that chanting slogans, displaying placards, and 'gesticulations' such as 'clenching of fists' were 'indicative of a demonstration or of disorderly behaviour'. 'It is one thing', they added, 'to have a group of people gather to hear a person or persons speak, but quite another when people come together for a specific cause' (*South China Morning Post*, 14 February 2001).

On another occasion, I had gone to Speakers' Corner and had criticised the government for banning four seven-year-old Muslim girls from school because their parents insisted that they wear their headscarves. I was accused of speaking on a religious matter and was duly prosecuted and fined. The penalty was more that 2,000 Singapore dollars which automatically disqualified me from running for elections for five years.

Lee Kuan Yew insists that allowing citizens to gather freely and speak would result in pandemonium. As a consequence, gatherings of any sort in a public place are prohibited. Six protestors who had wanted to gather outside the US Embassy in Singapore were arrested before they could even make their way to the venue ('Two Women Stage', 2003), a forum to discuss the situation on Burma among Asian activists was banned (Singapore Democratic Party, 2003), an application to stage a march to mark the UN International Day for Elimination of Violence Against Women was rejected ('Anti-Violence Events', 2003), a request for a protest against Singapore's media by a local NGO, Think Centre, was denied ('Permit for Singaporean', 2001), a forum to discuss homosexual issues was disallowed ('Police Refuse Permit', 2000), and so on.

In 1999, I had stood in the middle of Raffles Place (the heart of Singapore's central business district) at lunchtime and addressed a crowd. I repeated the event the following week. I was prosecuted for both acts and jailed. In 2002 I attempted to hold a May Day rally outside the Istana, the President's official residential and Prime Minister's office. A bunch of police officers were on hand to greet me and hauled me away before I could begin my speech. I was again prosecuted and jailed for five weeks.

Not only are citizens prohibited from organising meetings in public places, they are also not allowed to produce, distribute or exhibit any film, video recording, or material with visual moving pictures that have a political end to them.

And what constitutes a 'political end?' The Films Act states that any moving visual material is directed at a political end if its subject-material is related to any election or national referendum in the country, or contains 'partisan or biased references' to any political matter such as election candidates/election issues, the government or opposition, a member of parliament, a 'current policy of the Government or an issue of public controversy', a political party in the country, or any body 'whose objects relate wholly or mainly to politics in Singapore' (*Films Act* (Singapore), chapt. 107). In other words, no material criticising the ruling party.

The Films Act was passed by the government when the Singapore Democratic Party produced a 20-minute video documentary introducing its platform, criticising certain government policies, and proposing alternative ideas. The video was submitted to the Censorship Board for approval. It was then that the Minister for Information and the Arts stopped it, banned the video and then introduced legislation that henceforth outlawed the production of such material.

But even if one had the intention of making political comment through the visual medium, it would be almost impossible to raise funds for it. The Political Donations Act bans political organisations from receiving funds from the international community. This piece of legislation was passed because the Open Singapore Centre (OSC), an organisation that I had established together with Jeyaretnam to promote transparency and democratic accountability, managed to obtain some funding for its work from an international foundation, which was hitherto a perfectly legitimate exercise. Days later, the government introduced the Political Donations Bill which among other things banned political organisations in Singapore from obtaining funding from overseas bodies (the bill was pushed through parliament in less than two weeks). Of course, the question of what constitutes a 'political organisation' was left entirely up to the discretion of the Minister for Home Affairs. The OSC and Think Centre, another organisation that discusses human rights and democracy issues, were subsequently named as political organisations and therefore prohibited from receiving overseas funding.

Furthermore, under the Political Donations Act, the government disallows anonymous donations to political parties and political organisations for any one year that exceed S$5,000 (approximate US$3,000) (*Political Donations Act* (Singapore), chpt 236), knowing full well that Singaporeans are too fearful to give financial support openly. The already constricted space within which political society operates has thus been tightened further.

Closing off the Internet

Much has been made about the use of the Internet as a liberating force within authoritarian systems. The ease with which transfer of information through the electronic medium occurs makes it extremely difficult, if not impossible, for governments to exercise censorship effectively.

Or so the theory goes. In Singapore the Internet use is one of the highest in the world. Yet it has had a minimal impact on the political scene in Singapore. One of the reasons is that the government does not advocate an outright ban on the dissemination and discussion of political material, if only because such a tactic is unsophisticated and would do irreparable damage to the strategy of presenting Singapore as an information centre. Instead, as with the mainstream media, the PAP relies on a mixture of legislation and intimidation to force Internet users to exercise self-censorship.

In 1996, the government stipulated that political parties, religious groups, and other organisations that wanted to put up their own websites needed to first obtain a permit from the Singapore Broadcasting Authority (SBA), ostensibly because it wanted to prevent 'objectionable content' from entering cyberspace. The operative term, 'objectionable,' was deliberately left undefined, to allow the state to determine what is and is not fit for public consumption. An opportunity came during the general election at the end of 1996, during which the SDP used its website to post information and biographical data about its candidates. The party immediately received a letter from the SBA demanding the removal of the offending Web pages (Letter from the Singapore Broadcasting Authority to the Singapore Democratic Party, 27 December 1996). In 2001, the government announced that it would introduce new regulations to 'guide responsible use' of the Internet by political parties during elections (*Straits Times*, 11 June 2001).

Such censorship, however, is not possible on websites whose origins are not within Singapore. For such websites, persuading users to curb their own behaviour on the Internet is much more effective. In 1999, a law student complained to the police that someone with an account in the Ministry of Home Affairs had illegally entered her account. The incident was widely reported in the local newspapers, ending with the service provider, SingNet (a subsidiary of SingTel), apologising to its 200,000 subscribers for allowing the Ministry to scan their files without informing them: 'On hindsight, we should have considered the impact of this exercise on you and been more sensitive to your needs' (*Straits Times,* 3 May 1999).

The intrusion was, according to the management, for purposes of 'virus-detection scanning' (*ibid*). In the meantime, the subscribers scrambled to check their files and messages to see whether they had been engaging in any communication that was less than politically correct. Since then, numerous people have told me that they would not visit some of the websites that carry material explicitly critical of the PAP. When they do happen onto such sites, they try not to remain for more than a few minutes, just in case Big Brother is on active duty.

From time to time, expressions of anxiety surface about the possibility that the government tracks the activities of Internet users, especially on newsgroups and chat rooms. These messages 'warn' other users that the authors have been questioned and harassed by the authorities for posting critical comments or providing damaging information about the government. The veracity of such messages is difficult to ascertain. Even the motive must be questioned – the authors could be pro-establishment individuals or groups intending to sow fear in the Internet community, thereby promoting greater self-censorship.

In 2003, the police raided the homes of two Internet activists and confiscated their computers files. Mohd. Zulfikar and Robert Ho had separately posted articles about Lee Kuan Yew and the appointment of his family members to key posts in government-run businesses. The police later announced that Zulfikar was under investigation for criminal defamation, an offence that carries a sentence of up to two years' imprisonment ('Police Investigate Muslim', 2002). Zulfikar left the country, seeking political refuge in Australia ('Muslim Activist Seeks', 2002).

Conclusion

One of the main reasons why Singapore does not show up more significantly or frequently on the international human rights radar-screen is because of the PAP's well-developed public relations campaign. Another reason is because it is hard to believe that a city as technologically modern as Singapore can be so primitive in its political development. An Asian human rights organisation described

> Few States fly as far under the international community's human rights radar as Singapore. A prosperous, in many ways Western-style nation, Singapore is barely mentioned at the United Nations Commission on Human Rights. Occasional references to conscientious objection to military service and the death penalty aside, the Singaporean delegation sit smugly while their Asian neighbours face a barrage of NGO, and often State, criticism. Singapore is no better than its neighbours – in many ways, it's worse. It is the Cuba of Asia (but without the crushing poverty or damaging economic sanctions). Indeed,

> Singapore enjoys Western-style economic prosperity. There can be no argument – flawed, as it is – that civil and political rights cannot be afforded in Singapore. Denials of civil and political rights in Singapore are simply of governmental policy. (SAHRDC, 2002)

Whatever the cause, it remains essential that the international community pays more attention to the situation in the island-republic. Developing countries, especially those with autocratic leaders, increasingly view Singapore as a model where modernisation can take place without any serious disruption to authoritarian control. China's leaders, for example, are big admirers of the Singapore Way. The thinking is based on the age-old concept of keeping the people's stomachs full and heads empty. If citizens are kept busy trying to make money they will have little time to do anything else, including getting active in politics.

When the government throws in punitive measures to further discourage political activity, controls the flow of information, and encourages self-censorship the resultant effect is a level of docility among the citizenry that is unhealthy politically, socially, and even economically. One need only look at the failed experiment that was Indonesia under the reign of Suharto. Driven by unprecedented growth of the GDP, Suharto's human rights abuses and the suppression of democratic development meant that corruption and cronyism became rampant and endemic. When the economy started to unravel, society came apart at the seams because there was not a political system or culture to ensure a peaceful transition of leadership.

The economic cracks are only starting to appear in Singapore. If the country is to avoid some of the grief that have befallen other countries, it is wise that we in Singapore and those in the international community make greater effort to remedy the political deficiency and human rights violations in the city-state.

References

Amnesty International, 1997, *J B Jeyaretnam—the Use of Defamation Suits for Political Purpose Report*, 15 October, (web.amnesty.org/library/Index/ENGASA360041997?open&of=ENG-SGP) accessed 10.02.2005.

Amnesty International, 2004, *Amnesty International Report 2004*, (www.amnestyusa.org) accessed 11.02.2005.

'Anti-violence Events Banned in Singapore', 2003, AP, 24 November.

Asia Watch, 1990, *Silencing All Critics: Human Rights Violations in Singapore*, An Asia Watch Report.

Asiaweek , 10 March 2000, 'Ong Teng Cheong: Extended Interview'.

Chee, S. J., 1998, *To Be Free: Stories from Asia's Struggle Against Oppression*, (Melbourne: Monash Asia Institute).

Chuang, P. M., 2001, *New Legislation Won't Hurt Media Hub Ambition Much,* BTOnline, 20 April, (http://businesstimes.asia1.com.sg) accessed 05.02.2005.

Committee to Protect Journalists, 2000, *Singapore 2000: Country Report*, (www.cpj.org/attacks00/asia00/Singapore.html) accessed 11.02.2005.

Films Act (Singapore), chpt 107, Singapore Statutes Online, (http://statutes.agc.gov.sg/) accessed 05.02.2005.

Freedom House, 2004, *Freedom in the World 2004: The Annual Survey of Political Right and Civil Liberties*, (www.freedomhouse.org/research/index.htm) accessed 11.02.2005.

George, T. J. S., 1974, *Lee Kuan Yew's Singapore*, (London: Andre Deutsch).

Gupte, P., 2004, *Letter from Singapore*, 11 September, (www.pranaygupte.com) accessed 10.02.2005.

Haas, M., 1999, *The Singapore Puzzle*, (Connecticut: Praeger).

International Commission of Jurists, 1997, 'Singapore Judiciary Bows to Executive in Defamation Suit', 2 October.

'Jeyaretnam, Declared Bankrupt, to Lose Seat', 2000, Reuters, 6 May.

Leggett, C., 1993, 'Singapore's Industrial Relations in the 1990s', in G. Rodan (Ed.), *Singapore Changes Guard*, (Malaysia: Longman Cheshire).

McKay, R., 1990, *New York City Bar Association Report*, October.

'Muslim Activist Seeks Australian Refuge', 2002, Reuters, 24 July.

'Permit for Singaporean Press Protest Rejected', 2001, AP, 28 February.

'Police Investigate Muslim Group Over Alleged Defamation', 2002, AFP, 3 July.

'Police Refuse Permit For Gay And Lesbian Forum', 2000, AFP, 24 May.

Political Donations Act (Singapore), chpt. 236, Singapore Statutes Online, (http://statutes.agc.gov.sg/) accessed 10.02,2005.

Reporters Without Borders, (http://www.rsf.org) acessed 10.02.2005.

Rodan, G., 1989, *The Political Economy of Singapore's Industrialization*, (New York: Forum Enterprise).

Singapore Democratic Party, 2003, 'Dictators in Burma Have Good Friends in Singapore', Articles and News, 17 December 2003, (www.singaporedemocrat.org/news_display.php?id=421) accessed 05.02.2005.

'Singapore Responds to International Press Ranking', 2004, AP, 17 November.

'Singapore to Keep Records on Speakers', 2000, AP, 9 May.

'Singapore Toughens Trade Unions Act to Prevent Repeat of Pilots' Saga', 2004, AFP, 20 April.

Singapore Workers Relatively Underpaid, 1999, BTOnline, 14 July (http://businesstimes.asia1.com.sg) accessed 10.02.2005.

South China Morning Post, 14 February 2001, 'Police Call for Order at Speakers' Corner', Hong Kong.

Straits Times, 7 February 1998, 'Tang Liang Hong Declared a Bankrupt', Singapore.

Straits Times, 13 March 1999, 'Foreign TV Stations: Same Rules Apply', Singapore.

Straits Times, 3 May 1999, 'SingNet Apologises Via E-Mail', Singapore.

Straits Times, 11 June 2001, 'New Rules to Guide Use of Net at Hustings', Singapore.

South Asia Human Rights Documentation Centre (SAHRDC), 2002, *Singapore: Asia's Gilded Cage*, Human Rights Feature, 17 April, (www.hrdc.net/sahrdc/hrfeatures/HRF55.htm) accessed 10.02.05.

Today, 14 December 2000, 'Is Speaker's Corner for demos?', Singapore.

'Two women stage brief protest outside US embassy', 2003, AFP, 15 February.

KULWANT SINGH

The Resolution of Property Rights of Refugees and Displaced Persons and Ethnic Crisis Management: Bosnia Herzegovina and Kashmir Compared

Introduction

Various international human rights instruments, both universal and regional, have recognised the right to property as featuring among the fundamental rights of persons. Examples are provided by the Universal Declaration of Human Rights, 1948 (Article 17(1)) and the American Declaration of the Rights and Duties of Man, 1948 (Article 23). Although these instruments are not legally binding, they establish universal and regional rules, which have become rules of international customary law and, as such, are considered obligatory in the doctrine and practice of international law. Moreover, the interdependence and indivisibility of all human rights is nowadays unquestionable and, in this context, the importance of property ownership, as a contributory factor towards securing peace and economic and social development of a state, is assuming growing significance.

Do the refugees and displaced persons, whether in Jammu and Kashmir (J&K) or in Bosnia and Herzegovina (BiH), deserve to be treated differently? In both of these cases, people left their homes under circumstances of compulsion, got segregated on ethnic lines and fled to areas where they found the secure environs of their own ethnic group dealing a severe blow to the very basis of democratic institutions which stand on the firm foundation of secular principles. The approach to resolve this important issue in case of J&K has been that of total apathy on the part of India and Pakistan and the international community (IC) as well, leading to a state of perpetual uncertainty and confusion. The resultant discontent has found its expression in over a decade and a half long regime of terrorism in the area that has got the potentialities of nuclear confrontation between the two South Asian neighbours. The intervention by the IC in BiH has exhibited some encouraging results. This has been made possible because of the sustained and cooperative efforts of the IC representing one of the most intensive programmes of peace implementation missions ever. History is witness to the fact that unresolved property disputes do not simply disappear over time but remain a potential source of tension for decades. The resolution of property rights, therefore, becomes a vital component of a peace-building effort undertaken anywhere in the world.

The position in Jammu and Kashmir

The roots of present turmoil in J&K go back to the discriminatory politico-administrative regime established by erstwhile rulers from 1846 to 1947. The autocratic rulers created and practised a discriminatory regime that was biased against *Kashmiris,* particularly the Muslims, who constituted a majority of population in J&K. The Muslims, the *Ladakhis* and the *Baltis* were practically disqualified from military service and those who got recruited to military were *Dogras, Dards* and *Punjabis*. In fact, the *Dogra Rajputs*[1] dominated every important position in the army as well as the State administration.

The majority of people in J&K were agriculturists having small land-holdings. The revenue was collected in the form of kind, especially in Kashmir and Ladakh regions inhabited by non-*Dogras*. Yet another discriminatory practice directed against the majority of population was the ban on the slaughter of cow, wild or domesticated, an act treated as a cognisable offence under Ranbir Penal Code, 1932 (Sec. 297–A) and non-bailable under the State Code of Criminal Procedure, 1933 (Schedule–II). Under the State Arms Act, only *Dogras* and *Rajputs* could own and use firearms. The list is too long to be enumerated here. The fact remains that majority of population laboured hard under *Dogra* rulers.

Partition of India in 1947 envisaged a scheme under which the British Indian Provinces were to be divided into two dominions, India and Pakistan, whereas the princely States[2] were required to accede to either of the two dominions by signing an Instrument of Accession.[3] The ruler of J&K was interested in retaining the independent character of his State but the invasion by Afghan tribesmen in October 1947 changed it all. He executed the Instrument of Accession with India on 26 October 1947, which was accepted by the Governor General of India on 27 October and on the same day Indian troops landed at Srinagar to contain the onslaught of tribal invaders into the State.

The signing of the Instrument of Accession, the tribal invasion from across the border and the resultant mismanagement of ethnic crisis created generated the conditions J&K is passing through these days. J&K got divided *de facto* into two parts, two thirds with India and one third with Pakistan.[4] The partition process flared up communal disturbances in the State leading to an intense military engagement between the two countries. There was large-scale death and destruction on both sides and a massive displacement of population both within and outside J&K. The issue of J&K was referred to the UN Security Council (UNSC),[5] which passed two resolutions asking Pakistan to withdraw its troops from the territory of J&K while India could retain a small contingent of its forces to facilitate the holding of a plebiscite under UN observation.[6] There has been no implementation of these resolutions of UNSC so far. J&K remains divided between India and Pakistan and the refugees and displaced persons continue to be deprived of their homes and, thus, their right to property.

Immediately after the declaration of ceasefire, Property Commissions were set up at different places in J&K that functioned for a short while through their field staff: the Rehabilitation Commissioners, Rehabilitation Officers, etc. Those Commissions did award compensation, in some cases, to refugees and displaced persons where an application detailing the location, nature, estimated value, and so forth of the property was filed before a Rehabilitation Officer of the area of refuge. The application was then to be forwarded to the Rehabilitation Officer of the area where property was actually located, who in turn, would verify the claim after physical verification of property. The applicant would be awarded a paltry sum upon the receipt of the verification report. The Property Commissions were later disbanded and the Evacuees Property Department, created under The Jammu and Kashmir State Evacuee's (Administration of Property) Act, 1949, took over the administration of evacuees' property (Sec. 2(d)) left by the evacuees (Sec. 2(c)).

The J&K Displaced Persons (Permanent Settlement) Act, 1971 provides for the permanent settlement of displaced persons (Sec. 2(a)) in J&K. Under the Act, the State government has been authorised to transfer any evacuee land (Sec. 2(b)) to such displaced persons for agricultural purposes. Ironically, in no case could a refugee or displaced person be restored his/her property, as the *de facto* border so created continues to remain in place making it difficult for the people to cross over and claim back property they owned before the division of J&K.

The position in Bosnia and Herzegovina

The war in BiH (1992–1995) exhibited almost similar patterns, such as partition of the country and displacement of people both within and outside its borders. A total of 2.7 million people were displaced from their homes, 1.2 million being internally displaced within BiH.[7] In addition, the country once hosted between 30,000 and 40,000 Serb refugees from Croatia and Bosnian Croats expelled from Serb-held territory during the conflict. The turmoil in the Federal Republic of Yugoslavia (FRY) at its height in 1999 pushed into BiH 21,500 Kosovo Albanians, 21,000 Sandzak Muslims, beside 31,000 other persons, including draft evaders and deserters from FRY. BiH declared its independence on 3 March 1992 and became an internationally recognised State on 22 May 1992. Soon after the declaration of its independence, it plunged into a long and terrible war. The fall of Srebrenica and of the self-styled Serb state of Krajina in Croatia in the summer of 1995, and subsequent Serb losses in Bosnia, combined with a massive NATO bombing campaign, heralded a new age in Western engagement in the Balkans.

The internationally brokered agreement was negotiated by representatives of the parties involved in the 1992–95 war in BiH, including the neighbouring Republic of Croatia and FRY, at US-led talks at Dayton, Ohio, USA. The Dayton Peace Agreement was finally signed in Paris, France on 14 December 1995. The Agreement is formally referred to as the General Framework Agreement for Peace (GFAP). The prime aim of the Agreement is to provide the population of BiH with an opportunity to rebuild their lives together in peace and prosperity and commit themselves to creating a State which will bring them together within a social and political framework and, in turn, enable the country to take its rightful place in Europe.[8] An early and important objective of the peace agreement is to create secure conditions for the safe and orderly return of refugees and displaced persons to the places of their choice.[9]

Forms of ownership

In Bosnia and Herzegovina

Basic components of Yugoslav social order and organisation were the social ownership of resources of production and power in the hands of working people, which was manifested through a rather developed system of social self-management and associated labour. Under such socio-economic conditions, property relations were manifested through the following basic forms (Institute of Comparative Law, 1977: 108).

i) Social ownership

The Constitution of the Socialist Federal Republic of Yugoslavia (SFRY) and the Constitutions of Republics and Autonomous Provinces guaranteed social ownership as a basic form of ownership, which represented the material basis of Yugoslav socio-political system. No citizen or individual had the right to appropriate or distribute the social means of production or property on any ground (Basic Principles of the SFRY Constitution, III). Under the then-existing system of social management there emerged a specific criterion defining the nature and kind of objects of social ownership and the manner of their use. All objects of social ownership were deemed not to possess equal importance for the society, therefore, separate legal regimes were propounded to manage such social resources. The goods of general interest, basic and other resources of associated labour and of collective consumption were the objects of social ownership. It was not permitted to constitute the right of property over such objects (Arts. 12, 81 and 85).

ii) Private ownership

The right of ownership of citizens and of civil law entities represented, in terms of its content and form, a specific kind of property law. Citizens were guaranteed right of ownership over both movable and real property (Arts. 78 and 79). The foundation of right of ownership was generally the personal labour of holder of that right. It included the right to dispose of the object of ownership, subject to limitations imposed by the Constitution or by any law in force in relation thereto. The right of ownership of residential houses and dwellings in favour of citizens, associations of citizens and other legal entities was guaranteed specifically under Article 78 of the SFRY Constitution. The Law on Housing Relations, 1984, in force in the former Socialist Republic of Bosnia and Herzegovina, regulated the rights and responsibilities of the owner of an apartment, whether socially or privately owned (Art. 1). A person in possession of a socially owned apartment had the right to use the apartment permanently and freely but his/her right therein was only an occupancy right. The person was prohibited to sell, buy or in some other way transfer or acquire an occupancy right (Art. 11). That right could be exercised over one apartment only and the prohibition applied not only to the occupancy-right-holder personally but also to other members of her/his family (Art. 12).

iii) Occupancy right

The occupancy right[10] entails, *inter alia*, the right to use an apartment permanently. Although an occupancy right cannot be equated with a building lease, a premium lease, or private ownership, it does contain several elements of these forms of ownership. It has a permanent character as it is granted for an indefinite period of time and cannot be terminated except in certain specific circumstances enumerated in the still applicable SRBiH Law on Housing Relations, like, the non-use of an apartment for an uninterrupted period of more than 6 months without any justifiable reason in law[11] or in the Law on Abandoned Apartments. Although an allocated unit cannot be bought or sold by the occupancy right holder, yet a child or other member of family living with him/her can, pursuant to Article 21 of SRBiH Law on Housing Relations, obtain the occupancy right after his/her death or on the termination of occupancy right on other grounds. An occupancy right is established *de jure* as soon as the holder of right to allocate occupancy right issues a decision granting occupancy right to an individual.

In Jammu and Kashmir

Under the laws in force in J&K, only private ownership over immoveable/real property is recognised that vests in the owner an absolute right in the object of ownership. The immovable property that does not vest in any natural or legal person, vests in the government unless proved otherwise. All other forms of right to property are subsidiary to and flow from this basic right. The private ownership can be acquired by any of the modes recognised by the J&K Transfer of Property Act, 1920, *viz.*, sale, lease, gift, will, exchange, etc. An interesting feature of the right to property is that only a 'permanent resident' of J&K (J&K Constitution Act, 1957, Sec. 6) can acquire this right and other citizens of India cannot claim it.

The restriction is so strict that if a female from J&K marries a person who is not a permanent resident of the State, she loses her status of being a permanent resident and becomes incapable of acquiring the right of ownership in any immovable property in J&K.[12]

Article 19(1)(f) of the Constitution of India, as extended to J&K, guarantees the right to property to permanent residents and is non-derogable. Article 19(1)(f) read with Section 6 of the Constitution of J&K, confers the right to property even on those who had crossed over to Pakistan or the Pakistani-administered part of J&K (POK) during the communal disturbances of 1947. To give a more concrete shape to the right to property and the right to return in favour of refugees and displaced persons, the J&K Legislature has passed The Jammu and Kashmir Resettlement Bill. As the Governor did not assent to the Bill, it is pending approval before the Parliament of India, a procedure necessary to make it an enforceable law.

Property Law Implementation Plan (PLIP)

PLIP was conceived in October 1999 for bringing together all property related activities of different agencies and for formulating a coherent and goal oriented strategy directed toward securing the implementation of right to property. It involves collaborative efforts between different international agencies comprising Office of the High Representative (OHR), UN High Commissioner for Refugees (UNHCR). Organisation for the Security and Cooperation for Europe (OSCE), UN Mission to Bosnia and Herzegovina (UNMIBH) and Commission for Real Property Claims (CRPC) working in cooperation with other organisations, like, Stabilisation Force (SFOR), the Council of Europe and the European Commission, to resolve all outstanding claims by the refugees and displaced persons to repossess their property. By insisting on strict adherence to the requirements of law, it ensures de-politicisation of the property return process by treating it as a technical procedure for the implementation of individual claims and also its institutionalisation by creating effective legal and administrative structures to deal with the claims in a standardised and professional manner.

Operational mechanisms under PLIP

i) Political intervention strategies

PLIP contains different operational mechanisms to deal with obstacles in the implementation of the right to property. The monitoring and supervision operations conducted with the aid of the OSCE, UNHCR and OHR field network (Focal Point Scheme), ensure that the domestic mechanisms for resolving property claims operate uniformly throughout the country. PLIP structure has developed a standardised system of reporting violations of property law by local officials. Field officers keep running files on implementation issues in every municipality and wherever there is abuse of process or refusal to implement law, non-compliance reports are filed. PLIP regional structure then develops an appropriate intervention strategy in response thereto that may include a recommendation to the High Representative to exercise his Bonn powers, sparingly of course, to dismiss the erring official. Before making any such recommendation, an effort is made to promote domestic remedies, such as, appeal, administrative review, dialogue, persuasion, etc.

Local police are obliged to support eviction process by being present at every eviction, by using force wherever necessary and by bringing criminal charges against those who obstruct eviction process. On occasions, UNMIBH has appointed International Police Task Force/European Union Police Mission (IPTF/EUPM) monitors as special advisors to the local offices of Ministry of Refugees and Displaced Persons (OMI) to monitor, advise and report on the working of Housing Office. The presence of special advisor creates a feeling of security both for displaced persons claiming their property and for the Housing Officials who are subjected to different forms of pressure.

ii) Capacity-building

Institutional capacity-building involves empowering the local structures at Entity, Cantonal and Municipal level to take ownership of the implementation of right to property. The international organisations through cooperative programmes offer training seminars to the concerned officials familiarising them with details of law and their responsibilities there under. Placement of Data Entry Clerks in municipal housing offices to create chronological databases and information exchange programme initiated by OSCE, etc., has helped local authorities remarkably to work more effectively in relation to return process ensuring an impartial application of law.

Efficacy of property law implementation also depends upon judicial reform envisaging the availability of domestic remedies. Commendable work has been done by an Independent Judicial Commission established under the auspices of OHR for the implementation of judicial reform strategy providing for judicial review wherever the domestic remedies fail.

iii) Housing space

In many places around the country, there continues to be a genuine shortage of housing space. Under the existing property laws, administrative authorities are required to assess whether the current user of claimed property is entitled to an alternative accommodation, and if so, to find an accommodation. PLIP closely coordinates with Reconstruction and Return Task Force to maximise availability of housing space and assists donors in targeting housing reconstruction activities in the localities where reconstruction can offer an immediate boost to return process and also free up space to create a cycle of returns. Some municipalities have already started to channel funds from local budgets into small and precisely targeted repair works showing the signs of ownership of return process.

iv) Current phase

The current phase of implementation has focussed on cases of 'double' or 'multiple occupancy'. The amendments of 4 December 2001 to property laws have made the chronological processing of cases obligatory. These amendments tightened the conditions for claiming alternative accommodation and put a burden on the temporary occupants to demonstrate that they had taken all possible measures to seek repossession or reconstruction of their pre-war property. Funding of alternative accommodation projects in municipalities that have demonstrably done well to provide alternative accommodation and especially the directing of reconstruction funds to destroyed villages wherefrom people have been occupying properties in towns, started a long chain of repossessions.

Implementation of the right to property

GFAP established BiH as a state comprising two entities, the Republika Srpska and the Bosniak-Croat Federation, each with a high degree of autonomy. It guarantees the highest level of internationally recognised human rights and fundamental freedoms as provided in the European Convention for the Protection of Human Rights and Fundamental Freedoms and its Protocols and the other international agreements enumerated in the Appendix to Annex 4. Article 1 of Annex 7 details the right to property as one of the basic human rights inherent in every citizen of BiH. The Constitution of BiH (GFAP, Annex 4) recognises the right to property in its Preamble, Article II (3) (k) and Article II (5) which deal specifically with the right of the refugees and displaced persons to return to their homes of origin and to have them restored the property of which they were deprived during the hostilities since 1991.

i) Law on abandoned apartments

Ethnic cleansing during the war was reinforced by a complex set of legal measures adopted to make the return process extremely difficult for displaced people. From the crudest methods, such as forcing them to sign away their homes under duress or in exchange for exit permits, to the more complex administrative system of reallocation of abandoned property, law was used by all the parties to enforce segregation of population. Each of the wartime regimes adopted 'abandoned property' laws to erect permanent barriers to return. For instance, in the Federation, original occupants were given seven days, if within the country, or fifteen days, if abroad, to repossess their apartments or else lose their right altogether. Temporary permits to use abandoned property were then issued arbitrarily even to those who were not in genuine need. Authorities also made extensive use of pre-war law on obligation to use a socially owned apartment to get the right to apartment cancelled by a decree of court if the occupant did not use the apartment for more than six months (Law on Housing Relations, 1984, Art. 47).

Achieving reform of property laws has been one of the most strenuous campaigns conducted by IC. Despite opposition from local authorities, OHR was finally able to repeal abandoned property laws in April 1998 in the Federation and in December 1998 in Republika Srpska, establishing an administrative claims process enabling refugees and displaced persons to apply to local authorities for the repossession of their properties. The property law reform did not end there. The High Representative, making use of his Bonn powers, amended property laws on a number of occasions to strengthen the right to return, to tighten administrative procedures and to harmonise laws between the Entities. The legislative reform has strengthened occupancy rights to the point where they are now functionally equivalent to ownership. Court decisions cancelling occupancy rights have been revoked and jurisdiction thereon transferred to administrative authorities, newly granted occupancy rights converted into temporary permits, new rules governing the right of current user to alternative accommodation introduced, tough measures adopted against multiple occupancy and misuse of housing space, and reasonable controls imposed over the privatisation process to prevent wrong beneficiaries from taking advantage.

In order to assess the effectiveness of measures taken so far by the IC to keep the return process going and to make the right to property meaningful for refugees and displaced persons, the data collected exhibit that in BiH, up to the end of August 2004, a total of 215,810 claims, including 97,217 for socially owned property and 118,593 for private property had been filed and 200,689 positive decisions, 87,948 pertaining to socially owned property and 112,741 pertaining to private property, issued by the authorities in favour of claimants. At the same time, 13,637 negative decisions on contested/occupied property, including 8,928 for socially owned property and 4,709 for private property were also issued. But all the claimants, in whose favour a decision to repossess the property had been issued, could not be put into actual possession of the property. The data further showed that a total of 200,034 cases, 87,410 pertaining to socially owned property and 112,624 to private property were closed where the properties had been vacated and/or sealed and/or repossessed and/or the occupancy right holder or the owner notified that s/he could repossess. The overall implementation ratio of the property laws in BiH till the end of August 2004 was 92.69 per cent.

In J&K, the properties left behind by people while fleeing their homes during the communal disturbances of 1947, included houses, bungalows, flats, annexes, shops, godowns, water mills, garages, dilapidated buildings, orchards, agricultural and non-agricultural lands, while the ones allotted temporarily to displaced persons who crossed over to the Indian part of J&K included residential plots, commercial buildings and lands, office complexes, agricultural lands, trees, hutments and watchman huts. Most of the properties left behind by evacuees and allotted temporarily to others are located in Jammu, a region that witnessed the maximum displacement of population. Those allottees have not been vested with an absolute right of ownership over such properties but are mere occupancy or tenancy right holders. The sad part of the story is that the Evacuees Property Department is riddled with corruption and many of the evacuee properties have been subsequently sold to or permanently allotted in favour of influential persons or those who could pay for the same.

The data available with the Evacuees Property Department, Jammu, show that in all 32,000 families[13] migrated from POK in 1947,[14] of which 31,600 settled in different parts of India, including the Indian part of J&K. The government of J&K did not invite any claims for compensation in lieu of the properties left behind by migrants as POK has always been considered an integral part of India and under illegal occupation of Pakistan. Out of those 31,600 families, 22,700 were allotted agricultural lands and 3,600 residential properties in the districts of Jammu, Udhampur and Nowshera whereas 5,300 were settled in other parts of the country. In order to mitigate the hardships of those families, the government issued an order on 24 June 1960 for the payment of *ex-gratia* rehabilitation assistance to them. Formal registration of displaced persons for the said purpose started in 1960 and continued up to 7 August 1962. During this period, 31,619 families were registered and cases of 9,500 rejected on the ground that: i) they did not migrate between September 1947 and December 1950; or ii) the head of family did not migrate with the family; or iii) the family did not stay in a refugee camp; or iv) the monthly income of the family exceeded 300 rupees (US$ 6). Grievances of the displaced families whose cases were rejected have now been looked into by the government and a relief package of 2500 rupees (US$ 50) per family, provided their monthly income does not exceed 300 rupees (US$ 6), announced on 9 August 2000.[15]

The present turmoil in J&K has again forced about 350,000 people to migrate from their homes to safer areas both within and outside the State, leaving over 90,000[16] dead, over 40,000 orphans and over 20,000 widows. Many of the properties left behind by these migrants have been deliberately destroyed, forcibly occupied or even bought under coercion or on the basis of fake legal documents adding yet another dimension to the 'right to property' issue pending resolution for long in J&K.

Conclusion

The nature of international crisis and management thereof has grown more complex in the post-cold war era. The traditional international crises originated in an interstate conflict, involved adversaries and centred on peace and war, whereas today's non-traditional crises may emerge from an intrastate conflict and include players who are not adversaries. The crisis management previously focussed on state actors with the primary goal to avoid war without relinquishing interest, while it must now involve a number of players, including the state actors, non-state entities, and international organisations with the objective of preventing crisis, terminating hostilities, or negotiating a long-term settlement. Managing a non-traditional crisis may also involve diplomatic peace-making beside a host of peace support operations, like peacekeeping, peace-enforcement, and peace-building. Perhaps no crisis has been more synonymous with the complexity of the post-cold-war security environment than that in BiH where the international intervention, to an outside observer, appeared to be haphazard, confused, insufficient or even counter-productive. It is, in fact, a reflection of the evolution of parameters of a new collective security arrangement taking shape globally today (Sloan, 1998).

Strengthening of the national human rights institutions would ensure the internal stability and external viability of BiH as a state. The willingness of BiH and Entity governments to co-operate with the existing human rights institutions and to implement their decisions and reports is a test of their claim to respect human rights as a member of the Council of Europe. Moreover, the return of refugees to areas where they are an ethnic minority is crucial if BiH is to be re-established as a successful multi-ethnic society and if it seriously intends to participate in the Stabilisation and Association Process offered by the EU, in return for compliance with certain conditions, including, among others, the return of refugees and displaced persons to their homes of origin. Lasting peace and stability in south-eastern Europe will only become possible when democratic principles and values have taken roots throughout and a firm foundation laid for the transition of region as a whole to a peaceful and democratic future.

The IC might not have experienced the whole range of non-traditional crises management tools in BiH but the lessons learnt there may prove helpful in formulating policy guidelines and in establishing an institutional framework for the resolution of the J&K stalemate. An early return of refugees and displaced persons to their homes and a proper management of a pending ethnic crisis may bring peace and progress to that part of the world.

Endnotes

1 Members of the community of rulers of J&K.
2 There were approximately 564 Princely States at the time of partition of India.
3 See The Government of India Act, 1935 and The Indian Independence Act, 1947.
4 Out of this 1/3rd portion, 27,000 square kilometres territory of J&K has been handed over by Pakistan to China.
5 Security Council Verbatim Reports: S/P.V. 227, p.31, as reproduced in Security Council Official Records, Third Year Nos.1–15.
6 Security Council Document: S/651, 17.01.1948; Security Council Verbatim Reports: S/P.V. 236 and S/P.V. 237.
7 Statement by Sadako Ogata, United Nations High Commissioner for Refugees, at the Peace Implementation Conference for Bosnia and Herzegovina, London, 9 December 1995.
8 *Conclusions of the Peace Implementation Conference, London,* 8–9 December 1995, para 1.
9 *Ibid.,* para 23.
10 *Constitution of SFRY, 1974,* Article 164.
11 *The Law on Housing Relations, 1984,* Article 47.
12 The High Court of J&K, while disposing of a group of petitions, has recently recognised the right to immovable property in favour of a woman married to a non-state subject provided certain conditions were fulfilled. It is pending appeal before the Supreme Court of India.
13 These figures relate to families, generally the extended ones, who stayed in and were registered at refugee camps set up by the authorities.
14 The figures pertaining to the families/individuals who migrated from Indian part of J&K to POK or Pakistan are not included.
15 Information provided by the Minister of State for Home, Government of India, to the Parliament (*Lok Sabha*) on 14 May 2002. Source: Press Trust of India.
16 The conservative estimates published by the Government of India/J&K State put the number of dead as 90,000 that include 30,000 civilians and 60,000 militants. This figure does not include the number of security personnel killed during the present turmoil. See, ‘Kashmir Violence Takes Its Toll’ in *The Times of India,* 10 July 2003.

References

Anand, A. S., 1994, *The Constitution of Jammu and Kashmir Its Development and Comments*, (Delhi: Universal Book Traders).

Arechaga, E. J., 1967, 'The Background to Article 17 of the Universal Declaration', *Journal of International Commission of Jurists,* 2: 34–35.

Birdwood, Lt. Col. Lord, 1952, 'Kashmir Dilemma', *Fortnightly Review* (August) (London).

Institute of Comparative Law, 1977, *Guide to the Yugoslav Legal System*, (Beograd: Servis Saveza Udruzenja Pravnika Jugoslavije, Proleterskih Brigada).

Office of the High Representative, October 2000, *Bosnia and Herzegovina Essential Texts*, (Sarajevo).

'Kashmir Violence Takes Its Toll', *The Times of India*, 10 July 2003.

OSCE Press Release, 'OSCE Announces Process on Illegal Occupancy Rule', 14 December 1999.

PLIP., (www.ohr.int) accessed 10.11.2004.

Robertson, A. H., 1968–69, 'The United Nations Covenant on Civil and Political Rights and the European Convention on Human Rights', 43, *British Year Book of International Law*, 21: 28–31.

Silber, L. and Little, A., 1996, *The Death of Yugoslavia*, (England: Penguin Group and BBC Worldwide Ltd.).

Sloan, E. C., 1998, *Bosnia and the New Collective Security*, (London: Praeger Publishers).

Starr, R., 1967, 'International Protection of Human Rights and the United Nations Covenants', *Wisconsin Law Review*: 863–866.

KIIKPOYE K. AARON

Human Rights Violation and Environmental Degradation in the Niger Delta Region of Nigeria

Introduction

Oil exploration in Nigeria began in 1938 when Shell D'Archy was granted exclusive right to prospect for oil by the colonial state. However, oil was first struck in 1956 but production in commercial quantities began in 1958 in Oloibiri and subsequently at Afam, Bomu and Ebubu, all in the Niger Delta region, which is home to several of Nigeria's minority ethnic groups.

From an initial daily production capacity of 6000 barrels (Owabukereyule, 2000) amounting to 1,820,305 barrels of oil that was exported in 1958 (Okorobia, 1999: 397), Nigeria now has a daily production capacity of 2.6 million barrels of oil. Its actual daily production is 2.142 million barrels, in line with the Organisation of Petroleum Exporting Countries' (OPEC) quota allocation (*The Guardian* October 3, 2004). At current global prices, Nigeria's annual earnings from oil exports is put at $40 billion (Douglas et al., 2003).

Since the production of oil about 46 years ago, the oil resources of the Niger Delta have financed the phenomenal transformation of some sections of the Nigerian society and translated to stupendous wealth in the hands of corrupt military oligarchs and their civilian collaborators. The vast earnings from oil, especially during the oil boom years, elevated profligacy in government circles to an art: Nigeria paid the salaries of civil servants on one occasion in far away Grenada in the 70s (Owugah, 2000:106). Indeed a top government functionary boastfully declared that money was not Nigeria's problem but how to spend it (Ihonvbere, 1994).

But what has oil meant for the Niger Delta? From all indications, oil has meant for the indigenes of the Niger Delta, wrenching poverty, occasioned by human rights abuses, in particular, the economic, social and cultural rights (ESCRs) of the region's inhabitants. Specifically, the 'right to health' and the 'right to a healthy environment' recognised in Articles 16 and 24 of the *African Charter on Human and Peoples Rights* have come under severe assault by the ecologically unfriendly practices of oil transnational corporations (TNCs). In addition, state laws and policies as they relate to petroleum resources, expropriate the indigenous peoples of the Niger Delta of their 'right to their natural resources', which contravenes Article 21 of the *African Charter*. Essentially fisherfolk and farmers, ecological devastation threatens not only their lives but their livelihoods as well. But to what extent does the violation of the human rights of the Niger Delta people brought about by the environmentally harmful practices of oil TNCs and state laws and policies which expropriate the resource rights of the region's inhabitants lead to further environmental degradation? This is the key question explored in this chapter.

That the petroleum development activities of oil TNCs in alliance with the Nigerian State have led to gross human and environmental rights abuses is an established, well-known and well-documented fact (Sagay, 2001, Environmental Rights Action/Friends of the Earth Nigeria, 2000; Owabukereyule, 2000; Owugah 2000; Human Rights Watch, 1999; Clark et al., 1999; Social and Economic Rights Action Centre, (SERAC) 1995, Agbonifo, undated). As well, that the environmental degradation occasioned by the activities of oil exploration and exploitation TNCs has resulted in adverse effects on resource flows and material well-being of the region's inhabitants is also well established. Indeed, ruling in a case brought before the *African Commission on Human and Peoples Rights* (ACHPR), by the Social and Economic Rights Action Centre (SERAC) on behalf of the Ogonis, one of Nigeria's oil-producing minority ethnic groups in the Niger Delta region, the *African Commission* held that the Nigerian government should compensate the Ogoni people for abuses against their lands, environment, housing and health caused by oil production and government security forces (Lobe, 2002:1).

What appears to be inadequately captured in the literature is the potential of further environmental degradation as a result of the human rights violation occasioned on the Niger Delta people by the activities of oil TNCs and state policies that expropriate the resource rights of the people. This is the gap that this study aspires to fill. I argue that the ecologically harmful processes of exploitation of the oil resources of the Niger Delta by oil TNCs and petroleum development laws and policies of the Nigerian state violate the human rights of the region's inhabitants and that attempts to reactivate or re-assert their lost rights lead to further environmental degradation. Deprived and poor without much to show as producers of wealth on which the entire nation depends and reduced to 'benefiting' mainly from compensation for oil pollution, there has been a phenomenal increase in incidents of sabotage-related oil spill in the Niger Delta region.

By arguing that sabotage has played a significant role in recent pipeline ruptures, we do not seek to serve the agenda of petro-business in which sabotage is used as a sufficient justification for non-payment of compensation to victims of oil pollution. To do so not only blames and criminalises the victim, for the victim need not be the saboteur, but also does not promote understanding of the objective conditions that propel men to indulge in such potentially high-risk tasks of pipeline ruptures with long-term implication for destruction of the environment. If the reader comes away with the impression that environmental degradation in the Niger Delta is directly caused by oil TNCs or indirectly by oil-generated material conditions of poverty, then an aspect of the aim of this chapter would have been achieved.

The rest of this paper is in four parts. In the first part, we examine the Niger Delta people and their environment. Particular attention is paid to the pre-oil state of their environment. A section follows this on the crisis of environmental degradation in the Delta. The third part seeks to highlight the dynamics of the interconnectedness between human rights violation and environmental degradation and in the fourth and final part; some reflection and conclusions are drawn.

The Niger Delta people and their environment

The Niger Delta has been a victim of avoidable problems imposed upon it by the Nigerian state and its oil partners, most appropriately described as an 'outlaw oil industry' (Clark et al., 1999: 23). One such avoidable problem created for it by the state is the very definition of what constitutes the Niger Delta. Understood during the colonial and early post-colonial periods to be more or less conterminous with the administrative divisions of Ahoada, Brass, Degema, Opobo, Ogoni, Western Ijaw and Warri, which are in the current three minority states of Rivers, Bayelsa, and Delta, its definition has now been made quite elastic to incorporate nine states; just about any state with the smallest quantity of oil. This politicisation of interpretation of the Niger Delta is attributable to the ascendancy of oil as Nigeria's chief revenue earner and the desire by States to be classified as 'oil-producing states', bearing in mind the implication this has for revenue allocation (ERM, 1997: 7).

But the fact remains that the externalities of exploration and exploitation activities of oil TNCs impact more on the peoples and environment of the six core states of the Niger Delta: Rivers, Bayelsa, Delta, Akwa Ibom, Edo and Cross River. Not accidentally, the struggle for environmental, land and resource rights and the conflict generated by this have been more pronounced among the people of these states. For our analysis, the Niger Delta shall be restricted to these states.

Located in the southern part of Nigeria, the region is 'inhabited by some 1600 long settled communities' (SPDC 1999). It is Africa's largest and the World's third largest mangrove forest, 'the most extensive fresh water swamp forest in West and Central Africa and most of Nigeria's remaining primary forest concentration of high biodiversity and centres of endemism' (ERM, 1997; SPDC, 1999). Apart from this rich natural resource base, the region is home to 20 billion of Africa's proven 66 billion barrels of oil reserves and gas reserves of more than three trillion cubic metres (ERM, 1997: 196).

Primarily fisherfolk and farmers, the Niger Delta people, until the discovery and exploitation of oil in 1956 and 1958 respectively, exploited the resources of nature from their land, water and forest to meet their needs. Owabukereyule (2000: 6) citing records of the Federal Office of Statistics, notes that as at 1985, crop farming and fishing accounted for all forms of economic activities by indigenous peoples of the Niger Delta region. In exploiting nature, however, this was done in an environmentally sustainable manner, a fact Owugah (2000: 108), attributes to their awareness of 'the critical position of the environment to their sustenance and that of future generations'. Largely rural, they sourced their drinkable and domestic water from unpolluted streams and rainwater that posed no health hazards. To this day, the rural folks of the Niger Delta, lacking piped-borne water, still meet their water needs largely from the same sources. The quality of such water now cannot be said to be the same, what with the wide-scale pollution by the oil industry. The ecological devastation occasioned by the activities of oil exploration and exploitation have meant that TNCs have rendered their land, water and forest useless. This has adversely affected resource flows and livelihoods. Okorobia (1999), citing the Niger Delta Basin and rural Development Authority (NDBDA) sources, observed that there has been a progressive decline in fishing yields. Beyond their livelihoods, the very lives of the inhabitants are at issue, given the critical link between the natural environment and human survival. To appreciate how awful things have become, an account of the onslaught unleashed on the Niger Delta environment and peoples by the oil TNCs in collaboration with the Nigerian state will facilitate our exposition.

The crises of environmental degradation in the Niger Delta

Ever since the discovery of oil in Oloibiri in 1956, it can be argued that the Niger Delta environment has known no respite. Though apologists of *petro-business* often capitalise on the paucity of scientific studies to obfuscate the reality of extraction of oil on the Niger Delta peoples and their environment, there is a growing consensus among scholars, international rights NGOs and observers that the activities of oil TNCs have adversely affected the environment of the Niger Delta (Isichei and Standford, 1976; World Bank, 1995; Ibeanu, 1997, 2002/2003; Human Rights Watch, 1999; Clark et al., 1999; Owugah, 2000). Indeed, given the recklessness of oil TNCs in the Delta, even the most casual observer would come to the inescapable conclusion that their activities are a threat to lives and livelihoods. In a recent report, the UNDP (2004) for instance, notes that 'oil exploration in the southern most riverine areas of the country has resulted in severe damage to lakes, rivers, groundwater, soils, plants, animals, forest and fisheries of the region'.

To be sure, the activities of oil TNCs in the region do not conform to international standards. Until recently, petroleum exploration and exploitation activities were not preceded by Environmental Impact Assessments (EIAs). And with a 'rentier' state, that is, a state dependent on the collection of rents and royalties from foreign firms as its major source of revenues, hamstrung by its overwhelming involvement in the petroleum sector, it is no accident that the environmentally harmful practices of oil TNCs could at best be condoned or at worst be left unchallenged.

At the root of the mismanagement of the environment by big oil and the state is the modernist/positivist perception of the environment as 'something external to be exploited for present needs' (Ibeanu, 2002/2003). This perception, essentially of colonial origin still dominates the thinking of big business and the state in the exploitation of the resources of the Niger Delta region, several years after formal termination of colonialism (Agbonifo, undated; Ibeanu, 2002/2003). Our appreciation of the crises of environmental degradation would be enhanced if we examine the specific manifestations of the phenomenon in the Niger Delta.

Oil-generated environmental problems begin from the exploratory phase of petroleum development. The exploratory phase entails the boring of 3–6 m holes for the seismogelite explosive shots (Sagay, 2001). In detonating the dynamite, its particles are not only introduced to the soil with adverse effects on soil quality but the blast may actually scare away animals, making hunting less rewarding.

As earlier mentioned, because environmental and social considerations rarely figure in the calculus of big oil pursuits, causeways and canals constructed to facilitate their operations 'affect the hydrology of the seasonally flooded fresh water swamps and brackish water of the mangrove forest [...] killing off crops, destroying fishing grounds and damaging drinking water supplies' (HRW, 1999:7). Ibeanu (2002/2003:40) citing Mitee (1997), points out two incidents in this regard:

> Shell constructed a narrow road through the Ogoni town of Dere to link its oil well. This completely destroyed the drainage system of the town, leading to severe flooding. To date, the community is still seeking compensation for thirty-nine years of suffering. In Gbaran, Shell also constructed a road to link its installations with a major road from Yenagoa to Mbiama. As a result, water flows to a large section of timberland was cut off and 1,000 acres of forest simply atrophied and died.
>
> Apart from such forest destruction and biodiversity loss is effluent discharge and disposal of untreated waste into the land, air and water of the Niger Delta. According to Ibeanu (2002/2003) drill cuttings, drill muds and fluids composed of barides and bentonite clays are known for their stunting effects on the growth of plants. When they seep into water, aquatic life becomes endangered. The dumping of untreated drilling and refinery waste, which contain toxic chemicals, leads to land, water and air pollution. As well, brime from oilfields contaminates water and renders it unfit for human consumption. Dumping of toxic, non-biodegradable by-products of oil processing, hurts, not only livelihoods but lives as well. Cadmium, mercury and lead, contained in refinery effluents, at some high concentrations are known to be responsible for some metabolic malfunctions in humans. Yet, these are not isolated cases – they are routinely released into the environment of the Niger Delta with every recklessness and impunity.

Further, oil spill has become a regular feature of the extractive activities of oil TNCs in the Niger Delta. In 1996, Ake (cited in Owugah, 2000), had put the annual average of major oil spills in the old Rivers and Delta States at 300. Towards the close of that decade and by the beginning of the twenty first century, that figure had proved a gross underestimation. The number of incidents attributed to sabotage for the year 2001 was as high as 900 (*The Tide* 21 July 2001). Da Costa (2001) reports that Shell alone accounted for over

200,000 barrels of crude oil spilled into the Niger Delta environment for the five years preceding 2001.

When spills occur, farmlands, forests and bodies of water are rendered useless. To make matters worse, clean-up operations are unduly delayed either as a result of insensitivity of oil companies or by community people who may prevent company operatives from gaining access to the scene of the incidence presumably to allow for more spills so as to earn more compensation. At Aleibiri, Ibeanu (2002/2003) reports that a spill which occurred on 18 March 1997 was not attended to until 6 months later, when youths numbering about 10,000 had to stage a protest. In January 1998, a Mobil offshore facility ruptured and released over 40 barrels of oil into the marine environment of the Niger Delta. This attracted over 1,000,000 claims for compensation from individuals and communities. Out of this, Mobil accepted only 106,000 claims, restricting its liability to oil producing communities, whereas by the very nature of marine pollution, the spills were taken to distant, non-oil producing communities.

Even more damaging to lives and livelihoods of the Niger Delta is the gas flaring. Though it appears economically rational to flare gas as a result of a mild penalty that this practice attracts, its long-term destructive consequences on the lives, livelihoods and property of the region's inhabitants are simply ignored by the state and oil companies. It should be mentioned that gas flaring is prohibited or reduced to environmentally less harmful levels in the home countries of oil TNCs that operate in the Niger Delta and even in some Third World countries. As Table 1 below shows, Nigeria has the unenviable distinction of being the nation that flares more gas than any other in the world.

Until the Nigeria Liquefied Natural Gas began the processing and marketing of gas in 1999, Nigeria flared 95 per cent of its associated gas. Some of these flare sites are located just about 100 metres away from homes and they have been burning for 24 hours for over 40 years. Ibeanu (2003) reports that in 1983 alone, the Anglo-Dutch oil giant, Shell, flared over 483 million cubic metres of gas from its oil wells at temperatures up to 1,400 degrees centigrade.

Table 1: Percentage of gas flared by some gas and oil producing countries

Country	*Percentage*
Nigeria	76 per cent
Saudi Arabia	20 per cent
Iran	19 per cent
Mexico	5 per cent
Britain	4.3 per cent
Algeria	4 per cent
Ex –USSR	1.5 per cent
USA	0.6 per cent
The Netherlands	0 per cent

Source: Sagay (2001)

Though its full, destructive extent on the Niger Delta people and environment has not been determined, a report prepared by a US non-governmental delegation on a field trip to the Niger Delta concludes that its impact on 'the local ecology and climate, as well as people's health and property is evident' (Clark, et al., 1999: 5). Acid rain, which is a direct consequence of gas flaring, the report adds:

> [It] not only deprives people of drinkable rainwater and stunts crop growth (as we found in Eket and other communities in Akwa Ibom State) it is also affecting people's homes. In Iko, Eket and Etagbabiri, we were told that zinc roofs, which formerly lasted 7 – 10 years (and were a good alternative to labour-intensive thatched roofing), are now destroyed within one or two years by acid rain. This has led many homeowners to resort to asbestos roofing, which although more resistant to acid rain, is also hazardous to health.

Apart from gas flaring, another dangerous feature of the operations of the oil TNCs lies in pipelines. Pipelines are old and they criss-cross the landscape of the Niger Delta. In some cases, they are laid in front of people's homes without regard to the fact that a pipeline could explode and occasion harm, not only to lives but to the environment as well. The resultant fire from pipelines that exploded in Jesse Town in October 1998 left in its trail the destruction of a whole community and death of its inhabitants.

But what is the implication of the above account on the human rights of the Niger Delta people? It is to this we now turn.

Human rights violation and environmental degradation: the dynamic of their interconnectedness

Though in theory, and by the United Nations' 1948 *Universal Declaration of Human Rights*, human rights are indivisible and interdependent, at the level of praxis there has been a general tendency by Western nations and even international rights groups to accord the Economic, Social and Cultural Rights (ESCR) a second class status, paying more attention to the classic civil and political rights. Indeed, in their 1993 World Conference on Human Rights in Vienna, Western nations agreed that all the rights in the Universal Declaration are indivisible and interdependent. In spite of the acceptance of the indivisibility and interdependence of human rights, Lobe (2002), observes that 'Washington has tended to treat ESC rights as privileges [rather] than core rights'.

However, if developments in the past few years are any guide, it can be reasonably argued that there has been a shift in focus, in particular, to the environment, which is pivotal to human survival. Thus international and environmental law experts, meeting under the auspices of the United Nations Development Programme and the United Nations High Commission for Human Rights, in January 2002, took the position that 'environmental protection constitutes a precondition for the effective enjoyment of human rights and that human rights and the environment are inter-dependent and interrelated' (Earthjustice 2002:1).

Yet, whether environmental rights should be given separate, codified status in national and international legal instruments remains a subject of intense scholarly contestation. Anderson (1996) cited in Diaz (2000), for instance, argues that existing rights protected under international instruments and domestic constitutions, if sufficiently mobilised could provide a basis for environmental protection and that to create new, specific, environmental rights would be 'superfluous and at best, counterproductive'. Diaz (2000), while conceding that such a mobilisation of existing rights may help, points out that they may fall short in meeting this end.

Against the background of a flagrant abuse of environmental rights in the Third World by big business and the state, it may be imperative to insist on the need for specific legal norms which directly relate to the environment. After all, these countries are signatories to the relevant international conventions and covenants, yet little regard is paid to the environment in their business arrangements with big business. Perhaps an examination of the interconnectedness of environmental and human rights abuse may strengthen the point being made.

Nigeria is signatory to the African Charter on Human and Peoples' Rights. Articles 16 and 24 of the African Charter recognise the 'right to health' and the 'right to a healthy environment' respectively. As alluded to above, ecological devastation occasioned by the activities of oil exploration and exploitation of TNCs has brought about land degradation, fertility loss, fisheries depletion, biodiversity loss, and slow and steady death by poisoning of the region's inhabitants through contamination of air, food and water sources.

Although it serves the agenda of petro-business to dismiss the health consequences of their ecologically unfriendly practices to humans as 'exaggerated', pointing out the lack of 'independent research' (Harmon 1997) a report to the Dyfed-Powys Health Authority of Wales on the effects of the Sea Empress Oil Spill of 16 February – 16 March, 1996, on the health of the population of Pembrokeshire, is quite insightful. These symptoms include headache, nausea, sore eyes, runny nose, cough, itching skin, shortness of breath, with twenty-one percent of exposed persons experiencing weakness and twenty-three percent feeling generally ill.

If the health of the inhabitants of Pembrokeshire, whose drinkable water sources may not have been affected, was so adversely affected by a single incident of oil spill, then the case of the inhabitants of the Niger Delta, who have mainly depended on routinely polluted water sources for over 40 years, may be better imagined. Ekpo, cited in Sagay (2001) reports that about 180 people were reported dead, two months after the 'Funiwa 5' blowout of 1980, which was the first major recorded oil spill in the Niger Delta.

Further, the 'right to land and natural resources' of the Niger Delta people has been grossly violated by petroleum development policies and practices. Although land and resource rights of indigenous people are not part of the fundamental human rights contained in the Nigerian constitution, there is a growing consensus among experts on human rights and international environmental law that 'the right of indigenous people to control their land and natural resources' should be adopted by nations as a substantive environmental human right. This right is contained in Article 14 of the 1994 Geneva Draft Declaration of Principles on Human Rights and the Environment produced by a group of experts on human rights and international environmental law and was immediately added as an annex by the UN Special Rapporteur on Human Rights in her report (Diaz, 2000). Besides, Article 21 of the 1981 African Charter on Human and People's Rights, to which Nigeria is a signatory, recognises that 'all peoples shall freely dispose of their wealth and natural resources' and that such rights should be exercised in the 'exclusive interest of the people' (Shelton, 2002).

Even if such recognition has never been formally provided for in Nigerian constitutions, it can be inferred that the enjoyment of such rights was implied in the revenue allocation formulae that guaranteed, for the wealth-producing regions, a substantial amount of their wealth during the colonial and early post-independent periods. However, the ascendancy of crude oil, found in the minority states of the Niger Delta region as the nation's main revenue earner, brought about a progressive deprivation of the Niger Delta people of their land and natural resource rights.

Elsewhere I have argued that the ascendancy of the Niger Delta oil as the life-blood of the Nigerian economy occasioned a formalisation by the Nigerian state of the deprivation of indigenous people of their right to land and natural resources (Aaron, 2003).

As it relates to the Niger Delta people, there are two aspects to land and resource rights deprivation. First, the Nigerian state, usually controlled by people from the majority ethnic groups, has, through various obnoxious laws and policies expropriated the land and resource rights of the Niger Delta people. Indeed, it can be argued that this was not only made a state policy through the 1978 Land Use Act (Decree no. 6 of 1978) which vests land ownership on the state but was actually written into the various post-independence constitutions in which the Niger Delta people were either unrepresented or under-represented in the processes of constitution making as a result of their minority status. Thus, Article 40 (3) of the 1979 Constitution; Article 42 (3) of the 1989 Constitution; Article 47(3) 1995 Constitution provide that 'all minerals, mineral oils and natural gas are the property of the Federal Government'. The current Constitution is even more brazen in its deprivation of rights to indigenous people. According to it: 'The entire property in, and control of all mineral oils and natural gas in, under or upon any land in Nigeria or the territorial water and the exclusive economic zone of Nigeria shall vest in the government of the Federation'.

Further, the recent Supreme Court ruling on resource control which deprives the oil-producing states of benefits from off-shore oil has made an already bad situation worse. Thus, while the deprivation of the Niger Delta people appears immoral, it is at least, legal.

Second, the oil transnationals, through the ecological devastation attendant with oil exploration and exploitation activities, have rendered the land of the Niger Delta people unproductive (Human Rights Watch, 1999; Owugah, 2000; ERM, 1997). Gas flaring, in which, as noted, Nigeria occupies the unenviable position of being the number one country in the world, is believed to have a negative impact on species composition of vegetation (Isichei and Stanford, 1976). Thus, it could be argued that the unsustainable use of land and natural resources of the Niger Delta has rendered their land useless. At this point, our exposition may be enhanced if the dynamics of oil in Nigeria's political economy is examined.

Since the production of oil in 1958, when it accounted for only 1 per cent of national revenue, to date oil has contributed several billions of dollars to Nigeria's foreign exchange earnings. Tamuno (1999:11), citing *Time* sources, put the figure earned during 1974 – 1999 at about $300 billion. The July/August edition of the National Agenda (1995) reports that in 1990–1993 alone, Nigeria earned at least $199.3 billion. Today, oil and gas resources from the Niger Delta account for over 85 per cent of the nation's GDP, over 95 per cent of foreign exchange earnings, over 90 per cent of the national budget and 80 per cent of the nation's wealth (Owugah, 2000; Tamuno, 1999: 32; Obadan, 1996: 59; Countrywatch,www.countrywatch.com/cw-topic). It is with the oil, and lately gas resources of the Niger Delta, that important national projects have been executed, including the third mainland bridge in Lagos, the building of a new federal Capital Territory, the construction of a 38 billion Nigerian Naira stadium in Abuja and others.

Paradoxically, this significant contribution to national revenue by the oil-bearing communities of the Niger Delta region has not translated to any transformation of the region. The words contained in the Willinks Commission report of 1958, set up to look into the fears of the minority ethnic groups that 'The Niger Delta is poor, backward and neglected', remain the fitting description of the state of the Niger Delta except to add that the ecological devastation unleashed on the region is life-threatening (I-IDEA, 2000; Ibeanu, 1997; World Bank, 1995).

Largely shut out of the nerve-centres of power, where important decisions concerning their oil wealth and well-being are taken as a result of their minority status, and deprived of any tangible benefits as producers of wealth, the Niger Delta people feel marginalised and alienated from their vast oil and gas resources. Indeed, the Niger Delta represents the greatest paradox of all time: the region produces the wealth of the nation but it remains the most neglected region in the country. On some critical indicators of well-being, the region lags quite behind (1-IDEA 2000:50).

How did the region get to this state of affairs? At independence in 1960, Nigeria ran a three-region federal structure dominated by the majority ethnic groups of the Hausa/Fulani, the Ibos and the Yorubas in the North, East and West respectively. The North produced groundnuts and cotton, the West, cocoa and rubber and the East, palm oil. A principle of *derivation*, in which the resource-producing regions retained 50 per cent of their earnings, was adopted as the basis for revenue allocation.

However, the advent of crude oil found in the minority region of the Niger Delta as the nation's major revenue earner changed all that, as derivation as a revenue allocation formula witnessed a progressive decline from 100 per cent (1953), 50 per cent (1960), 45 per cent (under Gowon in 1970), 20 per cent (under Murtala who was assassinated, and his immediate successor, Obasanjo, in 1975), 2 per cent (under Shagari in 1982), 1.5 per cent (under Buhari in 1989) to 3 per cent (under Babangida). Recently, the 13 per cent Constitutional provision has been implemented by the Obasanjo administration. Even so, there is widespread allegation that through the application of offshore/onshore dichotomy, the states actually receive 7.5 per cent, and not the 13 per cent constitutional provision.

Aware of these injustices, due largely to the consciousness-raising activities of NGOs, environmental rights activists, youth, and opinion leaders, the people of the region have expressed their protest in various forms, including seizures of oil company workers, vandalisation of oil equipment and killings of security operatives. As Ifeka (2001) notes: 'Frustrated by the exclusion from the benefits of the oil economy, militant youths attack oil installations. These angry subalterns believe that their communities own and should take control of the natural resources in their vicinity'.

Recently, in what coincided with the nation's forty-fourth independence anniversary, a militant Niger Delta group which has been fighting for self-determination and control of resources by the Niger Delta region threatened to blow up oil installations in the region on October 1, 2004. Most incidents of petroleum pipeline vandalisation can be contextualised as a struggle to re-acquire their lost human rights.

But how does this struggle to reacquire their lost human rights lead to further environmental degradation? As pointed out earlier, there has been a phenomenal rise in incidents of petroleum pipelines rupture in recent times. Most of such incidents are attributed to sabotage. The Anglo/Dutch oil giant, Shell, for instance, reported that 60 percent and 80 percent of its incidents of oil spills was caused by sabotage for the years 1996 and 1997 respectively (HRW, 1999: 82). In 1999, the company attributed 50 percent of its incidents of oil spill to sabotage (SPDC 1999), while in the year 2000, 40 percent, still a significant proportion, was accounted for through the same reason (SPDC 2000).

Industry-wide statistics indicate that in 1999, 542 incidents of pipeline rupture were recorded, out of which 497 were confirmed by the joint inspection team to be clear cases of vandalisation. During the first six months of 2000, 400 incidents were reported. Based on this figure, the Pipelines and Product Marketing Company, a subsidiary of the state-owned oil company, projected that by the end of that year, 764 cases of pipelins vandalisation may be recorded. This was to be a gross underestimation: about 900 cases of pipeline vandalisation were reported by the end of the year (*The Tide*, July 26, 2001, pp.1 and 2). Without doubt, this is quite a sharp contrast from earlier patterns of pipeline rupture – between 1976 – 1996, the oil industry in Nigeria recorded a total of 4,835 incidents of pipeline rupture which resulted in the spillage of approximately 2,446,332 barrels of crude oil out of which about 1,896,930 were lost to the environment. Out of this 4,835 incidents, only four percent was attributed to sabotage, other factors being blowouts, equipment failure and corrosion.

The official explanation is that petroleum pipeline vandalisation is the handiwork of criminals, usually indigenous contractors and local chiefs who expect to be awarded clean-up contracts, or the evil machinations of detractors determined to derail the democratic project in Nigeria. Such explanations are not only simplistic but they serve the agenda of government and petro-business. They not only criminalise and blame the victim, but they also foreclose the possibility of alternative interpretation of the motive behind the acts. Without doubt, criminals may have carried out some incidents of pipeline vandalisation, but accepting crime as a major, or the only, explanatory variable conceals more than it reveals. For instance, it conceals the fact that clean-up contracts in the Niger Delta are rarely awarded to natives. Further, even if the Niger Delta contractors and chiefs were to be held culpable for sabotage, the explanation does not help us to understand why they suddenly came to the realisation that such criminal acts are necessary for pecuniary benefits. Also, the Niger Delta people were the worst victims of state terror during the dark days of suffocating military authoritarianism. It therefore becomes difficult to understand why they would easily offer themselves as willing disciples of anti-democratic forces, determined to derail Nigeria's nascent democracy, however imperfect it may have been.

Contrary to the official explanations, I insist that petroleum pipeline vandalisation should be contextualised as an aspect of the struggle to re-acquire a lost human right: 'the right of indigenous people to control their land and natural resources' – a right the Niger Delta people have been brutally deprived of by the Nigerian state and oil transnationals. Since they cannot find redress in the legal system, and against a background of institutionalised deprivation, the people have resorted to 'benefiting' from 'source' what they cannot get under the existing legal and revenue allocation formulae. Thus, it is now usual for communities not only to delay reporting incidents of pipeline rupture but also to prevent oil company officials from gaining access to the scene of pipeline ruptures. This is done, ostensibly to allow for more oil to spill, since the more the spill the higher the amount of expected compensation. The Ekakpamre oil spill of 17 September 1999 and the Otuegbe oil spill of 2 October 1998 as reported by Shell bear out our explanation.

In what appears to support our argument, Okoko (1994) cited in a study by the Environmental Resources Managers (ERM 1997), *The Niger Delta Environmental Survey* (1997) reports that:

> In some cases, there is a correlation between disturbances and sabotage-induced spills: certain communities which recorded a disproportionately high number of disturbances within a specific time period, equally recorded a disproportionately high volume of oil spilled. A correlation between disturbances and the allocation of community assistance projects is also noted; communities where there were disturbances were often rewarded with the provision of community assistance projects. Many oil companies responded to community requests only after violent confrontation.

Sadly, this pattern does not appear to be changing. Most recently, the Isaka community in the Niger Delta region has been given a generating plant by the Nigeria Liquified Natural Gas, following the rupture of a gas pipeline in that community. The inference to be drawn from the above is that pushed by the stark reality of poverty and institutionalised deprivation occasioned by state policy and environmentally unfriendly activities of oil TNCs and pulled by expected 'benefits' from compensation for oil spill, some people in the Niger Delta in their bid to re-acquire their lost land and resource rights may sometimes be complicit in or condone the activities of people that may lead to pipeline rupture.

Thus, the struggle to re-acquire their lost human rights brought about in the first place by environmental degradation by the activities of oil TNCs leads to further environmental degradation. The reality then is that the environment of the Niger Delta remains the common victim – a victim, in the first instance, of despoilation from the externalities of oil exploitation and a victim, in the second instance, of the survival concerns of a brutally deprived people whose desperation sometimes leads to further environmental degradation. This vicious circle of environmental degradation may be represented in Figure 1:

Figure 1. Vicious circle of environmental degradation in the Niger Delta

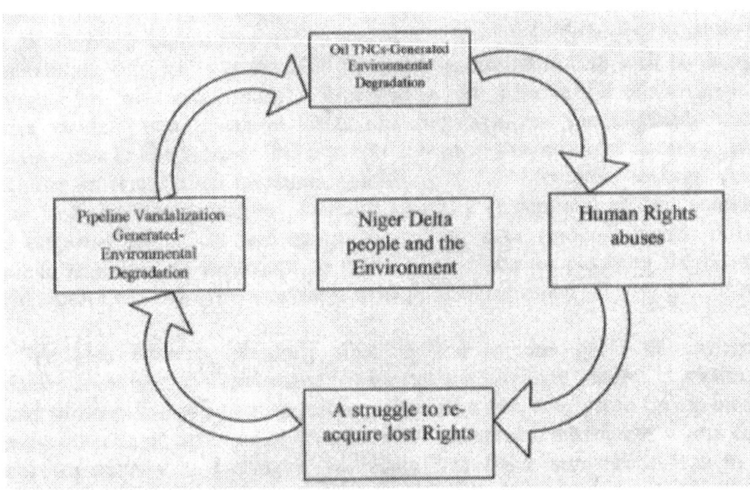

This brings into clearer relief the emerging consensus that human rights abuses lead to environmental degradation and environmental degradation leads to human rights abuses (Ksentini, cited in Diaz, 2000).

Reflections and conclusions

Over the past 40 years, state policy and ecologically unfriendly activities of oil TNCs have greatly violated the human rights of the inhabitants of the Niger Delta region of Nigeria, in particular the 'right to health', 'right to a healthy environment' and the 'right to the natural resources of indigenous peoples' recognised by some international legal instruments to which Nigeria is a signatory. Due mainly to the interdependent, interrelated and indivisible nature of human rights, such violations have negative implications for the enjoyment of the right to life, livelihood, housing, peace and development of the region's inhabitants.

We observed however that civil society groups, environmentalists and scholars neglect the critical link between institutionalised deprivation and poverty of the Niger Delta people occasioned by state policy and the environmentally degrading practices of oil TNCs and further environmental degradation. This study demonstrates this linkage.

We argue that the environmentally degrading practices of pipeline vandalisation, easily attributed to crime or anti-democratic elements, determined to derail Nigeria's nascent democratic project by apologists of petro-business should be seen for what it is: an aspect of a larger struggle by the Niger Delta people to regain a lost human right – 'the right of indigenous people to control their land and natural resources' – a right the Niger Delta people have been deprived of by the policies and practices of a 'rentier' state and an 'outlaw oil industry'.

While our evidence may not be conclusive, it is perfectly logical to argue that the environmentally unfriendly practice of pipeline vandalisation may well be an aspect of the struggle for 'resource control'. This conclusion is borne out of the frequency of pipeline vandalisation in recent times, the post-pipeline vandalisation reaction of community people in a manner that prevents company workers from access to scenes of the incident for remediation measures, presumably to allow for more leakage, which may translate to higher compensation. Coming against a background of the consciousness-raising activities of NGOs and environmentalists, over resource rights, it becomes difficult to separate this behaviour of some Niger Delta people from the clamour for resource control which has become most strident in recent times.

We also observe, painfully, that as this vicious circle of environmental degradation continues, the environment becomes the common victim: a victim, on the one hand, of despoilation by a rent-seeking state and an apparently mindless, profit-driven oil industry and on the other hand, by a brutally deprived and pauperised inhabitants whose desperate concerns for survival and struggle to regain lost rights sometimes lead to further environmental destruction.

The way forward for petroleum development in a people and environmentally-friendly manner is to build a community of interest among the key stake-holders – the oil-producing communities, the state and big oil. Specifically, if petroleum development policies and practices do not hurt the environment, lives and livelihoods, and if the indigenous peoples' resource rights are respected through an equitable revenue sharing formula, it would be logical to expect undisrupted petroleum production and distribution. By inextricably tying the interests of the key stakeholders, a balance could be struck between profit-seeking and respect for human and environmental rights. The realisation of such a vision necessarily calls for the deconstruction of the post-colonial state; an overcentralised state, privatised by big business and which has been unable to rise above class, personal, sectional and other special interests, is bound to make the realisation of such a vision impossible. This necessarily calls for a re-invention of the principles of federalism which were operative when Nigeria's economy was driven by resources of the majority ethnic groups.

References

Aaron, K. K., 2003, 'Human Rights Violation and Petroleum Pipelines Vandalization in the Niger Delta Region of Nigeria', *The Nigerian Social Scientist*, 6(2): 14–20.

Agbonifo, J., (undated), 'The Colonial Origin and Perpetuation of Environmental Pollution in the Post-Colonial Nigerian State'.

Brume, 2000, 'Oil pipelines Vandalization: The Wayout', paper delivered at the Annual Dinner of the National Association of Niger Delta Professionals, Bauchi, December.

Clark, H., et al., 1999, 'Oil for Nothing: Multinational Corporations, Environmental Destruction, Death and Impunity in the Niger Delta', A US non-Governmental Delegation Trip Report, 6–20, September.

Da Costa, 2001, 'Oil Pollution In Nigeria', (www.greennature.com/ articles 266.htm\) accessed 25.01.2003.

Diaz, A., 2000, 'Human Rights, Environment and Development: With Special Emphasis on Corporate Accountability', Human Development Report 2000 Background paper, (www.undp.org/ hdro/hdrs/2000/English/Dias2000.html) accessed 25.01.2003.

Douglas, O., Kemedi, V., Okonta, I. and Watts, M., 2003, 'Alienation and Militancy in the Niger Delta: A Response to CSIS on Petroleum, Politics and Democracy in Nigeria', *Foreign Policy in Focus Special Report*, 1 July.

Earthjustice, 2002, 'Human Rights and the Environment: Developments – Issue Paper for the Fifty-Eight Session of the United Nations Commission on Human Rights', Geneva 18 March – 26 April.

Environmental Resources Management, 1997, *Niger Delta Environmental Survey Phase 1, Report*, (Lagos: ERM).

Environmental Rights Action/Friends of the Earth Nigeria, 2000, 'The Emperor Has No Clothes', Report of the proceedings of the conference on the peoples of the Niger Delta and the 1999 Constitution, held in Port Harcourt 2–4 November, 1999, (Benin: ERA/FoEN).

Harmon, Z., 1997, 'World Bank, Big Oil and the Niger Delta', (http.www.waado.org/Environment/Oil Companies/World Bank-Bigoil.html) accessed 11.03.2003.

Human Rights Watch, 1999, *The Price Of Oil: Corporate Responsibility and Human Rights Violations in Nigeria's Oil Producing Communities*, (New York: Human Rights Watch).

Ibeanu, O., 1997, 'Oil, Conflict and security in Rural Nigeria: Issues in the Ogoni Crisis,' African Association of Political Science, *Occasional Paper Series*, 1 (2), Harare.

——, 2002/2003, 'Democracy, Environment and Security in Nigeria: Reflections on Environment and Governance in the Post-military Era', *Annals of the Social Science Academy of Nigeria*, 14 & 15 December 2002/2003: 35–48.

Ifeka, C., 2001, 'Oil, NGOs and youths: struggles for resource control in the Niger Delta', *Review of African Political Economy*, 87: 99–140.

Ihonvbere, J. O., 1994, *The Politics of Adjustment and Democracy*, (New Brunswick, N.J.: Transactions Publications).

I-IDEA, 2000, *Democracy In Nigeria*, Continuing Dialogue(s) for Nation-Building, Capacity Building Series 10, Stockholm.

Isichei A. O. and Stanford W. W., 1976, 'The Effect of Waste Gas Flares on Surrounding Vegetation of South Eastern Nigeria', *Journal of Applied Ecology*, 13.

Lobe, J. 2002, 'People versus Big Oil. Rights of Nigerian Indigenous People Recognized', (www.africaaction.org/docs02/nig0207a. htm) accessed 01.03.2003.

National Agenda, Lagos, July/August 1995.

Obadan, M., 1996, The Nigerian Economy and the External Sector, *CASS Occasional Monograph*, No. 8, (Lagos: Malthouse Press).

Okorobia, A. M., 1999, 'A History of the Underdevelopment of the Eastern Niger Delta, AD 1500–1993,' PhD dissertation, Department of History, (Port Harcourt: University of Port Harcourt).

Owabukereyele, W. S., 2000, 'Hydrocarbon Exploitation, Environmental Degradation and Poverty in the Niger Delta Region of Nigeria', paper presented at the Lund University, Lumes Programme, Lund, Sweden.

Owugah, L., 2000, 'The Political Economy Of Resistance in the Niger Delta', in Environmental Rights Action/Friends of the Earth Nigeria, 2000, 'The Emperor Has No Clothes', Report of the proceedings of the conference on the peoples of the Niger Delta and the 1999 Constitution, held in Port Harcourt 2–4 November, 1999, (Benin: ERA/FoEN).

Sagay, I., 2001, 'The Extraction Industry in the Niger Delta and the Limits of International Law,' ANPEZ Centre for Environment and Development Annual Lecture, 15 November, Port Harcourt, Nigeria.

Shelton, D., 2002, 'Human Rights and the Environment: Jurisprudence of Human Rights Bodies', *Background Paper No. 2*, Joint UNEP-OHCHR Expert Seminar on Human Rights and the Environment, 14–16 January, Geneva, (www.unhchr.ch/environment/bp4.html) accessed 01.03.2003.

SPDC, 1999, *People and the Environment Annual Report.*

——, 2000, *People and the Environmental Annual Report.*

Tamuno, T., 1999, 'The Niger Delta Question', A public lecture organised by the Rivers State College of Arts and Science and the Rivers State University of Science and Technology, Port Harcourt, 30 September.

The Guardian, 3 October 2004.

The Tide, 26 July 2001.

Thisday 12 July 2001.

UNDP, 2004,' Challenges of Poverty Reduction and Environmental Sustainability in Nigeria', *The Guardian*, 23 August.

World Bank, 1995, 'Defining an Environmental Strategy for the Niger Delta', Volume 1.

Part IV
Activating Particular Rights

GERARD GOGGIN AND CHRISTOPHER NEWELL

Reclaiming Civility: Disability, Diversity and Human Rights

> Fear of difference is an infantile disorder. It is common in kindergartens. However, it survives and flourishes long thereafter. Diversity is threatening to people who suffer from this disorder. They like things packaged in a safe, familiar presentation. This is so whether the challenge of difference comes because the other has a different skin colour, an unusual religion, a distinct sexuality different from the majority, sits in a wheelchair, or manifests some other genetic disability or difference [...]
>
> Justice Michael Kirby (2005)

> We have made some legitimate gains in terms of physical access but the real problem is yet to be fully addressed. Negative attitudes towards people with disabilities are rife in the community. If we are to achieve any sense of true emancipation, we must fight attitudinal barriers to equal participation in all aspects of community life. Nothing is really going to change until we do [...] Our lives are governed by legislation. Carers refuse to handle our bodies without the protection of latex [...] our bodies remain the property of those who lift, dress and wipe. Women with disabilities continue to be sterilised and when we do reproduce, over one third of our children are removed from our care. Quite often, our pregnancies are terminated against our will. We are raped by institutional staff and yet forbidden to engage in consensual sex. Our finances are managed and our lifestyles are regulated by duty of care.
>
> Kathleen Ball (2001)

> Disability is perhaps the area in which the importance of recognizing the indivisibility and interdependence of human rights and fundamental freedoms, as both [the International Covenant on Civil and Political Rights and the International Covenant on Economic, Social and Cultural Rights] do, is most evident and sharp.
>
> United Nations (2004)

At the borders of citizenship

On Monday 2 April, 2001, Shahraz Kiane[1] set himself alight in front of Parliament House, Canberra, Australia. On 26 May 2001, nearly three months later, Kiane died in Concord Hospital, Sydney, of massive infection and an acute abdominal problem due to extensive burns to most of his body. According to available sources, including a report by the Australian Commonwealth Ombudsman (2001), Kiane set himself alight himself because of his utter frustration with an unsuccessful five-year struggle to bring his wife and three daughters to Australia. The prime reason why the Australian government would not grant his application was because one of the daughters, Anum Shahraz Kiane, had a disability.

Mr Kiane had travelled to Australia alone, and was accepted as a refugee by the Department of Immigration and Multicultural Affairs (DIMA) and granted a Protection Visa on 21 October 1996. A Pakistani, he applied for the visa on the basis of persecution from religious leaders arising out of his support and friendship with Ahmadis in his country. At that time, his application included his family: his wife, Ms Talat Yasmin and their three children, Asma, Anum and Afia. This was declined and in March 1998, Kiane made a different application for his family to join him, this time under the newly created 'split family' provisions. In July 1999 the application was refused by the decision maker because the middle daughter, Anum, did not satisfy, nor were they prepared to waive, the 'health criterion'. The decision hinged on an opinion from the Medical Officer of the Commonwealth, which stated that one of the children, eight-year-old Anum, failed to meet the health requirements due to a range of medical problems including cerebral palsy, which would be too costly.

When the case was finally raised with the Ombudsman, he issued a highly critical draft report. Yasmin lodged her new application on 14 September 2000. After three followup inquiries by the Ombudsman, the Department advised on 29 March 2001 that 'there was a problem with Ms Yasmin's application as the projected health care costs had increased' (Commonwealth Ombudsman, 2001: 17). Three days later Kiane made his own tragic protest to the officials concerned.

Nearly three and a half years later, the Australian Federal Department of Family and Community Services published its annual calendar to coincide with the International Human Rights Day. For the cover of the calendar, it chose a photo of Rophin Morris, a twelve-year-old boy with autism. Rophin has lived with his family in Canberra since they emigrated to Australia a decade earlier. The family's application for permanent residency was rejected by the government because of Rophin's disability (Guerrera & Tomazin, 2004: 10).

The question of migration and refugee policy are matters of fierce contemporary debate and go to the very deepest issues about how we define citizenship – whom we value and embrace as a member of our community, whom we reject or cast out, and how we make the decisions and impose our values. Disability is deeply other, and people with disabilities are very often marginalised, discriminated against, impoverished, and excluded. The worth of our very existence is routinely called into question in contemporary conceptions of bio-technology, ethics, health, and science. Despite the gravity of the situation of hundreds of millions of people with disabilities around the world, they are not often considered under the banner of human rights. Unfortunately this is the case with migration also, something very much controlled by domestic governments concerned to safeguard national sovereignty, and the situation of refugees, in which the interplay of international and national governance is highlighted.

In this chapter we seek to redress this situation and make a case for the importance of activating the particular rights of people with disabilities as something that enlarges our general conceptions of human rights. First, we note some of the features of disability, and explain the importance of understanding its social, cultural and political nature. Second, we briefly theorise disability and human rights, critiquing rights discourse which seeks to individualise and pathologise those who are its subjects, we discuss how disability has featured in international human rights instruments and examine the development of an International Convention on the Protection and Promotion of the Rights and Dignity of Persons with Disabilities ('the disability convention'). Finally, we broaden our focus beyond the legal arena and point the need for a comprehensive approach to the activation of human rights for people with disabilities.

Becoming disabled

When we think about disability, we realise it is ever present, yet largely hidden from our social gaze. We write this piece with a deep awareness of the ever-pressing nature of disability found in two recent world events.

In the first place, the largely unremarked creation of disability via the invasion of Iraq – which has not just occasioned much killing, but an age-old different dimension of terrorism, the creation of disability amongst those who are outside of our moral community. A rare exception is found in the images of Ali Ismail Abbas, a twelve-year-old Iraq boy, who was gravely wounded by a US bomb, with loss of both arms, and burns (sixteen of his family members were killed in the bombing). His predicament was given wide coverage in Western media, with his shocking injuries shown widely in television footage and press coverage: 'Ali's agony puts human face to suffering of war' (*Sydney Morning Herald*, 12 April, 2003); 'Limbless Iraqi boy offered help' (9 April 2003). The *London Evening Standard*, which launched an appeal with the Red Cross, and a number of other papers, to raise money for victims of war in Iraq, called this image the, 'picture that will stay with us […] the image that refuses to leave the retina no matter how many times you blink, is of 12-year-old Ali Ismaeel Abba' (Pearson, 2003).

Abbas was eventually airlifted by the US to Kuwait for surgery, and all of the benefits of high-quality Western medicine and hospital care. In many respects, the focus on this boy saw disability utilised as a political tool. For the most part, audiences around the world were disturbed at his injuries, and comforted that this person, who became an exemplary individual, received treatment. There are profoundly ethical questions regarding the circulation and avid consumption of such images of people with disabilities – going to the heart of questions of cultural representation – that we would wish to note here. Yet the ongoing creation of disability amongst the tens of thousands of civilians and military, mostly Iraqi, but involving the coalition also, was not fundamentally addressed in the same movement, if at all. The treatment of this human being partakes of the narrative of the benevolence of the West towards its others; but also of the deeply rooted narrative of benevolence of society towards the deserving pathetic poor, among which disability is particularly constituted (see Jones, 2003).

An interesting juxtaposition with this situation, made by human beings, is found in the late December 2004 tsunami, which devastated many Asian-Pacific nations, especially Indonesia, Thailand and Sri Lanka. Yet there is a sense in which this colossal earthquake and tidal wave swept over the entire Western world, as many of us, immune to the daily statistics of death and suffering in the non-Western, identified strongly with the appalling loss of human life here – in large part, we would suggest, because of the way that the media told the tale, focussing on the heroic stories of many westerners or narrating that story in ways which touched our sensibilities. What is not being told is the emerging, colossal nature of impairment, which has been created. The impairment has been not just created through the tsunami; but through the underlying social conditions of these countries. For instance, the lack of readily available food, water, infrastructure, health care, ways of supporting people through mental and physical trauma and distress.

Disability is largely hidden in the narration of world events. Despite the fact that one in five of the global population is identified by UN agencies as in some way having disability, the sheer numbers by themselves do not foster a social demand for understanding the social reasons for why so many people develop impairments, and the structural and political dimensions to disability. Largely constituted in popular culture as 'special needs' and in accordance with physically obvious stereotypes, despite hidden impairment being far more common than people in wheelchairs, disability is even hidden in the identification and counting of population groups. Given this situation, we should hardly be surprised that disability is hidden in the enactment of human rights.

After all, disability for most is known as an objective fact – you are either disabled or not disabled – a fixed life sentence, a catastrophe, or even tragedy, which in similar ways to an ancient Greek tragedy remorselessly works its way through our lives, influencing their every aspect. Yet disability is a tragedy that does not culminate in any grand conclusion. It is just an ongoing tragedy, without a denouement. It makes sense, then, that we commonly refer to the death of a person with multiple disabilities as a 'merciful passing' or 'blessing'. The tragedy we know of as disability is defined as medical fact: from the diagnosis of disability at the pre-embryo implantation or pre-natal stage, identification of disability in children, early adult acquisition of disability through accidents, right through to the onset of a variety of disabilities later in the life cycle. We 'know' if a person has disability because this is commonly felt to be their defining attribute, with medical discourse closely defining our lives. Very often we refer to people as 'quadriplegics', 'diabetics', 'deaf', 'mute', a 'dwarf', or as a 'Down's syndrome'. As an individual tragedy disability is located in the person who is its bearer. He or she is subject to a life sentence of suffering pain, discomfort and loss of functioning. As the word 'disability' suggests, a person with disability is the opposite of someone with 'ability'. To be a person with disability is to deviate from the 'normal': to be a deviant who needs to be helped and managed.

This dominant 'medical' model of disability as biological certainty, individual pathology, deficit and loss to be diagnosed and managed by modern medicine, is challenged by new social, cultural, and political approaches. For example, British theorists of the 'social model' of disability propose a distinction between 'impairment' and 'disability'. Impairment is the bodily dimension, whereas disability is what society makes of someone's impairment. Disability is not 'natural' or 'given'; rather, it is the social processing, relations and meanings attaching to the impaired body and mind. Disability is no more an unarguable biological 'fact' than is gender or race; in fact, disability interacts intimately with the categories gender, race, ethnicity, class and sexuality, being integrally involved in the production of these social 'facts' and power structures.

From various standpoints, including poststructuralist and feminist theory, the critique of the social model has explored its limits in both social constructionist and historical materialist variants (among many discussions see Corker and Thomas 2000). Lived embodiment of impairment, and the stubborn and painful ways in which reasserts its challenges to its symbolization in language and society, is a leitmotif in much theory. Our own position seeks to acknowledge the sociopolitical nature of disability, as does the social model, but also to move beyond this to incorporate accounts of cultural, ethical and spiritual dimensions also (accordingly, we draw on theorists such as Snyder, Brueggemann & Garland-Thomson, 2002; Meekosha, 2003).

Within disability studies and the disability movement, many have sought to draw upon notions of human rights and a rights discourse. Arguably the pre-eminent organisation of, and for, people with disabilities at an international level is Disabled Peoples' International, formed because people with disabilities did not have an adequate voice in the global organisation Rehabilitation International, dominated by nondisabled providers. In so many areas, DPI and linked national organisations across the globe affirm the pre-eminent message of the disability rights movement 'nothing about us without us', with these organisations formed to provide 'a voice of our own' (Driedger, 1989). Such organisations have sought to introduce the perspectives of people with disabilities across the wide diversity of domains in which human rights are discussed or activated – for instance, across the areas nominated in the Universal Declaration, such as housing, the right to found a family. A number of scholars have also sought to theorise disability in terms of human rights (for example, Armstrong & Barton, 1999; Basser & Jones, 2002).

Sadly there has had largely been a disconnection between the academic and activist accounts of disability and human rights. In part this reflects the disadvantage experienced by people with impairments in gaining access to education. Yet there is an emerging theorisation that highlights the difficulties, complexities, and especially the challenges for international law.

In the process of activating the human rights of people with disability in this way, there have been difficult challenges posed to dominant understanding of 'human', 'rights', and 'human rights'. This in a world where disability is regarded as inhuman, subhuman, or second-class, even amongst those who consider themselves liberal, progressive, and well-educated. Christopher, for example, often finds a disturbed reaction when speaking about disability at human rights conferences. The explicit and tacit message seems to be in accordance with the dominant views of disability: 'better off dead than disabled', 'thank god I don't have a disability', 'disability is about the other rather than us'. Yet, the message of disability activists found in the text of their arguments, and in the sub-texts of our bodies and minds, is not only that disability is part of diversity but it can be positive, sexy, dare we suggest, desirable to live with impairment. Deaf people who are a socio-linguistic minority utilising sign language as their first language find it beautiful to be deaf, and indeed do not see themselves as having disability or loss. Yet, those of us in the dominant hearing world desperately want to sanitise their genes and lives, or seek a technological cure found in a variety of artefacts. From the cochlear implant through to genetic diagnosis, and even the routine use of genetic knowledge in ways that need to be properly understood as eugenic, society is routinely engaged in denying the full dignity of so many we identify as having disability. Paradoxically in the name of rights, therapy and, of course, the over-riding discourses of health and care. Of course, we feel so much better when we talk about and do unto the deviant lives and bodies of those that routinely disquiet, disgust, profoundly disturb our comfortable notions of what it is to be human, and a right to a very narrow, non-disabled future.

We also recognise that human rights organisations talk about disability, and have a disability component, but for the most part, disability is not central to their activities. Much of the work of human rights organisations is based predominantly around the thematic conventions such as the International Covenant on Civil and Political Rights and the International Covenant on Economic, Social and Cultural Rights. Hence the importance of establishing a thematic convention on disability.[2] In addition it is rare to find such organisations employing people who live with impairment and are part of the disability rights movement in leadership positions. Too often people with disability are clients rather than experts on their own lives. As this book goes to press, the globally reaching UK-based organization Disability Advocacy in Action (DAA) has been forced to close, not able to attract funding for its work on disability and human rights. Yet we suspect that if its aims were in terms of fostering a miracle cure, and in accordance with medical and charitable discourse, the situation would be very different.

Activating disability in international human rights

A critical social and cultural understanding is important for understanding the development of international practice and law on activating the human rights of people with disabilities. Article 25 of the 1948 Universal Declaration of Human Rights states that each person has 'the right to security in the event of unemployment, sickness, disability, widowhood, old age or other lack of livelihood in circumstances beyond his control'. The Universal Declaration was consolidated with the development of two key human rights instruments, the 1966 International Covenant on Civil and Political Rights and the International Covenant on Economic, Social and Cultural Rights. However, the six core human rights treaties of the UN, that include these three treaties, were 'drafted without regard to disability', according to the UN Special Rapporteur on Disability, Bengt Lindqvist.[3] The three instruments are referred to as the Universal Bill of Human Rights.

In 1971, the General Assembly proclaimed the Declaration on the Rights of Mentally Retarded Persons. In December 1975 it adopted the Declaration on the Rights of Disabled Persons, which states that all persons with disabilities are entitled to the rights stipulated, without respect to race, colour, sex, language, religion, political or other opinions, national or social origin, state of wealth, birth or any other situation (UN, 2004). The culmination of decades of work, which initially started with a welfare paradigm, heavily focussed on rehabilitation and prevention of disability, occurred with the International Year of Disabled Persons in 1981. In 1982 the General Assembly adopted the World Programme of Action concerning Disabled Persons, revolving around three areas: prevention; rehabilitation; and equalization of opportunities (UN, 2004). Later that year it made recommendations on the implementation of the World Programme, and proclaimed 1983–1992 the United Nations Decade of Disabled Persons.

The International Year of Disabled Persons, the Decade of Disabled Persons, and the World Programme of Action were important steps in advancing the rights of people with disabilities. This international articulation of the importance of human rights did provide a persuasive framework for national governments to consider their role. Progress was slow, however. In 1987, midway through the International Decade, the Secretary-General issued a report finding that 'much progress has been made in increasing awareness on the significance of disability and its human consequences, but that much more needs to be done' (UN, 2004).

In 1992, the General Assembly appealed to governments to observe 3 December of each year as the International Day of Disabled Persons. In 1993, the Standard Rules on the Equalization of Opportunities for Persons with Disabilities were adopted by the General Assembly. The rules included a monitoring mechanism to support their implementation, and the appointment of a Special Rapporteur (Bengt Lindqvist 1994–2003; Hessa Al-Thani from 2003) who would establish a direct dialogue between member states, local non-governmental organizations and other intergovernmental bodies in order to implement the Standard Rules. In the same year the World Conference on Human Rights reconsidered universally recognized human rights instruments in light of contemporary issues and adopts the Vienna Declaration and Programme of Action. The Conference recognized that 'all human rights and fundamental freedoms are universal, and thus should unreservedly include persons with disabilities' (UN, 2004). In 1994, the Committee on Economic, Social and Cultural Rights took a significant, revisionist step in assuming the responsibility for disability rights.

> The Covenant does not refer explicitly to persons with disabilities. Nevertheless, the Universal Declaration of Human Rights recognizes that all human beings are born free and equal in dignity and rights and, since the Covenant's provisions apply fully to all members of society, persons with disabilities are clearly entitled to the full range of rights recognized in the Covenant. In addition, in so far as special treatment is necessary, States parties are required to take appropriate measures, to the maximum extent of their available resources, to enable such persons to seek to overcome any disadvantages, in terms of the enjoyment of the rights specified in the Covenant, flowing from their disability. Moreover, the requirement contained in article 2 of the Covenant that the rights 'enunciated will be exercised without discrimination of any kind' based on certain specified grounds 'or other status' clearly applies to discrimination on the grounds of disability. (General Comment No. 5, cited in UN, 2001, chapter 2)

The task of incorporating disability into the international human rights framework has been a protracted one. Work is now well underway on an International Convention on the Protection and Promotion of the Rights and Dignity of Persons with Disabilities. The idea of a convention gathered momentum since 2000 with its advocacy by a number of international disability organisations (Lindqvist, 2002, section 66). It was Mexico that proposed a draft resolution that was adopted on 19 December 2001. However, some governments have been slow to recognise the importance of such a convention.

As this book goes to press it is apparent that there has been significant developments in development of a meaningful convention, which now really has potential to make a positive difference. Yet, despite this we remain deeply concerned at the various aspects of the lives of people will remain untouched. In particular those aspects seen by powerful and especially transnational interests as costing too much or being unreasonable. A good case study was found in a recent disability meeting where we were talking about the convention and its location in New York. Christopher remarked that of course he could never have participated as his pre-existing conditions prevent him getting adequate health insurance cover, something which is legal in a variety of jurisdictions including Australia, where there is actuarial data supporting this. A significant discussion followed as to the various ways people with disabilities get around, evade or just lie about their conditions in order to gain cover. Much as we would like this situation to change we doubt that in his lifetime the UN Convention on Disability will mean Christopher can gain access to affordable health travel insurance in order to travel to the US without risk of inadequate access to health care. A significant proportion of the developing world does not have access to adequate health care as it is, and it will require a significant re-examination of the structural nature of disability in order for this situation to change. We would also suggest that while a positive dimension of the Convention work may well be to foster leadership in the UN by people with disabilities, leading to social change via opportunities for relationships with people with disability, it seems likely that those without stereotypical disability or who are regarded as too expensive to support are less likely to participate in such developments. A significant outcome may well be a furthering of the stratification already occurring whereby some people with impairments do better than others in society.

Disability rights: lost in translation?

We have sketched the trajectory of disability in the international human rights framework, especially as represented by the United Nations. We point out that genuine incorporation of disability into international human rights instruments has been slow and piecemeal, however that there is a significant 'twin-track' approach (Lindqvist) emerging that has the potential to marshal the resources of general human rights agreements and protocols as well as a specific disability rights Convention. To explore what guidance international consensus and standards might offer, we briefly return to our Australian case study of refugees with disabilities.

Throughout the Western world, a significant response by legislators to some of the experience of otherness felt by a variety of marginalised population groupings has been found in anti-discrimination legislation and an invocation of rights. In more recent years there has been a trend towards specific legislation tackling the incidence of disability. In the United States there was the *Americans with Disabilities Act* 1989; in Australia there has been the *Disability Discrimination Act* 1992 (Cth), as well as state legislation in the form of equal opportunity laws commonly outlawing discrimination on the ground of disability; and in the United Kingdom, the *Disability Discrimination Act* in 1995.

The Australian legislation provides a good case study in how such legislation actually can be significantly disabling, in addition to the clear ways in which it can enable and outlaw particular forms of discrimination. In the peroration to his second reading speech, then Minister for Health, Housing and Community Services, the Hon. Brian Howe declared: 'Our vision is a fairer Australia where people with disabilities are regarded as equals, with the same rights as all other citizens, with recourse to systems that redress any infringements of their rights [...]' (Howe, 1992).

In Australia the definition of disability used in the *Disability Discrimination Act* is quite extensive, though exclusions apply to key aspects of the lives of Australians with disabilities including migration, social security and insurance (where there are actuarial tables in existence to support discrimination). More than ten years since the *Disability Discrimination Act* came into effect, there is evidence of its positive role (HREOC, 2003).

However, there is also a marked lack of real change too. Many people with disabilities have difficulty actually being able to afford to use the legislation, especially since a constitutional challenge which resulted in a requirement for cases to be heard in the Federal Court rather than in the relatively more affordable, informal and flexible setting of a Commission hearing. There has been a slow and uneven process of developing and setting standards for non-discriminatory treatment of people with disability, due to weak provisions in the legislation but also lack of action and leadership by businesses, service providers, government agencies, and civil society actors themselves.

A major obstacle to activating human rights in Australia and elsewhere, and disability as part of this, is the caution, indifference, or outright hostility of national governments. Since 1996, Australia has had a conservative Liberal and National Party coalition government at the federal level (though it has had the somewhat more social democratic Labor party holding power in a number of state governments). In the September 2004 federal election, the Conservatives were re-elected for a further term of office.

The Liberal/National party coalition has steadily undermined, wound back, delayed or weakened specific human rights legislation, as well as much legislation, policy, and initiatives conducive to achieving human rights. It has been especially unsupportive of the lead national institution, the Human Rights and Equal Opportunity Commission. In the disability area, the government has refused to appoint a permanent commissioner since inaugural Disability Discrimination Commissioner, Elizabeth Hastings retired in 1997. More recently, the government has made an attempt to curtail the powers of HREOC to initiate action on instances of discrimination – a blatant attempt to diminish the independence of the Commission as the agency that would challenge discrimination.

Despite its continuing marginalization and downgrading, HREOC has persisted in championing human rights. An important recent area where it sought to exercise its powers was in the controversial area of detention of aslyum-seekers. This matter has been of great national significance, pivotal as it was to the government's re-election in 2001 and 2004. It is also of international importance, as repressive policies towards refugees have been gathering momentum around the world.

The Federal Human Rights and Equal Opportunity Commission (HREOC) conducted a National Inquiry into Children in Immigration Detention. The final report of the Commission's Inquiry was tabled in Parliament in mid-May 2004. In the report, HREOC found that Australian immigration detention laws 'create a detention system that is fundamentally inconsistent with the Convention on the Rights of the Child (CRC)' (HREOC, 2004: 5). One of HREOC's main findings directly related to disability discrimination

> At various times between 1999 and 2002, children in immigration detention were not in a position to fully enjoy the following rights: [...] (c) the right of children with disabilities to 'enjoy a full and decent life, in conditions which

ensure dignity, promote self-reliance and facilitate the child's active participation in the community' (CRC, article 23(1)) (HREOC, 2004: 6).

The HREOC Inquiry makes a strong case that Australia's treatment of children with disabilities in detention centres is a flagrant breach of human rights conventions and standards.

In the case of the Australian government at present, however, there is a threshold difficulty. Previously proud of its contribution to international human rights instruments and their monitoring, and also the development of the League of Nations and its successor in the United Nations, the present Australian government has been almost alone in the world in its slavish support for the exceptionalist position – not least in providing moral and material support for the United States. On a number of crucial resolutions, quite indefensible positions taken by US have been supported by one or two countries, most consistent of which has been Australia (we are not referring here to treaty body reform, which whilst formally started by Australia, among others, is now widely supported). Australia now reserves its right to choose what international agreements and bodies it will support, and has been openly critical of many existing and projected human rights initiatives. Indeed, Australia has been reluctant to extend even the most minimal protections to its own citizens overseas whose human rights have been abused, as in the case of two Australian citizens, David Hicks and Mamdouh Habib, held in the infamous facility at Guantanamo Bay.

In this context, it comes as no surprise that the Australian government simply rejected HREOC's invocation of the Convention on the Rights of Children as grounds for criticising abuses of the human rights of refugees with disability. The Australian government, like its US counterpart, now routinely rejects attempts by international bodies to suggest that they may be in breach of international obligations, let alone enforce international instruments. Depending on its final form, the international Disability Convention is likely to offer a much clearer framework on what constitute human rights for people with disabilities. Also it should provide much more unequivocal guidance for national governments and their citizens on what is and is not acceptable behaviour and policies. It will remain to be seen what national governments do with such a Convention. At the very least it promises to be a powerful tool for human rights activists. Just as the Convention has been contested in its international formulation, it will most certainly be contested in its various national and regional instantiations and incarnations (not be mention difficulties binding governments which contend with federalist systems).

Are people with disabilities human?

In our opening quote above, Michael Kirby, an internationally renowned jurist, reminds us of the fear of difference. We would contend that fear at the national and international level of law has yet to be addressed adequately. For people with disabilities, the exemptions and non-disabled accounts of what is reasonable in such law and legal decisions stand as a devastating commentary on the inadequacies of international human rights.

In 1993, the General Assembly of the United Nations recognised that '[i]n all societies of the world there are still obstacles preventing persons with disabilities from exercising their rights and freedoms and making it difficult for them to participate fully in the activities of their societies. (Resolution 48/96 of 20 December 1993, annex paragraph 15; cited in Lindqvist, 2002). While there have been many important improvements in the lives of people with disabilities over the intervening decade or so, we believe that the situation is still dire. The lack of real and widespread change is due not just to 'obstacles' that need to be removed, but to fundamental and deeply-cherished beliefs and ways of life relating to disability, deep social, cultural dimensions of everyday life.

Baden Offord has written eloquently about whether homosexuals are human, posing a question which many wish remained unuttered. Baden's conclusion is that 'homosexuals are human and that therefore homosexual rights are human rights'. 'Homosexuals', he reminds us, 'are human beings, after all' (Offord, 2003). In a shared spirit of inquiry and activism, we also wish to ask: 'Are people with disabilities human?'

This query seems to us a reasonable and apposite one, in face of the signs everywhere that many in our society, especially the powerful, regard people with disabilities as less than human – as subhuman. The policies and actions of the present Australian government, and those of many other governments and opposition parties around the world, as well as those of the still powerful institutions and influential actors regarding disability show many signs of being inexpressibly inhumane.

We too wish to emphatically declare that people with disability are human beings, after all. At a notional level, we hope most people – especially those professing a concern for human rights – would agree. So, if we have consensus on this point, how and why do we as a society continue to treat people with disability as subhuman? And how can we challenge such dehumanisation, and activate human rights of and for people with disabilities?

A central answer lies in the realization that a vision of an all-encompassing civil society rests upon a fundamental ethical question: who are the members of our moral community and whom do we routinely exclude? In our own country, those who live with disability are still not adequately represented in society – rarely to be found in leadership positions, in our cultural life (in performing arts, film, and television, for instance), and remain near invisible in prestigious posts in our schools or universities, government departments, and businesses. There is much evidence to suggest that the situation of people with disabilities in most other countries is similar.

Sadly this creation and perpetuation of disability as 'otherness' is even perpetuated in accounts of diversity and human rights, where disability is an awkward postscript. Human rights practitioners and institutions have a long way to go, we would suggest, before the rights of people with disabilities are accorded the respect and protection they deserve.

Yet not only are people with disability some of the most disadvantaged citizens, but in a whole range of ethical, political, social, economic and spiritual debates they provide an important litmus test as to whether or not we have a vision and a plan for a truly civil society – one which truly embraces diversity and where social policy lives out human rights. Rather than seeing disability as inherently uncivil, uncivilising and deeply distressing, we need to encounter disability as an inevitable, normal, and indeed positive part of the diversity of society to be celebrated.

In every aspect of society, the situation of people with disabilities provides us with a significant challenge to understand our lived values and even to dare to ask: how can we embrace people with disabilities as part of the human rights movement, of a just and civil society in general? The ethical and political challenge facing us all is not whether we should embrace people with disability within a vision of a civil society, but rather if in our social institutions, day-to-day ethics and human rights agenda we dare to do so.

Endnotes

1 Shahraz's surname is spelt in two different ways, Kayani and Kiane, and we use the latter unless quoting from other sources.

2 Our thanks to Rosemary Kayess for this point, and other helpful comments on this paper.

3 The official history of the United Nations and disabled persons is at (http://www.un.org/esa/socdev/enable/history.htm). The focal point for information on the United Nations and persons with disability is (http://www.un.org/esa/socdev/enable/index.html).

References

Al-Thani, H., 2004, 'Report of the Special Rapporteur on Disability to the 42nd Session of the Commission for Social Development', 4–13 February, (www.un.org/esa/socdev/enable/srcsocd42.htm) accessed 16.12.2004.

Armstrong, F. and Barton L. (Eds.), 1999, *Disability, human rights and education: cross-cultural perspectives*, (Milton Keynes: Open University Press).

Ball, K., 2001, 'We don't live in our homes, we live in our carers' workplace', *Link Magazine*, 10(4): 14.

Basser, L. A. and Jones M., 2002, 'The Disability Discrimination Act 1992 (CTH): a three-dimensional approach to operationalising human rights', *Melbourne University Law Review*, 26(2): 254–284.

Commonwealth Ombudsman, 2001, Report on the investigation into a complaint about the processing and refusal of a subclass 202 (split family) humanitarian visa application, Commonwealth Ombudsman Australia, Canberra, August, (http://www.ombudsman.gov.au/publications_information/reports_publications.htm#reports) accessed 30.06.2003.

Driedger, D., 1989, *The Last Civil Rights Movement: Disabled Peoples' International*, London: Hurst.

Guerrera, O., and Tomazin, F., 2004, 'A showcase disability family finds it is not welcome in Australia', *The Age* (Melbourne), 4 December, p. 10.

Howe, B., 1992, second reading speech on Disability Discrimination Bill, 26 May, House of Representatives, *Hansard,* (Parliament House, Canberra).

Human Rights and Equal Opportunity Commission (HREOC), 2003, *Don't judge what I can do by what you think I can't: ten years of achievements using Australia's Disability Discrimination Act*, HREOC, Sydney, (www.hreoc.gov.au/disability_rights/dont_judge.htm) accessed 30.06.2003.

——, 2004, *A last resort?: national inquiry into children in immigration detention*, (http://www.humanrights.gov.au/human_rights/children_detention_report/) accessed 30.06.2004.

Jones, S., 2003, '"Does he understand why war took place?"', *The Guardian*, 19 April, (http://www.guardian.co.uk/Iraq/Story/0,2763,939522,00.html) accessed 21.02.2005.

Kirby, M., 2005, 'Foreword', *Disability in Australia: Exposing a Social Apartheid*, (Sydney: University of NSW Press), pp. 9–12.

Lindqvist, B., 2002, 'Report of the Special Rapporteur of the Commission for Social Development on monitoring the implementation of the Standard Rules on the Equalization of Opportunities for Persons with Disabilities on his third mandate, 2000–2002', (www.un.org/esa/socdev/enable/disecn520024e1.htm) accessed 16.12.2004.

Meekosha, H., 2003, 'Communicating the Social: Discourses of disability and difference', *Australian Journal of Communication*, 3(3): 61–68.

Offord, B., 2003, *Homosexual Rights as Human Rights: Activism in Indonesia, Singapore and Australia*, (Berne: Peter Lang).

Snyder, S. L., Brueggemann, B. J., and Garland-Thomson, R. (Eds.), 2002, *Disability Studies: Enabling the Humanities*, (New York: Press of the Modern Language Association).

Pearson, A., 2003, 'The boy fighting tears that makes us weep', *London Evening Standard*, 9 April, (http://www.thisislondon.co.uk/news/opinion/articles/4258248?source= Evening%20Standard) accessed 21.02.2005.

Thomas, C. and Corker, M., 2002, 'A Journey around the Social Model', in M. Corker and T. Shakespeare (Eds.), *Disability/Postmodernity: Embodying Disability Theory*, (London: Continuum), pp. 18–31.

United Nations, 1989, Convention on the rights of the child, United Nations, adopted 20 November 1989, (www.unhchr.ch/html/menu3/b/k2crc.htm) accessed 28.08.2004.

——, 2001, *'Let the World Know': Report of a Seminar on Human Rights and Disability*, Almåsa Conference Centre, Stockholm, November 5–9, 2000, (http://www.un.org/esa/socdev/enable/stockholmnov2000a.htm) accessed 16.12.2004.

——, 2004, 'The United Nations and Disabled Persons – The First Fifty Years', United Nations Enable, (www.un.org/esa/socdev/enable/dis50y01.htm) accessed 16.12.2004.

Chantal Nadeau

Same-sex Domestic Rights and Nationalist Politics[1]

This chapter aims at offering a theoretical reflection on the issues of identity and governance that map the queer body as a national citizen. It asks, what are the implications of queer claims for equality in terms of human rights discourses and competitive claims regarding citizenship? Taking up from debates around same-sex marital and domestic institutions in Western democracies, my paper explores how lesbigaytrans' (lgbt) struggles for inclusion and equality cannot be excluded from the recent rise in Western democracy of alliances between nationalist claims and queer rights.

In this chapter, I suggest that the contentious alliances between democracy, citizenship and queer claims for equality are framed by an important vector that intimately affects how queer bodies are perceived and constructed as either meritorious or non-meritorious citizens: blood. I argue that the politics of blood (through the redefinition of rules of filiations, family and ethnicity) has been instrumental for nations such as Québec, France and the Netherlands in their recent decision to extend rights to lgbts over other *classes* of citizens. On one hand, blood is still a powerful dispositif of belonging, either to family (filiation), a nation (via citizenship and ethnicity) or even a species over another one (human vs. beast). On the other hand, and consequently, blood is a dangerous and effective political device to screen those who are not considered part of the family, a nation or a species. As political debates and legal struggles over custody rights, citizenship and human rights constantly remind us, blood still very much defines the boundaries between inclusion and exclusion.

In the specific context of gay rights, such politics of blood are far from 'innocent'. In fact, what can we find beyond blood? As I will demonstrate further in my discussion of Bill 84, blood influences not only how rules of filiation for instance 'work' for gay and lesbian families, it also validates how a democratic nation should rule whose lgbt people should be protected and included or excluded in the national project.[2] In order to illustrate how blood circulates as sexual and nationalist politics, I focus my analysis on two specific articulations of blood and queerness: (1) the humanisation of queerness; (2) the nationalisation of lgbt sexuality.

Given the current interest and symbolism attached to marriage in the struggles for equality, it comes with little surprise than civil union and gay marriage stand as a rich nexus to interrogate the crossings between queer rights and nationalist politics. Looking at some of the arguments that have emerged indiscriminately from community activists, legal experts, and governmental representatives in regards to recent decisions granting gays and lesbians equal rights regarding family and marriage, it appears to me quite clearly that not all queers are invited to join national citizenry: only those who are recognised as socially, politically, and *sexually* responsible. Such figures, I argue, are publicly revealed as the queer family wo/man. The figure of the queer family wo/man is constructed in rupture with the dominant representations of queers as party animals or sexy beasts. Contrarily to party animal figure/gay consumer of entertainment business attached to Gay Pride Weeks, Circuit Parties, etc., the queer family wo/man who is featured regularly in campaigns for equality, gives face (a human face) to queerness. Henceforth *being recognised as human* – a phenomenon that is contingent to the domestication of the wild sexy beasts – makes the moment of citizenship possible for gays and lesbians. This moment of citizenship is both represented and understood as legal and cultural: those queers that are human/ised are not only legally recognised but also culturally accountable, making them at once full participants in the reproduction of the nation. The goal of this chapter then is to unpack the uncanny sex and rights politics of Québec Civil union in order to better understand the complexities at work between democracy, queer sexuality and nation.

My interest in these articulations of sexuality, rights and nation is tied to the ways in which queer body and governance are channelled through the intimate bonds created between the state, the family and the sexual citizen in legislation such as Bill 84. I am fascinated by the ambivalent and often ambiguous nature of the alliances between the queer lobbies and state governmentality, more specifically regarding how these intimate bonds are informed by a nationalist conception of 'community' where modalities of inclusion and exclusion constitute a mixture of ethnicism, racism and heteronormativity. Two claims will frame my argument:

(1) Gay marriage, Civil Pacts of Solidarity (PaCS), and Civil Union totally fit a neoliberal scenario that democracy is better served within the borders of the nation (same-sex marriages, civil unions are only valid within state borders);
(2) Civil union institutes the idea of community of birth over community of election/choice. In this sense, the recognition of 'human' queer is conditional to the creation of an ethnic national subject. I will pursue my discussion on this latter point.

I: Queers as humans

Over the past six years, one could feel – rightly so – that almost everything has been said, analysed, dissected, reclaimed, trashed and celebrated about same-sex marriages, civil union agreements and other claims for equality formulated by queers or on behalf of queer citizens. On one side, words such as visibility, political equality, recognition, civil liberty, virtuous inclusiveness, fair distribution of resources, humanist legacy, ethical commitment toward the tradition of liberalism, come as strong arguments for queer advocacy lobby, queer activists, critics and sympathetic theorists who seek to defend more rights for queers. On the other side of the looking glass, many theorists have condemned quite eloquently the dangers that institutions such as marriage and the army represents in normalising queers (Warner, 1999; Berlant, 1997, 2002; Hallett, 1999; Duggan, 2001, 2002, 2003), concentrating most of their argument on the trade-off, or the downsizing of democracy to quote Lisa Duggan in *The Twilight of Equality?* (2003), that these struggles have necessarily brought up in the context of queer politics.

Those who are familiar with some of the rhetoric of claims for queer rights will notice – and for those of you who are not familiar will learn – a growing desire amongst queer advocates to frame those claims in the broader context of human rights for minorities. Under such an umbrella, states and nations have the moral obligation to protect queers because while members of a (in)visible minority they also are members of the human family and the national community, the latter being in fact an important argument in the ways that we understand the concept of citizenship. In this context, because of their inclusion to the human species, queers should be granted equal – or shall I say equivalent – treatment as any other human citizen. Concretely, it means that one of the pivotal and implicit dimensions of such rhetoric is to present queers who wish to marry for instance, as elevated to a human quality on the scale of progress, and as such they should deserve the same protection as any human in a state of injury (Brown, 1995).

The new human queer adds a different spin to a fundamental liberal principle; that the citizen of democracy is sovereign and master of her/his body. The former is less driven by the urges of his/her body (an amoral trait that belongs to the non-human, the sexy beast) than by a concern for moral good, a desire to 'participate' as a responsible body in the social order that has been constructed as normal. While the most avid supporter of human good could interpret this public benevolence towards lgbts as a sign of tolerance and empathy, I argue that the human quality of queerness is only imaginable and made intelligible in contrast to the beastly side of queer and, consequently, the threat that queers as sexy beasts represent for democracy.

For sake of clarity, I will now like to make an analogy between the queer sexy beast, the queer who is amoral and politically irresponsible (in other words, whose sexuality escapes the realm of normal) and Jacques Derrida's conception of *the rogue*. Derrida in *Voyous* (2002) uses the expression rogues [trans. of *voyous*] to designate those who defy and mock the law, those who are not subjected to the nation or the state, those who are seen to embrace debauchery and lust, while occupying the streets and ruling its economy. Borrowing from eighteenth- and nineteenth-century semantic interpretations of the rogue as not quite human (Rousseau, La

Fontaine), he also casts the rogue as a beast, a werewolf, and an outlaw that troubles the sovereignty of people. In this sense, as half-human, half-beast, surreal creature, whose presence is unmistakably a threat to the safety of the nation-state, yet whose appeal is unquestionably attractive and seductive to promoters – among which we should count politicians – the queer sexy beast is also a rogue who troubles the very idea that claims for equality are necessarily about meritorious citizenship. Rogue and beast are then closely tied to rules of democratic order, including rights.[3] In this sense, in my project, the beast is not only an animal it also embodies the unknown, the threat, the evil, and the amoral. It embodies the face of the nation because the beast exposes the fact that citizenship and democracy are still to become. Animals have a long history of standing in for sexual misconduct (cross-species and same species), starting with ancient Greek and early modern regulations over sexual offences, where bestiality went hand in hand with sodomy law and the proscription of cross-racial marriages, i.e. miscegenation. In this sense, my use of the concept of *beasts to mark the unfit queer* is not arbitrary: it responds to a specific history and politics that frame beasts as 'sex offenders' and beasts as either reasonable or non-reasonable beings.

The proscriptive boundaries between human and animal were considered moral – laws against sodomy, bestiality, homosexuality, unnatural sex, etc. – and material, laws and policies implemented to protect property (private and state-based) for and against animals. Such discourses also have roots in the history of democracy as well as in liberal thought, from Aristotle to Jeremy Bentham, to Montaigne and Montesquieu. For instance, we can retrace the bonds between beasts, democracy and sexuality in the work of the British philosopher and animal-rights activist Jeremy Bentham (1748–1832), for whom questions of sodomy (pederasty) and care for animals were as pertinent as those of property in deliberating on the rules and conduct of the responsible citizen (Ryder, 2000: 71–72). All this to say that debates regarding the value and merit of 'beasts' as responsible beings and their rights for inclusion into society are troubled by questions regarding their predatory status and threat to national safety and social order. To put it differently, the queer as human is in complete rupture with the queer as beast, a figure that has much to do historically and politically with the pathologisation and criminalisation of homosexual acts as being conceived inhuman (see the constant association between bestiality and sodomy). The human queer ceases to be a sexual stranger (to quote Shane Phelan) but a member of the liberal family: a wild consumer of goods (including rights) and a tamed producer of desires. Such constructions of queer as human not only conform to what is conceived as an intelligible model of meritorious citizenry but also consolidate a regime of values within which family, monogamy, merit and labour intertwine in the recognition of a meritorious status (vs. an identity).

However, instead of seeing the sexy beast and the domesticated pet as opposition, I treat them as necessarily constitutive of the ways that our Western liberal democracies are guided by logic where equality and citizenship is only possible under the predicament of merit and calculable risk. I would like to suggest very tentatively and with extreme care that such rhetoric of equality as meritorious and virtuous inclusiveness speaks to the growing tendency in queer claims for equality to monitor the others, the outlaws, the outcasts, the sexy beast that threatens the new social contract: i.e. the *new homonormativity* (Duggan, 2002). Ultimately, the ideal responsible queer citizen is the one who legitimates a heteronormative compulsory model of sexual exchange that excludes sexual irregularities and 'unnatural (i.e. beastly) acts' such as non-monogamy, multiple partner kinship, the refusal to embrace coupledom, etc. (Butler, 2002: 6).

It is no coincidence that a great deal of intervention and lobbyist strategies have been specifically aimed at deconstructing and marginalising the image of the queer as a species of its own kind who can't in any way follow the rules of good citizenry, the party animal by excellence. The irony is, while many welcome the instrumental value of the queer beast for the consuming culture – national and global (from entertainment to tourism to fashion) – its existence is still very much seen as toxic to democratic order, especially in debates and battles for the moral and political inclusion of queers into institutions such as marriage or civil unions. In other words, doesn't the value of Western liberal democracies itself become 'outlawed'/out ruled through the queer beast? I believe that claims for queer rights cannot be understood outside an analysis that takes into account how sexual practices situated outside yet inside the state consolidation of partnership (couples and families) are subjected to control, censorship, restrictions, criminalisation, including what I called self-immunity, i.e. the control by queers of queer misbehaviours. To clarify, I wish to challenge the assumption that all rights for queers are necessarily progressive and discuss instead how queer claims over family rights and same-sex marriages can be an effective vehicle of nationalist rhetoric. Considering the recent shifts and gains in Western Europe and North America around same-sex domestic partnerships (from civil union in Québec, to Civil Pact of Solidarity, known as PaCS in France, to same-sex marriage in Holland, Belgium and now in Canada and Spain, I ask the two following questions:

(1) How do conservative and progressive views of sexual citizenship, nation, and conceptions of the human emerge within new geographies of lgbt politics?
(2) How do same-sex domestic institutions fit into a nationalist agenda? These concerns constitute my link to the second part of my discussion.

II: Civil union and the citizen within

In a conjuncture where the legalisation of gay marriage seems to monopolise the public space and to be the defining political 'it' for lgbts in North America and Europe – more so with the recent vote in June 2005 by the Canadian government to legalise marriage between same-sex partners – it might seem obsolete to discuss what other legal forms of intimacy are on offer in the debate about queer rights. I believe however, that it is necessary to dissect the genealogy of recent legalised arrangements for lg couples such as Québec's Bill 84 (L.Q. 2002, c.6) voted in 2002, in order to get a keen understanding of the strange bedfellows that exist between the state and its queer citizens in 2005. My discussion of the Civil Union in Québec (Bill 84) will be framed along the following argument: blood still haunts the strategies of recognition of specific forms of cultural belonging and democratic recognition.

On 7 June 2002, the government of Québec legally sanctioned the right for same-sex couples who are residents of the province to enter into civil unions. The new legislation, entitled appropriately *Act instituting civil unions and rules for establishing new filiation*, a.k.a. Bill 84, constituted a major reversal for a government that only six months earlier was fairly hesitant to support claims forwarded by gay and lesbian advocacy groups to extend parental rights and the recognition of filiation to same-sex domestic partners.

The result of a concerted collaboration between various same-sex advocacy groups – more importantly the all powerful Association des mères lesbiennes du Québec, the new institution of 'civil union' gave same-sex and common law partnerships the same rights and obligations under the law as heterosexual marriages, *de facto* legalising a third form of domestic partnership (after married couples, and common-law spouses). As Justice Bégin stated in his introduction to the Bill: 'People will continue to live together, but from now on, they (namely lesbian and gay couples) will be able to do so legally, with all the love that they have for each other, particularly towards children'. While the usual suspects are included, such as health insurance, a new tax status, and rights to benefits after dissolution of the union or death (inheritance and access to family heritage), the most interesting and surprising element of the Bill is in fact the inclusion of the thus far contentious issue of filiation, an issue that has direct consequences for gay adoption and queer parental rights – including second-parent adoption. Ironically, filiation was a provision that was excluded in earlier laws extending rights to same-sex couples (such as Bill 32, passed in 1999 by the same government, and earlier drafts of Bill 84), and only the restless pressure of the Lesbian Mother Association of Montreal and the Gay and Lesbian Coalition, both strong supporters of Parti Québécois and its nationalist agenda, made this filiation provision possible. For the first time in its history (though not in Canada, since Nova Scotia had already passed a similar bill the same year), the Québec government had specified the conditions under which 'rules of filiation' apply to same-sex partners, providing an official response to how queer filiation works before the state and the court. As Justice Bégin explained in the preamble to the law: 'The civil union is a way of giving equal rights to all the children of Québec' (Chouinard, 2002: 15). Hence, the civil union fulfils two goals: providing the official means by which equality for queers may take a legitimate and socially recognisable form; and maintaining filiation at the core of state's survival.

The desire to clarify how queer filiation works before the state while creating a third category of intimacy indicates the extent to which sexual regulation continues to be central, not only to the production and reproduction of citizens, queer or otherwise (as Butler, Foucault, and A. M. Smith have suggested), but also to the needs of a productive nation. Within the framework of civil union (and I could easily say same-sex marriage), the human queer is entitled to recognition and responsibility like any other citizen of the nation, yet that very status of human queer is contingent to coupling and family (Stychin, 1998).

The culture and market of status and entitlement that Bill 84 provides for same-sex domestic partnerships provokes major questions about the very nature of the ties between the state, sexuality and who gets to be invited into citizen-land. As Elizabeth Povinelli reminds us, this is an ongoing debate for democracies, particularly when it comes to retrace the kinship rules and social status that contracting members hold. As she rightly puts the question: 'Who should be included and excluded from the ranks of blood and money, property and inheritance, love and affection, and sex?' (Povinelli, 2002: 219) To be really suspicious of the growing attention paid by the state to queer rights, I would argue that as to who should be included, what should matter here is: first, the constitution of a new class of citizens legally fit and economically valued in the production of national wealth (families and couples); and second, the regulation and close monitoring of those who persist to be wild, the non-meritorious citizens, the sexy beasts who disturb the liberal society, yet whose presence is vital for establishing the paradigms of desirable bodies. Here, again blood is central not only because it feeds kinship rules (even through porous lines), but more importantly because it still stands as the main screening (discriminatory?) factor to set citizenship status.

Let me be clear here. Same-sex marriage, PaCS, civil union, *like heterosexual marriage* are all legitimated by the state on the very principle that they contract any two individuals unrelated by blood, regardless of sexual orientation. This is even more ironic given the fact that historically, blood has been the stigma that has kept queers from being ruled and included into civil society. My claim is that, because it challenges the boundaries between sex and status, filiation stands as a political and social strategy espoused by both the state and lgbt couples in order to reassert the centrality of legal forms of domestic love and intimacy in the construction of the national body. At the intersection of sexuality, the nation and the queer citizen, filiation entrenches two complementary forms of 'transmissible' social status: firstly, the entitlement for lgbt to the status of 'couple', to that of a democratic family, and secondly, the recognition of a sexual intimacy that until now has fallen outside the realm of democratic marriage. In other words, legislation that favours filiation reshapes the sexual borders of the national community through the reinvention of blood relationships that reduce queer identities to questions of value and exchange. These blood relationships are not necessarily biologically informed, but are nevertheless tied to the entitlement of a social class of citizens who are socially constituted by their consent to inclusion in existing structures of family and national community.

When Québec voted for the civil union in 2002, it spelled out the first time the conditions under which 'rules of filiation' apply to same-sex partners and queer families. What I find interesting and compelling in the civil union is the fact that one of the most vigorous arguments raised by right conservative lobbies and advocates to keep queer couples from being recognised as spouses before the state – the famous issue of reproductive sex – was finally addressed and answered in the very preamble of the law. In other words, filiation as defined by Bill 84 thwarts the traditional biological predicament because it extends parental rights to non blood-related spouses. Yet, it is grounded into status since it is contingent to family ruling and property provisions. To put it another way, the civil union is reconnecting with a seventeenth century understanding of heredity as matter of entitlement and status.

As Michael McKeon (1995) explains in 'Historicizing Patriarchy: The Emergence of Gender Difference in England, 1660–1760', before heredity came to signify bloodlines, genetic purity and the institutional process of managing legal descent (or lineage) in the nineteenth century (more precisely in the 1820s in France), it was strictly a matter of economic status, an entitlement to power through status conferred through property or 'titles'. The transformation of heredity into a matter of bloodlines at the turn of the century by policymakers, reformers, social scientists, and medical authorities naturalised what was once understood as an economic status into an exclusively biological trait. Hence, the hereditarily 'fit' citizen came to dominate the public sphere and liberal discourse at the turn of the nineteenth century.

While today our common legal and cultural references to filiation are still shaped by a nineteenth-century biological construction of heredity, we are now witnessing a tendency in gay and lesbian discourses around family rights to make blood less a question of biological essence than a matter of entitlement to filiation and inheritance (i.e. access to property). Through the civil union, blood now stands for *le sang-loi, the blood that forces the law* through claims of equivalent citizenship. The blood that forces the law is the same blood that extends rights and access to the polity for the queer citizen. It is a blood that makes noise, one that advocates for laws, privileges and responsibilities to constitute the new rules of filiation. It is a blood that allows for the constant measurement, monitoring, and self-monitoring of the good will, the good health and the good faith of those who embrace the status, values and norms that continue to inform the prominent model of good citizenry. It is a blood that excludes the rogue, the beast, the non-meritorious citizen; it is blood that constructs queer citizenship over and within the sex wars that marked the 1990s for lgbts. It is a blood that maintains a moral and quasi-evolutionist (species) classification; and under this ruling of national blood, not everyone can receive a visa to good citizen-land: only those who belong to the human species. But which kind of human queer can come for the Q of Québec? In this culture of 'civilized union', naturalist and hygienic considerations (the self-regulation of sexual practices) establish which queer becomes the desirable citizen. In this way, sexuality comes to be intimately constituted as a definite marker of responsibility, recognition and self-regulation: responsibility towards the distribution of 'domestic' resources; recognition of new sets of blood ties that are not necessarily biologically defined, yet that are socially normalised, regulation of misfit behaviour that could jeopardise the state of the union and the status of the queer citizens.

However, what makes me the most anxious before this circus to normalise the queer blood type (and I have hinted to it a couple of times since the beginning of my discussion) is the ways that queer groups and lobbies also participate in this (blood) screening. For instance, when queer American columnists (Rotello, Sullivan) or conservative, queer organisations adopt a right-wing moralist rhetoric that goes nowhere, such as monogamy = clean blood, public sex = tainted blood, it is easy for me to roll my eyes. However, the discourse carries a different weight when the outcry comes from a group like ACT-UP who in its press release posted on Advocate.com (13 October, 2003) vilifies the myth of the sexual outlaw among gay men for being responsible for the rise of unsafe practices in the gay community across the states. While there is a clear need to worry about the incidence of unsafe sex on the ongoing spread of HIV/AIDS, by reducing the sexual outlaw to a reckless sex perpetrator, ACT-UP completely obliterates the cultural importance of the politics of sexual outlaw for queers in the history of democratic battles.

Many see in the gesture toward 'homo/queer' inclusiveness (if not assimilation) in Western democracies as a way of revamping a naturalised heteronormative model. Yet, beyond the comfort of a new homonormativity, I believe that what must be challenged and questioned are the pernicious outcomes of this citizenship economy where dubious patriotism and questionable display of ethnocentrism expose the contentious links between blood and nationalism. When Equal Marriage, a private advocacy forum, reminds us constantly about the tradition of tolerance, diversity and inclusiveness of the Canadian people, one has to wonder if what is actually the issue is giving face to the Nation or giving face to queer rights. While this latter example seems extreme, the tendency to nationalise queer struggles for equality is certainly a disturbing reality amongst the various lobby groups active in Western democracies.

I concur with Lauren Berlant (1997) when she argues that what drives a declining democracy made ostensibly vulnerable by the supposed 'threat' of migration waves, is the deep (and mistaken) belief that citizenship ultimately comes down to a matter of private rights shared by members of the same association and protected under one nation (a position that was put forward by the late Dutch gay politician Pim Fortuyn, yet disturbingly recycled by the gay America global corporation gay.com in the weeks following the murder of this 'admirable politician and queer hero'). [4] This conception of citizenship as bound to the creation of a community of blood is primarily shaped by the *privilege* of entitlement to specific rights: the rights that are reserved exclusively for members of the family/community, for those who are already members of the – national – wedding (Berlant, 1997). The growing desire expressed by so many gays and lesbians to become blood sisters and blood brothers (as fellow citizens) only magnifies how much historically blood has been a troublesome site for queers: traditionally as a marker of shame (in relation to psychological and pathological diseases, and recently regarding prohibitions over fit blood donors), and now as a foundation to rethink questions of lineage, inheritance and recognition.

If in my chapter I have addressed mostly the relationships between democracy, citizenship and rights in terms of meritorious couple and family queers, I also believe that those relationships by far exceed the comfort of 'domestic' intimacies. For instance, we need to scrutinise how pro-gay legislation fits in a political and cultural system that seeks to control and police reproduction rights for women while extending family rights to its meritorious couples and families. For the former it means new and intrusive rules to screen the private and public access to abortion (if the US comes first, Québec is also guilty by making it more and more difficult for women to access 'therapeutic' abortions), for the latter it runs from increasing tax breaks for assisted technologies of reproduction to a wide range of legislation that accommodate dual parental leaves, state intervention in day care system, etc. Yet more importantly, I am interested in understanding how same-sex rights discourses tell us about access for citizens and non-citizens to local and global mobility and how they affect the constitution of another salient form of domestic environment: the nation. In this sense, the debate of same-sex legislation and policies shares in many instances a disturbing commonality with that of immigration and the mobility of population and desirable bodies. This issue becomes increasingly alarming knowing how a significant number of countries that extend similar rights to same-sex couples and families (France, Australia, Great Britain, Germany, US, Canada, The Netherlands) have restricted policies towards desirable immigrants and residents' mobility.

Further, if we consider that in Québec, The Netherlands and France for instance, the queer lobby has historically made alliances with nationalist ethnicist political parties, the collusion and trading of rights between the state and its queer citizens is problematic because at the very core, it does allow progressive and conservative views to frolic happily in the same waters in the name of national preservation. It is from this contested terrain that the recent decision by the Supreme Court of Canada on 9 December 2004 to rule that same-sex couples are discriminated under the Federal Marriage Act should be understood. We need to move beyond the apparent progressive anti-discrimination argument and the politics of inclusion, and to situate such 'breakthrough' into a more complex process of assessing who gets to be citizen of the nation, a process where issues and values such as sexual morality and ethnic cohesion are always already encrypted with normativity and a sense of entitlement for those who somehow manage to fit in and perpetuate a system of equality based on the meritorious value of its citizens.

Endnotes

1 The ideas expressed in this paper matured within the following venues: the Canadian Association for American Studies 'Contention and Authenticity' Conference in Winnipeg, Manitoba, 17–19 October 2003, as well as a Public Guest Lecture delivered for *Rules: A Speaker Series in Communication, Culture and Law* sponsored and hosted by the School of Journalism and Communication/Department of Law, Carleton University, Ottawa, 23 February 2004. The author wishes to extend her gratitude to the organisers of these two

events Dr. David Churchill and Dr. Sheryl Hamilton. My deepest thanks to Angela Kouris for her contribution and restless support. Finally, this research has been made possible with the generous contribution of the Social Sciences and Humanities Research Council of Canada, Standard Research Grant Program.

2 In other words, my conception of blood owes less to biological determinism than to a powerful and effective *dispositif* through which stigmas towards unfit sexuality, race or ethnicity are legitimised and normalised.

3 Following Derrida's careful distinction, I shall mention here that, ironically, the term 'rogue' has been a defining marker of American international policies since 1945. The expression rogue state was rhetorically used by the American administration – and that up to Clinton's second mandate – to designate nations that constantly violate the spirit of international law: read, American interpretation of democracy. According to such rhetoric, rogue states were filled with rogues and beasts. Even if the expression was abandoned in White House briefings and discourses, its shadow is still prominent in the current Bush Administration.

4 For an in-depth analysis of Fortuyn's right-wing nationalist politics in the context of the extension of queer rights, see my article 'The Beast of Democracy: The sexual nationalism of Pim Fortuyn,' *GLQ: A Journal of Gay and Lesbian Studies* 12, no. 4 (September 2006) – forthcoming.

References

Berlant, L., 1997, *The Queen of America Goes to Washington City*, (Durham and London: Duke University Press).

——, 2002, 'Uncle Sam Needs a Wife', in R. Castronova and D. D. Nelson (Eds.), *Materializing Democracy: Toward a Revitalized Cultural Politics*, (Durham and London: Duke University Press), pp. 144–174.

Brown, W., 1995, *States of Injury: Power and Freedom in Late Modernity*, (Princeton, New Jersey: Princeton University Press).

Butler, J., 2001, *Antigone's Claim: Kinship Between Life and Death*, (New York: Columbia University Press).

——, 2002, 'Is Kinship Always Already Heterosexual?' d*ifferences: A Journal of Feminist Cultural Studies*, 13(1): 14–44.

Chouinard, T., 2002, 'Homoparentalité: Les enfants d'abord', *Voir*, May (23–29): pp. 14–15.

Clarke, E., 2002, *Virtuous Vice: Homoeroticism and the Public Sphere*, (Durham and London: Duke University Press).

Derrida, J., 1990, 'Force de Loi: Le "Fondement Mystique de l'autorité"/Force of Law: The "Mystical Foundation of Authority"', *Cardozo Law Review*, 11: 919–1039.

——, 2002, *Voyous*, (Paris: Galilée).

Duggan, L., 2001, 'Beyond Blood', *CLAGS News* XI (3): 1–2.

——, 2002, 'The New Homonormativity: The Sexual Politics of Neoliberalism', in R. Castronova and D. D. Nelson (Eds.), *Materializing Democracy: Toward a Revitalized Cultural Politics*, (Durham and London: Duke University Press), pp. 175–194.

——, 2003, *The Twilight of Equality? Neoliberalism, Cultural Politics, and the Attack on Democracy*, (Boston: Beacon Press).

Fassin, E., 2002, 'Same Sex, Different Politics: "Gay Marriage" Debates in France and the United States', *Public Culture*, 13(2): 215–232.

Fraser, N., 2000, 'Rethinking Recognition', *New Left Review*, 3 (May/June): 107–120.

Foucault, M., 1976, *Histoire de la Sexualité 1*, (Paris: Gallimard).

Goldstein, R., 2002, *The Attack Queers: Liberal Society and the Gay* Right, (London and New York: Verso).

Hallet, J., 1999, *Don't: A Reader's Guide to the Military's Anti-Gay Policy*, (Durham and London: Duke University Press).

McKeon, M., 1995, 'Historicizing Patriarchy: The Emergence of Gender Difference in England, 1660–1760', *Eighteenth-Century Studies*, 28(3): 295–322.

Nadeau, C., 2005, 'Sang-statut, sang-loi: le sang sans sexe (Notes sur l'union civile, les *queers* et l'état),' *Multitudes*, 20 (Spring 2005): 175–186.

Phelan, S., 2001, *Sexual Strangers. Gays, Lesbians and Dilemmas of Citizenship*, (Philadelphia: Temple University Press).

Povinelli, E. A., 2002, 'Notes on Gridlock: Genealogy, Intimacy, Sexuality', *Public Culture* 14(1): 215–238.

Ryder, R. D., 2000, *Animal Revolution: Changing Attitudes Towards Speciesism*, (Oxford, New York: Berg).

Salecl, R., 2000, 'Love Me, Love My Dog: Psychoanalysis and the Animal/Human Divide', in *(Per)Versions of Love and Hate*, (London and New York: Verso).

Schowengerdt, D. M., 2002, 'Defending Marriage: a Litigation Strategy to Oppose Same-Sex Marriage', *Regent University Law Review,* 14: 487–511.

Sloterdijk, P., 2000, *Règles pour le parc humain. Une lettre en réponse à la Lettre sur 'l'humanisme de Heidegger'*, (Paris: Mille et une nuits).

Smith, A. M., 2001, 'Missing Poststructuralism, Missing Foucault. Butler and Fraser on Capitalism and The Regulation of Sexuality', *Social Text*, 19(2): 103–125.

Stychin, C., 1998, *A Nation by Rights: national cultures, sexual identity politics and the discourse of rights*, (Philadelphia: Temple University Press).

Warner, M., 1999, *The Trouble with Normal: Sex, Politics, and The Ethics of Queer Life*, (Cambridge, Massachusetts: Harvard University Press).

Wintemute, R., 2000, 'Lesbian and Gay Equality 2000: The Potential of the Human Rights Act 1998 and the Need for an Equality Act 2002,' (Fourth Stonewall Lecture, 4 October 2000), *European Human Rights Law Review*, 6: 603–626.

Irene Watson

Internationalising, Humanising and Diversifying: The One Nation State

The colonisation of Australia and the final results of the legal doctrine *terra nullius* can be seen and felt in almost every aspect of our Aboriginal being. Aboriginal peoples have become less than two percent of the Australian population; how we come to this marginalised position and how we move on are questions I have struggled to investigate from within an Aboriginal horizon or Aboriginal worldview and in this limited space I will communicate some of my thoughts.

Human Rights – different things to different peoples?

The peoples of the world have different experiences of human rights. I am an Aborigine and to have the ability to retain that identity is for me what is fundamental to my humanity. However, existing human rights frameworks do not provide the basis or even the minimum standard for survival of Aboriginal peoples. To identify and to live as an Aborigine, to simply be in the identity of one's self – is a huge struggle. The nation state of Australia, in common with all other colonial states has failed to enhance the survival of first peoples of the land.

From a human rights framework, the question of survival is a matter of reconciling the immediate and essential needs of shelter, food and water, but when looked at from an Aboriginal perspective it takes on another dimension, that is, Aboriginal peoples also look to the question of the survival of future generations. The survival of Aboriginal peoples into the future embraces the idea of or the right to exist as Aboriginal peoples within an Aboriginal worldview, continuing to live in the spirit, culture and traditional practices of the ancestors. At the core of an Aboriginal worldview is the obligation to care for country, and to keep the land and its natural environment alive for future generations. The idea of reciprocity and sustainability is inherent in this relationship, for the country keeps us alive and we in turn honour this, we work to keep country alive for our lifetime but also for future generations.

Human rights as I understand them are also about human obligations, that is, we are obligated to come into country in a respectful way, and to honour land, first peoples and their laws. However, what is most simply stated has become the most difficult ideal to achieve, particularly as Aboriginal rights and worldviews are not recognised by the Australian state and the majority of its voting citizens.

The language of international human rights has so far failed to incorporate the concerns of Aboriginal peoples, and in particular Aboriginal relationships to country. Generally, human rights discourses are largely disconnected from the natural environment, but from an Aboriginal perspective, the human is integral with and connected to country, as are our laws and cultures of place. Nevertheless, the Australian state fails to work towards a greater recognition of the broader idea of Aboriginal rights; instead, it allows the misrepresentation of an Aboriginal right to grow and to be represented as an elitist or 'special' right held only by indigenous peoples. But the idea of Aboriginal exclusivity is not what Aboriginal peoples advocate.

For example, Biddy Lindsay, a 63-year-old elder of the Malak Malak people whose people have been living by the Daly River in the Northern Territory for generations, in responding to a proposal to take water from the river for the supply of the water-hungry southern states, said in her concern for the future of the river, 'We don't own the water. It's for everyone, so everyone should look out for it' (Murdoch, 2004). It is the bit about, 'it's everyone's responsibility' that seems the most difficult concept to convey, yet despite that difficulty the state and the media appear generally to portray the picture of Aboriginal rights as being elitist. Aboriginal peoples have never said that Aboriginal rights are exclusively for Aboriginal peoples, but rather that the right to good drinking water is a right for all of humanity. What is being called for here should not be dismissed as some narrow claim made by the world's indigenous minorities, but a claim that Aboriginal peoples are upholding for all humanity, that is, the right of peoples to sustain our connections to country while also honouring obligations to care for country. Shouldn't the right to a healthy and sustainable environment be the right of all peoples? Of course, it should, but with the rights to clean drinking water also come the Aboriginal obligations to ensure that these rights survive for the benefit of future generations as well. It is this Aboriginal right/obligation that has proven problematic in the framing of international human rights standards.

The country lives in the places of humanity

Aboriginal peoples bring challenges to the ideal of human rights, because we bring the awareness of the relationship between land and humanity, and the idea/reality that the destruction of the natural world is equally a destruction of the human. So what is the balance, and what are the possibilities for future generations to live a sustainable lifestyle? These are questions that currently confront Aboriginal peoples in Australia, and across the planet, yet they are questions more often than not ignored by states and powerful corporations.

What power do Aboriginal peoples have to effect decisions being made regarding the development of their lands? Are the results equitable in relation to Aboriginal peoples or are they lucrative and mostly beneficial for corporate developers? Aboriginal peoples' ability to care for country is inoperable while the power to determine vests with states that are influenced by transnational corporations. What powers of persuasion do we have; can we inflate the Aboriginal worldview into the general psyche of humanity, and thereby develop an ethic that cares for country?

One of the old people from the Coorong was recorded in the 1930s speaking to ethnologist Norman Tindale. In that recording, he spoke of the *krinkiri,* that is the white man, and of the impact his sheep and cattle had upon our land. He commented on the rate at which native vegetation covering the sand dunes had been stripped, leaving them to blow away and to uncover the ancient burial places of our ancestors. He said, 'just like ants, they are eating away until there is nothing left'. Our old people had seen nothing like it before, and my generation was born into a time where we knew nothing other than the stripped dunes of my ancestor's country. I hold concern for what future generations will come to witness. In the big picture of global devastation, this is a small story, but it conveys the same idea, that is, we are seeing the removal of Aboriginal peoples from their lands coinciding with huge impacts upon country. We have seen the ethic of caring for country replaced with one of disconnection. The sovereign lands of Aboriginal peoples have become the property of the Crown, and alienated as a commodity that is traded and sold. Our ability as Aboriginal peoples to hold together a sustainable environment falls to the 'democratic' process, and the recognition of Aboriginal rights falls prey to the majority. This is a majority who do not know us, a majority that the Aboriginal writer Thomas King asks, 'why do you not like us'?

One nation state

Aboriginal peoples, as in the past, continue to be removed from traditional lands. We have had no peaceful settlement, and the process of dispossession has never stopped. In a short space of time, the lands of Aboriginal peoples, once pristine, have been largely devastated. For example, the main river system of south-eastern Australia is being over-taxed by irrigators and is salting up. Originally its out-flow filled the Coorong, but now the lands of my grandmother are drying up. This picture of environmental devastation is repeated across Australia and across the globe and is not unique to the land of any particular people. At the same time, the possibility of caring for the land is over-ruled by ideas about the survival of the fittest, and in today's world, that is those who are economically powerful, and armed to the teeth with an arsenal of weaponry. What can Aboriginal peoples do, but to continue to struggle and protest against the devastation of human life which runs in parallel with devastation to the natural environment and the extinction of species? Yet, while the future looks bleak and the ending has been spoken of, I, like many other Aboriginal people, think in terms of cycles, not endings.

We struggle to uphold an Aboriginal worldview while the dominant worldview embraces ideas of evolving to an end point, to the one homogeneous state. But in this homogeneous nation state, what space do Aboriginal people occupy? Will they continue to experience the rates of over-representation inside the prisons, juvenile institutions, medical institutions, mental institutions, in zones of homelessness and poverty, unemployment, and as victims of violence and sexual abuse? Aboriginal peoples are over-represented in all areas of human rights concern. In the face of the damning statistics, does a social justice agenda exist in Australia to repair the human rights abuses suffered by Aboriginal peoples? No, not anymore. Instead, the state works towards implementing its policy of 'practical reconciliation', a policy which upon close examination reveals at its core assimilationist objectives, and the Aboriginal peoples call for the recognition of self-determination, land rights and reparation remains unheard. The Australian state and the majority of its citizens believe justice has been delivered, by the various mechanisms of *Mabo*[1] and native title,[2] but it has not.

In this returning assimilationist environment, what spaces exist for the advancement of our Aboriginal being? How do we live inside the one nation or one-size-fits-all space; do we become absorbed or can we modify the territory for Aboriginal people's development? What are the possibilities now that the Australian government has abandoned the principles of self-determination and cited them as a failed policy, as though the ideals of self-determination have become dirty words for dangerous conversations. The decline in the use of the term self-determination, has increased since 11 September 2001 and since the war on Iraq, to be replaced with the language of the oneness of nationhood, and ideals of plurality and co-existence have slid away from sight and earshot. During that slide, the principles of self-determination have been repudiated and criticised as being part of the cause of the Aboriginal problem (see Sutton, 2001). Also, while some Australian media reporting has denigrated the international advocacy for the recognition of Aboriginal peoples, arguing that the 'focus on the rights of Indigenous peoples is to the detriment of what goes on domestically', journalist Janet Albrechsten adds '[...] the policies of the International Decade of the World's Indigenous Peoples, based on self-rule with little accountability, have done more damage to indigenous Australians than the white missions of the 1930s did' (Albrechsten, 2003).

On that analysis, should Aboriginal peoples be fearful of gaining recognition of the right to self-determination? The 'road map' for Aborigines, our journey to self-determination, has hit a wash-out. The path is now demonised and held to blame for the violence and dysfunction within Aboriginal communities across Australia. Anthropologist Peter Sutton (2001), among other 'white experts', claims that violence is inherent in Aboriginal communities, but is it? Or is it a form of internalised oppression that is unique to the experience of those subjugated by colonialsim? As Sartre wrote

> If this suppressed fury fails to find an outlet, it turns in a vacuum and devastates the oppressed creatures themselves. In order to free themselves they even massacre each other. The different tribes fight between themselves since they cannot face the real enemy – and you can count on colonial policy to keep up their rivalries; the man who raises his knife against his brother thinks that he has destroyed once and for all the detested image of their common degradation, even though these expiatory victims don't quench their thirst for blood. (Sartre in Fanon, 1971: 16)

What is going on in communities is a form of internalised oppression-colonialism, which historically occurs when conditions within colonised communities have become so critical that the people within those communities are calling for protection. This call is then appropriated by the state and translated into a form of confirmation or legitimisation for past policies of assimilation and worse, legitimisation for a return to that of colonialism. The colonial predator returns re-invented as the saviour of poor 'backward black peoples' and assimilationist objectives are reinstated. If we refuse the racist hand of paternalism, we are then characterised as the ungrateful native, (ungrateful for the native title scraps) and in our 'ungrateful' and 'dysfunctional' state, we are further deemed in need of supervision and protection from our own. This is the impact of colonialism. When peoples are displaced, dispossessed, and left with only the colonial institutions, (remember the *Aborigines Acts* which controlled every aspect of an Aboriginal person's life were not repealed in most states until the 1960s) what opportunity have we had to reconstruct Aboriginal communities? None at all; yet there is a perception that for the past thirty years, Aboriginal policy has been framed by the principles of self-determination, and that the current problems and crises that exist in Aboriginal communities are a direct result of the failure of self-determination. The point is that we have never had the opportunity to savour the real taste of self-determination. The economic resources allocated by government to Aboriginal development were largely eroded before they reached communities on the ground.

The poverty of Aboriginal communities provides evidence for the failure of government to fairly and equitably re-distribute economic resources to where they were most needed. Was this failure to share equitably the economic resources of this country a failing of Aboriginal self-determination, or was it a failing of the Australian government? The inequitable distribution of wealth and the high levels of poverty and homelessness in the white community are also becoming endemic and yet Aboriginal communities are blamed for our position of abject poverty, and our failure to make self-determination work. Why is it that poor white communities are not blamed for their abject poverty in the same way that Aboriginal peoples are? This blame can be seen in the recent abolition of the Aboriginal Torres Strait Islander Commission (ATSIC)[3] and the return of the management of ATSIC programs to the Australian Federal government service providers. Will these governmental service providers be monitored, measured and evaluated to the same degree that ATSIC was prior to its dismantling? The Australian government's conclusion that the fault lies in Aboriginal hands is to say that Aboriginal peoples have had the power to change and improve our position. But did we really have the power and resources at hand and the autonomy to make it work? Could the same blame be laid at the feet of poor white Australians for failed delivery of their programs?

Losing my voice – or was I under an illusion?

We remain powerless in many ways; economic resources have never been allocated to provide all Aboriginal people with gainful employment, good housing, good education and good health. Instead, our control and power over our lands has been wrested away and since the original theft and invasion, all of our indicators of wealth have continued to decline. Instead of Aboriginal peoples and communities having some say over our lives, we have lived with policies of providing a buffet of opportunities for the players in the Aboriginal industry. Other disadvantaged groups also suffer in the same way; perhaps one difference is that when we focus on Aboriginal peoples, it is those Aboriginal peoples who joined the Aboriginal industry who are blamed for the failings of the government policy of economic rationalism. Blame is the price paid by Aboriginal people who seek to fit into the dominant paradigm. We can see this in the demise of the Aboriginal Torres Strait Islander Commission. Nevertheless, it copped the blame for failings in Aboriginal community development across Australia. The ATSIC body was initially presented as a model of Aboriginal self-determination and governance, but in reality, it was in the same form of other western bureaucratic institutions but it was also further limited and shaped by Australian government policy and economic rationalism. To argue that Aboriginal peoples have had the opportunity to develop self-determination in the body of ATSIC is a deceitful lie, but it is this lie which underpins the demonisation of the Aboriginal struggle for self-determination.

A critique of ATSIC was called for, but how do Aboriginal peoples put forward our criticism of bodies such as ATSIC without running the risk of the Aboriginal critique being mis-appropriated by the state, which might support policy shifts back to assimilation? This is exactly what occurred in the recent move of the Howard government to dismantle ATSIC. The Aboriginal position was obviously aiming to move forward and improve; instead, what occurred was that the Aboriginal critique was appropriated and then mistranslated for political agendas which are not our own. This Aboriginal critique I have named 'dangerous conversations', conversations that risk being appropriated, re-translated and contaminated by the state for its own political agendas, in this instance for the return to assimilation. Thus, the tension between the need to name what is true and the resulting danger of naming truths arises. Can the marginal risk ever speaking again? But what does it mean to not ever speak again? A genocide of voice.

To date, the destruction of the quasi-representative ATSIC model has not resulted in an improvement of the Aboriginal position, instead it has been replaced with an advisory panel of 'Aboriginal experts' handpicked by government.[4] The government view will preside over any advisory body, and the opportunity to expand Aboriginal aspirations has been denied. In the demise of ATSIC, Aboriginal peoples have come to know even more clearly than ever before that we have a very narrow space (and for most Aboriginal peoples the reality is there is no space at all) in which to negotiate for our survival as peoples. It is a difficult time for indigenous peoples to engage in discussions on our future rights, dreams and hopes, for I see that those conversations in the past (in relation to ATSIC, native title and reconciliation) have left us even more vulnerable. Those conversations were appropriated by the state to expand the myth of the ungrateful native (see Watson, 2004: 205; 2002: 253; 2001: 21).

We do not have the power to determine how our discussions or conversations will be framed by government and the media. For example, once Aboriginal people called for the improvement of ATSIC by focusing upon greater Aboriginal representation and Aboriginal community access to resources, those discussions were hijacked by the state and used to direct resources back into governmental service providers. This was not what Aboriginal peoples had advocated for, and as a result, Aboriginal community development has taken a step backward into the days of assimilationist practices of the past. The Aboriginal struggle for recognition of self-determination is no longer considered a remote possibility for serving as the vehicle for delivering justice to Aboriginal peoples, it has become a flickering and fading light.

Lost ground – is it redeemable?

We have lost extensive ground under the Howard Federal government, which has been successful in selling to the voting public its racist representation of Aboriginal peoples as being the cause of the problem. What the problem is that we have not in truth had the opportunity to speak. It is simply characterised as 'the Aboriginal problem'. Instead of engaging in truth talk, the state has adopted the populist language developed by the Aboriginal 'leader' Noel Pearson of 'taking responsibility' or of 'mutual obligation'. Yet how do the dispossessed, disadvantaged and poor rate in the ordering of mutual obligation, particularly when the state fails to house, feed and provide adequate health care? This idea of mutual obligation has effectively shut down the discussion of Aboriginal self-determination and the development of economic independence.

Future landscapes

How did we get here, and where is here? For humanity is in different places, as are human rights, which can be experienced in differing degrees (and for much of humanity not at all). For Australia, the spread of experience is diverse: it ranges from great wealth and comfort to the abject and fatal poverty of urban, rural and remote Aboriginal communities. There are solutions, Aboriginal laws prescribe a more caring and sharing ethic, such that the natural resources of this country would be equitably shared and also cared for the benefit of all life forms. However, what solutions will be invoked by the state? The socio-economic and political profile of Aboriginal peoples shows that very little has changed. Aboriginal communities may be now more impoverished than at any other time in our history; at least while bush foods remained available, one could get a feed, but there is very little accessible bush left these days. Aboriginal peoples in this country are starving like at no other time before. These are hungry times, as they are for one third of humanity.

While Aboriginal worldviews are all but erased, we work to survive within imposed structures such as ATSIC and native title, working within structures that were created not by us, or for us, but externally imposed upon us. We have had to fit in, while also trying to counteract the illusion crafted that these models are ours and of our creation, as though we made them. It is a strange idea; what resources did we ever have to make these institutions? We had no choice but to work with these structures or alternatively to disappear into spaces salvaged from the power and forces of colonialism. Imposed colonialist structures have never worked for us, and they are what I would argue is an aspect of underlying genocide, an impossible-to-prove subtle kind of genocide, a *terra nullius*, invisible genocide, not a form that is in your face. You just feel it, in a deeply inter-generational kind of way. The feeling never goes away, it just deepens. You swim against the tide of absorption, while absorption grows with the 'progress' of each colonised generation.

The power of the state has determined that we would get to this point in the journey, to this road block, where the caricature of the undeserving, untrustworthy, dangerous native would be returned to the protectorate of the Minister of Aboriginal Affairs. Will some be returned to the care of the mission protectorates of the past? And those not returned left to be absorbed, whitened and assimilated.

What of history – or is it all disappearing and coming to its own ending?

I grew up to understand history where the past, present, and future is the same. Time has no beginning and ending; there is a cycle of time and events.

But the dominant scientific view encased within evolutionary theories understands the world as moving from an evolutionary beginning and progressing through time to an end point. The history of humanity is seen with the same perspective. This dividing of time is something peculiar to western thought. With the coming of Cook, we were deemed pre-historic, and the history of Australia was seen to begin with the coming of the European, while Aboriginal tellings of history were deemed mythical, pre-historic and irrelevant.

The Australian colonies were seen as fundamental to the evolutionary process and the expansion and de-centering of European civilisation across the world. The displacement of the pre-historic native was seen as an inevitable aspect of the process of history. It was 'known' that 'world history takes account only of peoples that form a state' (Hegel in McCarney, 2000: 154). The doctrine of *terra nullius* was based on theories of evolution and 'the march of God in the world' (Hegel in Dallmayr, 1991: 321–346). Ideas of 'progress' are founded upon the disappearance of the 'pre-historic'. Aboriginal peoples in Australia have maintained a 200-year–long struggle of survival against these ideas of evolution, and our characterisation as 'uncivilised, irrational', peoples.

Now 200 years after the event, what is the response of those privileged by history to the idea of history beginning with the Europeans, their rational state and the rendering of all that had been before and that still lives in this land, as pre-historic? The idea of the evolved rational state is particularly interesting when considering the contribution that Fukuyama's work has made to the think-tank, which has supported the Presidency of George W. Bush. What similarities are there between the position of Aboriginal Australia and the claims made by Fukuyama that we have reached the end of history, having arrived at the high point of evolution in the US model of the democratic state?

Here it is important to consider the relationship between the idea of history as beginning and ending and our place as the pre-historic native. When our place in this end of history, is set against the Australian government's announcement that Aboriginal self-determination is a failed policy, I would suggest the Aboriginal place inside European history is as it ever was, that is outside of European history, excluded as pre-historic. This is the source of our othering.

Is there an ending? Is this the end road of expectations for greater human rights and justice? Would Fukuyama have us as arrived? And what would we expect upon our arrival? Are we even meant to arrive? The announcement by Fukuyama of the end of history justifies endings or the annihilation of peoples, laws and cultures that are different to the US liberal democratic model of state. The idea of evolution, progress reaching an end point in history is a 'nice' tidy way of containing humanity, its 'evolution' 'progress', and its finality as a species on earth. The idea thus reduces genocide to a sanitised container, where it becomes justified in the quest for progress. Fukuyama has redubbed evolution and progress in the name of the 'fully evolved state'; here the connection can be made, for genocide today is excused in the same way it was in Aboriginal Australia in earlier eras of colonial expansion when used to annihilate Aboriginal peoples. Today the same ideology is practised in the states' denial of our Aboriginal right to self-determination, as it is also in the states' invasion and colonisation of the Middle East.

Fukuyama tells us, that the good news is what comes with liberal democracy and its technology – 'Is the limitless accumulation of wealth, and an increasing homogenization of all human societies' (in Derrida, 1994: 60). But what will the cost to Aboriginal peoples of the limitless accumulation of wealth and the increasing homogenisation of human societies be? What kind of globalised genocides are planned, or are likely to occur, as a result of a Fukuyama-styled ending to history? For in the marking of an end to history, is there also the marking of an end to the cultures, ways of life and life itself, for much of humanity?

Is progress to an end point all that is left to think through or can we open minds to another way, to a way of knowing this world as of cycles, where there are no beginnings and endings, and in thinking this way, can we consider the possibility of human relationships and the land in a place of a continuing co-existence? Can we then think of building in this present a future, which embraces the diversity of the peoples inhabiting the planet? Can we afford not to?

Where does the idea of endings take us? To the end of the world, or the end of a certain concept of history? These are dangerous times, but they are also times for important beginnings, of returning cycles and through reflection, and meditation, we will return. Return to cycles of rebirth, for that is the law, the law of this Aboriginal place. I also know that respect, generosity, compassion and love, love of self, land and peoples, will return us.

Endnotes

1 *Mabo* v Queensland (1992) 175 CLR 1.

2 (Cth) Native Title Act 1993.

3 The Aboriginal Torres Strait Islander Commissioner, is a statutory body that was established by the Commonwealth government to administer Aboriginal services to communities across Australia.

4 The Indigenous Advisory Panel was established in late 2004 following the re-election of the Howard government in October.

References

Albrechsten, J., 2003, 'The decade of squalor', *The Australian,* 18 June.

Dallmayr, F., 1991, 'Re-thinking the Hegelian State', in D. Cornell, M. Rosenfeld, and D. Gray Carlson (Eds.), *Hegel and Legal Theory*, (New York: Routledge), pp. 321–346.

Derrida, J., 1994, *Spectres of Marx: the state of the debt, the work of mourning and the new international*, (London: Routledge), p 60.

Fanon, F., 1971, *The Wretched of the Earth*, (Melbourne: Penguin).

McCarney, J., 2000, *Hegel on History*, (London: Routledge), p. 154.

Murdoch, L., 2004, 'Hands off our Rivers, Top End Says', *The Age,* 25 November.

Sutton, P., 2001, 'The Politics of Suffering Indigenous Policy since 1970', *Anthropological Forum*, 11(2): 125–173.

Watson, I., 2001, 'One Indigenous Perspective on Human Rights', in S. Garkawe, L. Kelly and W. Fisher (Eds.), *Indigenous Rights*, (Sydney: Sydney Institute of Criminology).

——, 2002, 'Buried Alive', *Law and Critique*, 13: 253.

——, 2004, 'From a Hard Place to Softer Terrain', *Flinders Journal of Law Reform*: 205.

Contributors

KIIKPOYE K. AARON has a PhD in Development Studies, teaches Political Science at the Rivers State College of Education, Port Harcourt, Nigeria and is Co-Chair of THEDI-The Health, Environment and Development Initiative, an NGO. His research on the Niger Delta crises has appeared in leading national and international journals and book chapters. He has also published on Nigeria's enterprise reform, globalisation and the crises of democratisation in Nigeria. His current research interest is on rights abuses in the global South by Northern corporations and their effect on the Northern consuming public in a globalising world.

CHEE SOON JUAN is a neuropsychologist and was sacked from the National University of Singapore after he joined the opposition Singapore Democratic Party of which he is the Secretary-General. He has been repeatedly jailed for making public speeches without permits. He has also been the target of two defamation lawsuits brought against him, the latest by two former Prime Ministers of Singapore. He was a Fellow at the Monash Asia Institute, the University of Chicago, and the National Endowment for Democracy as well as the recipient of the Defender of Democracy Award 2003. Dr. Chee is also the author of several books and articles.

LARA FERGUS is a Researcher with the Australian Centre for the Study of Sexual Assault, and has been an activist for women's human rights for ten years. She has worked in both paid and voluntary positions with Amnesty International (AI), and is currently contributing research to AI Australia's *Stop Violence Against Women* campaign. She is also working with Women's Rights Action Network Australia on the production of a *Shadow Report* on Australia's implementation of the Convention on the Elimination of All Forms of

Discrimination against Women. She is doing a PhD at Victoria University on the subject of women and exile.

SAM GARKAWE is an Associate Professor at the School of Law and Justice at Southern Cross University, where he teaches International Law, International Criminal Justice, Human Rights and Victimology. Sam has published numerous articles in these areas, and is the co-editor of *Indigenous Human Rights*, (2001, Federation Press: Sydney). Sam has a MLaw from London University and is enrolled in a Doctorate of Law at Sydney University. His recent publications concern the rights of victims and witnesses in the International Criminal Court, and the South African Truth and Reconciliation Commission. Sam has been a visiting Professor at Hamline University's School of Law, Minnesota, and at Whittier Law School, California, and a Research Fellow at the Institute of Human Rights and Criminal Justice Studies, Technikon South Africa, Johannesburg.

GERARD GOGGIN is an ARC Australian Research Fellow in the Centre for Critical and Cultural Studies, University of Queensland, researching mobile phone culture and regulation. With Christopher Newell he is author of *Digital Disability* (Rowman & Littlefield, 2003) and *Disability in Australia: Exposing a Social Apartheid* (University of NSW Press, 2005). Gerard is also interested in human rights in the field of new media, and is editor of *Virtual Nation: The Internet in Australia* (University of NSW Press, 2004).

JIM IFE is Haruhisa Handa Professor of Human Rights Education and Head of the Centre for Human Rights Education at Curtin University of Technology, Perth, Western Australia. He was previously Professor of Social Work and Social Policy at Curtin University, and also at the University of Western Australia. He is a former President of Amnesty International Australia, and a former Secretary of the Human Rights Commission of the International Federation of Social Workers. His two areas of academic interest are human rights and community development, and his current work seeks to integrate the two.

MONICA MCWILLIAMS became Northern Ireland's Chief Commissioner of Human Rights in 2005. She was an elected representative in Northern Ireland from 1996 to 2003. She is the co-founder of the Northern Ireland Women's Coalition created to increase women's representation at the Multi-Party Peace Negotiations and is a signatory to the 1998 Good Friday Agreement. Monica was elected to the Northern Ireland Assembly and was Chairperson of the Human Rights Implementation Committee. In 2004, she returned to the University of Ulster as Professor of Women's Studies and Social Policy where she is a Research Associate with the Institute for Transitional Justice and INCORE. She has published widely on the impact of political conflict on women's lives with expertise in domestic violence. She holds a Doctor of Humane Letters from Lesley College, Massachusetts; and is a graduate of Queens University Belfast and the University of Michigan.

MICHAEL MORISON is a practising lawyer in the areas of Commercial Law, Litigation and Intellectual Property and a lecturer in the School of Law and Justice at Southern Cross University, Australia. He holds degrees in Humanities, International Studies and Law. He has a professional background in human rights and capacity-building in developing countries. His research and publishing interests focus on democratisation and post-conflict legal capacity-building. His focus is on South East Asia and in particular East Timor, Cambodia and Sri Lanka. He is currently working on a book on democratisation.

CHANTAL NADEAU is an Associate Professor of Communication Studies at Concordia University (Montreal) where she teaches queer theory, postcolonial studies and media criticism. Her first book *Fur Nation: From the Beaver to Brigitte Bardot* (Routledge, 2001) offers a re-mapping of Canadian history by reclaiming the centrality of beaver(s) in the sexualisation of the nation. Her current research addresses the intersections between queers, rights and democracy. She is working on her second book entitled, *Beastly Politics: Queers, Rights and Democracy* (working title).

CHRISTOPHER NEWELL, PhD, is Associate Professor, School of Medicine, University of Tasmania. He teaches, researches and consults in the areas of bioethics and disability studies. He is a person with disability and active member of the Australian disability rights movement. Recent books include *Digital Disability: The Social Construction of New Media* (with Gerard Goggin, Rowman & Littlefield, 2003); *From Out back to Out Front: Voices in Spirituality and Disability from the Land Down Under*, (Haworth Press, 2004) and (with Gerard Goggin) *Disability in Australia: Exposing a Social Apartheid*, (UNSW Press, 2004).

BADEN OFFORD, PhD, is Director of the Centre for Law, Politics and Culture; Chair of the Human Research Ethics Committee; and Senior Lecturer in Cultural Studies at Southern Cross University, Australia. His book, *Homosexual Rights as Human Rights*, (Peter Lang, 2003) won the George Duncan Memorial Award in 2005. He has published widely in human rights, sexuality, cultural diversity, belonging and citizenship.

ELISABETH PORTER, PhD, is INCORE Research Director. INCORE is a joint University of Ulster and UN University centre for international peace and conflict research (www.incore.ulster.ac.uk). She has also taught Politics, International Relations and Sociology at the University of Ulster, Flinders University of South Australia, the University of South Australia and Southern Cross University, Australia. She has published widely on women and peace-building, citizenship, pluralism, diversity and democratic dialogue. Her current research interests are on the ideas and practices that build and sustain peace, human security, inclusive citizenship and reconciliation in a post-9/11 global era.

KULWANT SINGH has a LLM and PhD in Law from the University of Jammu (J&K), India. At present, he works as Reader at the Faculty of Law and as Director of the Legal Aid Clinic, University of Jammu. He has done comparative study on Property Rights of Refugees and Displaced Persons in Bosnia and Herzegovina and J&K and made presentations on the subject at international seminars and conferences in Bosnia and Herzegovina, Italy, Sri Lanka and Australia. He has published extensively on different themes of human rights in journals of international repute.

CARL F STYCHIN is Professor of Law and Social Theory and Pro Vice Chancellor (Enterprise), at the University of Reading, England. His research interest is in gender, sexuality and law, including human rights, citizenship, transnationalism and globalisation with a particular focus on same-sex sexualities. He has published extensively in these fields, including three monographs and two co-edited collections, as well as numerous periodical articles.

IRENE WATSON currently teaches law at Flinders University and also works as a lawyer with the Aboriginal Legal Rights Movement in South Australia. She has published widely on indigenous legal issues, and her current research interests are on Aboriginal women and the law. Irene will commence work on a post-doctoral research fellowship with the University of Sydney in late 2005.

Index